Location and space in social administration

To Hélène and Alexandra

Location and space in social administration

Bryan Massam

Edward Arnold

© Bryan Massam. 1975

First published 1975 by
Edward Arnold (Publishers) Ltd
25 Hill Street, London W1X 8LL

ISBN: 0 7131 5776 3 Cased Edition
ISBN: 0 7131 5777 1 Paper Edition

Printed in Great Britain by
Billing & Sons Limited, Guildford and London

Contents

Preface

This book aims to introduce students to a selection of contemporary procedures for analysing the influence of space and location on the provision of public services. Substantive material from several disciplines is integrated under one subject heading, and I have attempted to present it in such a way that expertise in all fields is not a prerequisite for understanding the text. It is intended that this book will bridge the gap between a social value-oriented approach and one which relies more heavily on rigorous analytical techniques.

Several times in this book we evaluate the structure for providing public services in terms which consider distance and accessibility. While physical proximity often relates directly to the satisfaction which an individual derives from a service we should not overlook recent work on locating 'noxious' facilities. Further, we should consider public awareness and its influence on utilization patterns. Information may be available to all, but comprehension varies and some people do not take advantage of facilities and services to which they are entitled. Our analysis is frequently concerned with individual services, but ideally we should look at all the services which are associated with a particular location before we make statements about social justice, public welfare, and equity. Problems of analysing social well-being are of great concern to social scientists, and while we should not dismiss humanitarian values in our studies we would be wise to complement them with careful measurement wherever possible. This point was well made in the recent work by Smith (1973). He noted that if social well-being is to be improved procedures for evaluating alternate structures and systems are essential. One of the purposes of this book is to consider some procedures which examine the role of space and location, in an objective way, on the provision of public services. I hope this sort of work will aid in the planning process and the improvement of social well-being.

The book is divided into nine chapters. An overview of the topic is provided in the Introduction and this is followed by a review of the spatial form of service districts. Chapter 3 concentrates on the size of administrative units and here I draw on work from economics and public finance as well as geography. Chapter 4 reviews one of the most rapidly growing fields in human geography: allocation–location model-building. Theoretical and empirical literature is cited. In an attempt to evaluate some of the dynamic aspects which relate to the provision of social services, chapters 5 and 6 examine interaction within and among administrative units. The large-scale and long-term trends in the spatial organization of service districts are examined in Chapter 7. The penultimate chapter deals with some of the broader aspects of government, politics and administration and the final chapter offers a set of conclusions and suggestions for future work.

Many people have helped directly and indirectly in the preparation of this book. I would particularly like to thank Mike Goodchild for his assistance with allocation–location model-building, and Gerry Rushton and Gordon Ewing for introducing me to preference studies. I am also grateful for comments that were provided by Professor E. Soja and Dr N. Ginsburg on the Resource Paper on the Spatial Structure of Administrative Systems that was prepared in 1972. Gerry Rushton, Charles Monroe and Max Barlow kindly provided unpublished material. Diana Bouchard, my research assistant at McGill, has helped me enormously.

Bryan H. Massam

Acknowledgements

The authors and publishers gratefully acknowledge permission given by the following to reprint or modify copyright material:

The Association of American Geographers for Figures 2.6, 2.7, 5.7, 5.8, 7.7 and 7.8; Chapman and Hall for Figure 5.4; R. A. Whitaker, Department of Geography, University of British Columbia for Figure 7.2; the Canadian Association of Geographers for Figures 7.5a and 7.5b; J. Glasgow, Department of Geography, Clark University for Figures 6.4 and 6.5; Peter Haggett for Figure 7.6; Northwestern University Press for Figure 7.12; C. B. Monroe, Department of Geography, Pennsylvania State University for Figures 5.10 and 5.11; Prentice Hall Inc. for Figures 4.1 and 8.1; M. F. Goodchild, Department of Geography, University of Western Ontario for Figure 2.2.

1   Introduction

1   Overview

The division of the surface of the earth into territorial patterns is a dominant feature in the spatial organization of societies. The analysis of these patterns has attracted the attention of several disciplines and approaches, the former includes geography, anthropology, political science, biology, sociology and economics, and the latter ranges from abstract mathematical treatment of the shape of enclosed areas to the collection of empirical data on real-world administrative patterns. Attempts have been made to define the functions of territorial divisions and the relationship between spatial form and the function as it varies from place to place and over time. The decision-making processes which give rise to territorial division have also been examined, as has the sense of territoriality which is a common explanation of man's spatial organization and behaviour.[1]

In this book we will focus upon a particular type of territorial division, *the administrative area within a state*. While some of the ideas discussed may have broader implications within the field of spatial organization[2] and may apply to many types of territorial divisions these will not be developed here. It is widely recognized that all states, except the very smallest, are divided into smaller units for the purpose of internal administration.[3] Thus we must first examine the smaller spatial units and try to determine the precise reasons for their form and so add to our knowledge of man's organization of space. However, from a practical point of view, if we are to help in making decisions about the size, shape and number of administrative areas within a country we need to be able to define and measure the efficiency of a particular arrangement and to compare this with alternative spatial arrangements. The advantages and disadvantages of all possible spatial patterns should be known if a reasoned choice is to be made. Traditionally the decision-maker has relied heavily on his experience and on trial and error in defining administrative areas. Clearly geographers, among others, ought to help in defining areas by offering their knowledge on this subject to society to use as it deems most appropriate.

Administrative areas can be defined according to many functions, and they are restricted neither to rural or urban areas nor to developed or developing nations. Whether the problem is to define school districts in New York, health units in Botswana, milk marketing areas in Southern Ontario, voting districts in the UK or local government units in China it is essential that the decision-maker has access to various plans so that he may select one objectively, rather than on a purely intuitive basis.

With an increasing proportion of the world's population becoming concentrated in urban centres there is a pressing need to examine the spatial administrative structures which have been defined to delimit service areas of many public facilities such as fire and police protection, education, helath and welfare. Within the North American context Teitz has outlined the impact of public services on the lives of individuals. He deplores the failure of location theorists to give sufficient attention to public-determined facilities which play so important a part in shaping both the form of cities and the quality of life.

> Modern man is born in a publicly financed hospital, receives his education in a publicly supported school and university, spends a good part of his life travelling on publicly built transportation facilities, communicates through the post office or the quasi-public telephone system, drinks his public water, disposes of his garbage through the public removal system, reads his public library books, picnics in his public parks, is protected by his public police, fire and health systems; eventually he dies, again in a hospital, and may even be buried in a public cemetery.[4]

We should also note in passing that of three recent texts in urban geography,[5] only the one by Yeates and Garner makes a serious attempt to consider the role of the public sector in the organization and operation of a city.

Location theory in economics and geography has primarily been concerned with industrial, commercial and residential decisions. For a complete picture of human organization we need to develop theories to explain the location of public facilities. March and Simon (1958) discuss the

> great disparity between hypotheses and evidence. Much of what we know or believe about organizations is distilled from common sense and from the practical experience of executives. The great bulk of this wisdom and lore has never been subjected to the rigorous scrutiny of scientific method. The literature contains many assertions, but little evidence to determine – by the usual scientific standards of public testability and reproducibility – whether these assertions readily hold up in the world of fact.

At the moment there is a lack of solid theoretical basis to help us determine the size or location of public facilities and Teitz (1968) claims that 'rules of thumb have been developed, but for the most part without ways to evaluate the results or to stimulate investigation of new systems.'

It is clear that the supply of public services by governments contributes greatly to the overall welfare of society. The location of supply centres and the spatial demarcation of service areas strongly influences the efficiency of the services. If we are to use taxes and government investments wisely it is therefore essential that we have a clear understanding of the relationship between efficiency and the spatial attributes of the service system. This book is designed to help in this direction by introducing students to concepts developed in geography, economics, operations research and business management which consider the role of space and location in the provision of public services.

2 A basic classification of services

Though administrative areas can be defined for many different services it is possible to make a basic classification of types of services according to the general characteristics of the distribution system used. This allows us to treat groups of services by examining systematically the underlying principles in the particular distribution system.[6] Table 1.1 illustrates the scheme.

Table 1.1 A basic classification of services

Type	Distribution system	Examples of services
1	From many origins to few destinations; single or multiple-purpose journey.	1 Hospitals 2 Schools 3 Libraries 4 Clinics 5 Welfare offices 6 Voting areas
2	From few origins to many destinations; single-purpose journey.	1 Fire stations 2 Police stations
3	From few origins to many destinations; servicing several destinations on a single journey	1 Garbage collection 2 Mail delivery and collection 3 Police surveillance 4 Snow removal
4	Few central points which serve areas, linkages may be by physical transmission of goods or services, or by information networks including mail, telephone, radio or television.	1 Taxation units 2 Jurisdictional area 3 Pollution control 4 Planning districts

Table 1.1 distinguishes between the single-purpose journey and the multiple-purpose journey. For most purposes of analysis we assume that type 1 systems involve a single-purpose journey, for example to schools, hospitals, or voting booths, and thus when we examine the locational patterns of these facilities we are primarily concerned with the separation in space between the destinations and *each origin treated in turn*. On the other hand the type 3 system requires us to examine the accessibility of the origin to a set of destinations: the latter are not necessarily directly linked to the origin. In the first three systems the analytical procedures which have been developed depend upon precise information about the location of origins and destinations and a method of defining the accessibility of origins to destinations. This is usually the spatial separation of the places, the greater the distance between [points the lower the accessibility. A linear function of accessibility is normally used, which can be described symbolically as $A_{ij} = d_{ij}$. If we draw a graph of A

against d for several values of i and j, we would produce a straight line which goes through the origin. In words, the accessibility of origin i to destination j is equal to the distance between i and j. It is argued that accessibility is a measure of the cost of moving between i and j, therefore we replace A_{ij} and d_{ij} by a cost statement, call it C_{ij}, and it is this cost statement which is a basic ingredient in most analytical work on distribution systems. Recent work by Chaiken and Larson (1971) is largely developed from the analytical models which minimize d_{ij}. For example, we try to find the location for a destination, such as a school, so that the C_{ij} is minimum when we consider all the children the school serves. We are trying to minimize the aggregate cost of the distribution system by minimizing the distance which children have to travel to the destination. Precise details of this type of approach will be given in Chapter 4.

With regard to type 4 services, we may not have specific information on the location of origins or destinations but we have details of the configuration of the enclosed area. We know where the boundaries are. With this rather limited information we can still make objective statements about the spatial compactness of the area and depending upon the assumptions made regarding the distribution of origins and destinations within the area and the transportation system, for example, a rectangular grid, we can calculated the average distance between points.[7] We therefore have a set of procedures for examining alternate spatial forms for administrative units in terms of compactness measures and distance values, and this allows us to undertake objective comparative studies over space and time and also to evaluate the properties of different-shaped administrative areas. Attempts can also be made to search for relationships between the spatial properties of administrative areas and other attributes, specifically those concerning the function of the unit. This approach – to search for relationships between form and function – is now firmly established in the social sciences and is the basis of both predictive and prescriptive work.

To substantiate some of the general points mentioned above we will turn to four types of studies which are currently being undertaken. This summary will introduce the state of the art of analysing administrative structures. Later chapters will take up specific points and develop them in more detail.

The four types of studies are:

1   Those concerned with the role of decentralization in national and local development. The regional emphasis in these studies tends to lie in developing countries.
2   Rigorous analytical studies which investigate relationships between attributes of administrative areas and which serve as a basis for spatial reorganization of governmental units.
3   Studies which focus attention particularly on the provision of public goods and services in the urban environment.

4   Studies which are concerned with defining and determining conditions for the optimum distribution of goods and services, or for determining the underlying dimensions of the actual patterns of utilization within current administrative structures.

3   Decentralization and development

The first concerns itself with the problem of making 'further use of local authorities and other forms of decentralization involving participation of the people in the administration of services required locally for social and economic development' (UN Report, 1962). The emphasis is on developing countries, and recommendations are made regarding decentralization in rural communities (World Bank, 1972a). The UN study deals with various methods of administering locally general government functions and technical services, in the fields of agriculture, education, health, and social welfare. Appendix II of the report carries the ambitious title 'Optimum areas for Administration of Technical Services' and it deals with the services mentioned. After reviewing the highly centralized French educational system, the strongly decentralized US system and the compromise arrangement of the UK the study concludes that there is no such thing as an optimum area of educational administration in rural communities, and that fiscal, topographical, ethnographical, linguistic and historical factors forbid any valid generalizations. It would seem that if we are to use the term *optimum* then the at outset we have to define *optimum with respect to what?* We must also determine which constraints are operating. For example, do we want so to locate the schools that they have maximum accessibility to their pupils, given that financial constraints limit the number of schools which can be built, or do we wish to determine the best size of school so that the return on investment will be the highest possible. To attempt this we need measures of size of schools with respect to money invested and we also need to measure the performance of different-sized schools. The UN study does not offer procedures for either of these approaches though they are clearly of fundamental significance in making recommendations for optimum administration units. In the health service as in the educational service, comparative figures are used in making recommendations for the size of units and a list of norms are presented. Typical examples are shown in table 1.2. The practice of using comparative figures as

Table 1.2   Norm list for health services

1 nurse for 1,000–1,500
1 dentist for 4,000–5,000
1 general practitioner for 4,000–5,000
1 general surgeon for 20,000–30,000
1 gynecologist for 40,000–50,000

(*UN 1962, 121*)

a basis for defining goals appears fairly frequently and will probably continue until a more analytical foundation is built and precise relationships are known. National planners look at their neighbour in order to define goals and thus to provide a basis for policy statements regarding the standards required for the provision of public goods and services. It is suggested that optimum helath service units should be approximately 35 kms in radius and contain a population of 50,000. This claim is based upon the argument that the central hospital will be about one hour from the farthest patient and that a population of approximately 50,000 could be handled by the hospital. This unit could be subdivided to satisfy the norms listed in table 1.2. The polemic debate on the quality of services is glossed over. With regard to the administration of social services we are primarily concerned with three main categories of services:

1   counselling, where specialized personnel provides advice and guidance or informal education;
2   institutional care, where physical facilities are required in addition to specialized personnel for the performance of service;
3   economic assistance in the form of cash payments and, in some cases, of distribution in kind.

The report notes the dearth of available data on the subject and the lack of research on the requirements, not only for efficient administrative organization, but also for the operational efficiency of particular types of social services. Without basic facts it is not surprising that specific recommendations do not emerge. At one extreme the need for large areas is stressed in order to plan and to spread the risk and responsibility. At the other extreme the need for accessibility is regarded as important and thus the object is to produce small units with many administrative centres. The limited availability of personnel and capital often places severe limits on the number of centres which can be built with the expectation of operating effectively. The consequences of this are twofold. First, many people never receive the service because it is too far from them and second, the centres may be overloaded, the work-load per employee may be so high that long queues develop and the organization is likely to be operating under strain. Insufficient time may be given to clients and the quality of the service is not as good as it might be. The lack of operational definitions and data prevents specific recommendations being made for the description of optimum areas for the administration of agricultural services, though the report does make some generalizations. These reinforce our subjective belief that the question of optimum areas is influenced by many factors, particularly population density, the transport system, the educational level of the population and the personnel available. Yet again experience with administrative structures now operating is used to suggest norms, for example, 'in countries with small farms [undefined] one extension worker [work undefined] can effectively [undefined] serve from 600 to 1000 farmers'. The caveat, concerning the question of optimum areas that was cited above, is added, and we are left to ponder the wisdom of the stark figures 600 to 1,000!

It is clear that there is a feeling abroad that decentralization, the establishment of local administrative centres and service districts, together with the delegation of responsibility to these units, is a critical element in improving the welfare of a country. In the last five years a group of geographers have in response to this feeling suggested that there is evidence of decentralization in developing areas in the spatial diffusion of the trappings of social organization. Further, they state that this spatial pattern of diffusion can be regarded as a move towards modernization.[8] Valuable as this work may be in providing objective descriptions of spatial diffusion the basic questions remain unanswered. For example, what are the relationships between the size of the units, the location of the centres and administrative boundaries, the amount of authority that is to be delegated and, on the other side of the equation, the effectiveness with which the system operates?

4 Reorganization and rationalization

The second type of study we will consider has tackled some of these questions in an objective scientific manner. In this group we can consider the set of studies which were undertaken as Research Reports prior to the formulation of the final report on the Royal Commission on Local Government in England.[9] We will not examine these reports in detail at this point – some of the details will be taken up in later chapters – rather we will draw attention to their merits as we try to get some idea of the approaches that are being used to evaluate the characteristics of administrative patterns.

The Royal Commission on Local Government in England, usually known as the Redcliffe–Maud report tells us that there were (in 1969) approximately 1,200 units of local government in England, not counting parish councils and the Greater London authorities. The upper tier in the two-tier system consists of county boroughs and county councils of which there were 124. The second tier was made up of 227 non-county boroughs, 449 urban districts and 410 rural districts, which are known collectively as county district councils. The delegation of responsibility among these units has evolved from legislation passed towards the end of the nineteenth century and today we find many anomalies of size and function. For example, the population of education authorities ranges from 30,000 in Canterbury to almost 2·5 million in Lancashire; and of housing authorities from less than 2,000 in Tintwistle rural district to over 1 million in Birmingham. There is also considerable variation in size: for example, Bootle occupies 3,330 acres (1,348 hectares), whereas the Devon authority covers 1,612,372 acres (652,366 hectares). It was claimed that the administrative structure did not fit the pattern of contemporary life, and the purpose of the Commission was to make suggestions for a new structure which would perform efficiently a set of functions concerned with health, safety and welfare; would allow citizens full participation both at a broad level and a national level, and would consider contemporary patterns of life with regard to residential, employment, retailing and recreational facilities. The Commission's terms of reference clarify its role:

> to consider the structure of Local Government in England, outside Greater London, in relation to its existing functions; and to make recommendations for authorities and boundaries, and for functions and their division, having regard to the size and character of areas in which these can be most effectively exercised and the need to sustain a viable system of democracy;[10]

Good reviews of the report are provided in Wiseman (1970, Chapters 2, 3 and 5) and Hanson and Walles (1970, Chapter 10).

The commissioners complemented the opinions and views offered in briefs and interviews by a set of ten research studies. Each dealt with a specific problem area. For example, what is the relationship between the quality and quantity of local government services and the social characteristics and the size of the service area? For this Research Report a preliminary study was conducted and it concluded that population size, as a measure of authorities' size, explained only a small proportion of the differences between local authorities' provision of services. They examined education, health, welfare and children's services. Therefore, the specific task of the study was to measure attributes of the services for each administrative area and also to measure social, economic and demographic elements in the areas. The next step was a statistical analysis of the relationships between the two sets of variables. This is perhaps the most significant feature of the majority of studies in this series. The problems under investigation were defined so as to be amenable to rigorous analysis using statistical techniques. Further details of the empirical findings will be given in Chapter 3, when we will focus attention on the size of service districts and the cost and quality of services. But as a general point, if we are to improve our knowledge of administration, then one approach is via careful data collection and analysis. We can thus try to overcome the criticisms made by March and Simon and by Teitz.

5 The urban environment

Let us now turn to the third study area, the urban environment. While it is generally agreed that urban studies is one of the most diverse fields of academic interest, when we search the literature for good examples of contemporary work on the administrative structures of cities we turn increasingly to the work of political scientists. Some of the purely spatial elements are handled by geographers, and the major financial aspects are treated by economists but it is the political scientist who has had a significant influence on the development of systematic studies of municipal policies and the variables which are related to particular policies. One of the most recent statements is provided by Hawkins (1971). He used data from many US cities to make generalizations about urban

Table 1.3   Relationships and variables in urban policy research

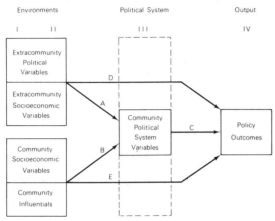

Note: Lines A, B, and C show environmental variables shaping system characteristics which in turn shape policy outcomes. Lines D and E show environmental variables directly affecting policy without sizable influence by system characteristics.

Examples of variables

1 Extracommunity variables	2 Community environmental variables	3 Urban political system variables	4 Urban policy outcome variables
1 Federal grants-in-aid	1 Racial, ethnic composition of population	1 Form of administration	1 Level of welfare expenditures
2 State laws on governmental structure	2 Economic base	2 Type of election	2 Level of taxation
3 National political party ties	3 Educational level	3 Type of election district	3 Level of general expenditures
4 State of national economy	4 Density of population	4 Council decision-making processes	4 Urban renewal program completions
5 Absentee ownership of local corporations	5 Population growth rate	5 Degree of governmental fragmentation	5 Fluoridated water supplies
6 Regional political values and culture	6 Activities of non-governmental elites	6 Attitudes of officeholders	6 Segregated School systems

(*Hawkins, 1971, 15*)

policy formulation. This approach is summarized in Table 1.3. Boaden (1971) uses the same approach when analysing data from County Boroughs in England and Wales on a variety of public services including education, personal social services, police, fire and libraries.

While it is true that much work must still be done on the direction, force and time lags between the sets of variables and policies, and also on the construction of logical hypothetical relationships, a good start has been made by Hawkins, Boaden and their fellow workers[11] in unravelling the complexities of administration in urban areas.

6   Distribution and utilization

The fourth area of interest is concerned with studies which examine the movements of goods on service between supply and demand points. The studies which focus primarily on the distributional attributes of administration have been treated in greatest depth, from a theoretical standpoint, within the field of operations research, and a selection of this material will be discussed in Chapters 4 and 5. Much of the work which has been developed in operations research on the distribution of commodities from origins to destinations has been done in the last five years. Though certain problems within the field of administration, such as the determination of a single location with maximum accessibility to a set of other points, have attracted the attention of mathematicians since the seventeenth century it is only recently that methods for solving fairly complex location problems have been discovered.[12] As I have already mentioned in this chapter the sort of location problems which can be tackled by operations research methods are most commonly those where origins and destinations have known locations, transportation costs are readily available and where the demand of the destinations and the supply of the origins are also known. With data for these elements in the service system is it possible to determine the cheapest way of satisfying the demand or the cheapest place to locate collection or distribution depots. It should be noted that thus far we have not considered variation of supply and demand over time or space. Nor have we considered the problems caused by congestion to movement between origins and destinations. These and other details will be examined in later chapters. Excellent summaries of the operations research approach to distribution planning is provided by Eilon et al. (1971) and Drake et al. (1972). We should note that this approach allows us to determine optimum allocations or locations, but the definition of optimum is usually in distance or transportation-cost terms. Optimum does not refer to satisfaction in its general and much wider context. This is a very difficult concept to define and measure and thus far has escaped successful empirical analysis though theoretical statements are available. The most famous is that of Vilfredo Pareto, the early twentieth-century Italian social thinker. Pareto's concept of optimality has been defined as the allocation of goods and services among a set of people in such a way that any shift in distribution would not improve distribution. This is a utopian theoretical ideal which may represent a goal for planners, politicians and the public but so far seems to defy empirical measurement.

Let us now turn to the work which has its roots in psychology and which focuses upon the utilization of facilities. Studies in this field are usually termed behavioural and their main purpose is to examine patterns of behaviour and search for underlying regularities. A recent study by Ross (1972) is a good example of this approach. He examined the patronage patterns of consumers choosing among alternative destinations. A scale of the relative attractiveness of the sites was derived from observed behaviour. By relating this scale to the sites' other attributes it is possible to determine the relative importance of certain attributes as perceived by the consumers. It follows therefore that the locational attribute of a facility, that is its accessibility to clients in distance terms, is only part of the problem of defining attractiveness for an individual client. He may patronize a facility which is not the one nearest him because he considers all its attributes, taken together, to be more attractive. He is setting the effort of travelling an extra distance against the greater satisfaction to be gained at the farther location. Work in this field, evaluating, measuring and defining precise scales for the attractiveness of sites, has just started to appear in the literature on location theory.[13] Clearly it is relevant to the study of service areas when not infrequently we have to consider the utilization patterns of public facilities.[14] While it is true that a facility in the private sector, such as a grocery store, will go out of business if utilization drops below a certain level, there is no such market mechanism controlling the inability of a public facility, such as a library, at a particular location. Yet obviously we must be concerned with utilization patterns if we are to choose sites from among a set of possible locations with the objective of giving as good service as possible to as many people as possible, within a fixed budget constraint. The non-spatial attributes of a facility are often closely linked to the degree of utilization of the facility and they must be incorporated into the more traditional models in geography which have been used to explain utilization. The latter have been developed primarily from the distance–decay hypothesis of human interaction.[15] This hypothesis suggests that distance is the critical variable in utilization and the models are not primarily concerned with patterns of choice behaviour.

Variables concerning origins, that is the clients, should also be considered in models which tell us something about the utilization rates of public facilities, such as hospitals, clinics, welfare offices, libraries and schools.

7 Conclusions

In the chapters which follow, we will examine in detail some of the major features of administrative areas, we should note here that essentially we are concerned with *de jure* units. These differ from *de facto* spatial units which are without formal boundaries. The examples of these units are given by Soja (1971): 'home areas, networks of interaction, domains, spheres of influence, hinterlands, buffer zones, no-man's land, cultural homelands, regions, neighborhoods, gang "turfs", and ghettos.' The *de facto* units play a significant role in human organization and these units often mesh together into formal units. Where there is a discrepancy between *de jure* and *de facto* boundaries we have the site of potential boundary conflict. Reorganization of administrative areas in developed or developing countries and in urban areas can give rise to conflict situations where closely knit non-formal units have been divided among two or more administrative areas. While the emphasis in this book will be upon manipulating specific variables such as, distance, costs, utilization rates and quantity of service which can be measured fairly readily, we should not overlook some of the more intangible variables which measure the strength of local ties and sentiment.

After this broad summary of the topic the next chapter will concentrate upon procedures for evaluating the spatial attributes of administrative areas.

Notes on further reading*

The best introduction to the field of spatial analysis of human organization is provided by Abler, Adams and Gould (1971). This book is rich in empirical examples and provides good clear statements on measurement problems, data and techniques.

Territoriality and its influence on social patterns is discussed in Soja (1971).

Details of quantitative techniques used for locating facilities are provided in the advanced text of Eilon *et al.* (1971). This book assumes a fairly high-level knowledge of mathematical concepts.

A good summary of empirical public sector location problems in New York is given in Drake *et al.* (1972).

One of the most significant recent publications by political scientists on the urban milieu is provided by Lineberry and Sharkansky (1971).

* A small selection of references for further reading will be included at the end of each chapter. Full details for each reference are provided in the bibliography.

Notes

1 Soja (1971); Massam (1972b); *Ad hoc* Committee (1965).
2 For a broad summary of methods of analysing spatial organization see Abler, Adams and Gould (1971).
3 This point is taken up by Pounds (1963).
4 Teitz (1968, 35–51).
5 Berry and Horton (1970); Yeates and Garner (1971); Carter (1972).

6 A first-class review of distribution systems is provided in Eilon, Watson-Gandy and Christofields (1971).

7 The average distance is often called the 'expected distance'; this is examined in Fairthorne (1965), and in Christofides and Eilon (1969, 437–443).

8 Some of this work will be examined in Chapter 7. This type of study is well exemplified by Witthuhn (1968); Riddell (1969); Hirst (1971, 90–98).

9 See also Johnson (1970, 17–21).

10 Royal Commission (1969, Vol. I).

11 See Lineberry and Sharkansky (1971).

12 Eilon *et al. op cit.*, (Chapter I).

13 Some of the most significant contributions have come from Rushton. See, for example, Rushton (1969, 391–400).

14 The utilization of facilities has also been treated in Isard (1960, 528).

15 A broad summary of distance–decay models in geography is given in Olsson (1965).

2 The spatial form of administrative areas

'Every political system is prominently if not
pre-eminently characterized by space'[1]

1 Introduction

For many years researchers have been concerned with the planar shape
of geographical distributions, and Whittington *et al.* (1972) have argued
that shape studies form the basis not only for classification but also for
an understanding of process. Proof of this belief is to be found in a large
body of literature in human geography which is devoted to describing
the geometrical properties of the distribution patterns of man and his
activities. From these geometrical properties we try to discover how
the particular spatial distribution came into existence and we also hope
to gain information on the way the functional attributes vary as we alter
the configuration of the distribution. For example, if we redefine boundaries for fire protection units what will be the precise effect on the overall
level of fire protection in the unit? The philosophical underpinings of
the shape–process argument have been examined by Harvey (1969) and
it is clear that there is not a one-to-one correspondence between process
and geometrical pattern: several different processes may cause the same
pattern and a particular pattern may be generated by more than one
process. The relationship between shape and metabolic activity is well
documented in biological literature (see MacMahon, 1973). However,
if we are to improve our understanding of the principles of the spatial
organization of administrative areas over space and time we need more
than qualitative descriptions of their form. For this reason we will examine a series of shape measures, both from theoretical and practical
standpoints. We will start by describing shape measures which have
been applied to administrative areas, and in a later section we will
show how certain of these measures can be used to evaluate the spatial
efficiency of a service district.

In this chapter we often refer to *pattern* and *shape*, and at the outset
we should draw the distinction between them. Hudson and Fowler
(no date) state that 'Formal analysis of pattern is hampered by a lack of
precision in its operational definitions. Pattern should not be confused
with shape as they each represent geometrical or geographical properties.'

These two authors suggest that any closed curve has a shape, and a
collection of points has a pattern. An administrative area or a service
district therefore has shape because its boundary is a closed curve which
circumscribes a two-dimensional surface. The area also has a pattern if it
encloses a distribution of one-dimensional objects. Points circumscribed

14

by a boundary can be considered, as in geometry, as being one-dimensional. Thus, the shape of an administrative area has two dimensions; to consider a pattern of points, such as origins (clients) and destinations (libraries) is to deal with one-dimensional objects whose pattern can be operationally determined using the distance or spacing of the objects with respect to one another. Therefore, pattern and shape can be separated by the relevant dimensions of the objects being studied. Conceptually shape and pattern are not related to the size of the area; I will discuss the size attribute of administrative areas in a later chapter. Here we will use shape and pattern measures in an attempt to capture the essential spatial properties of administrative areas and to provide descriptive evaluations of alternate configurations.

Most of the studies which derive geometrical measures of administrative areas assume that the space under examination is Euclidean and has the properties that parallel lines never meet, the shortest distance between two points is a straight line and that Pythagoras' theorem is appropriate for calculating the distance between points.[2] The assumption that real-world space can be treated as Euclidean has been criticized by several workers. In their view earth-space is made up of a surface of varying friction and the separation of points and the effort in moving from one to another is related to the frictional force of the intervening space. Points may be joined by a fast super-highway or a dirt track, and the straight line distance does not truly reflect the time, effort or cost of moving from place to place. Rectangular road patterns, traffic congestion and mode of transport all serve to produce earth-spaces of varying frictional qualities and sets of origins and destinations of varying degrees of accessibility.[3] Thus when we define administrative areas as having a certain shape, based upon Euclidean space assumptions, we should note the nature of the surfaces upon which the area is defined. In some recent studies of the shape of areas real-time or cost measures between origins and destinations have been used. However, as it is very rare to find that cost or time measures are not directly related to distances, the solutions to location problems which minimize distance are very close to ones that minimize cost or time. This is a significant point in the analysis of the spatial efficiency of an administrative area as will be shown later in this chapter.

We should also remember that there are two distinct types of administrative areas. The first contains a distribution system with a characteristic transportation network. In some ways this is like the outline of a leaf with the veins making the linkages within the boundary. The second contains pieces of space which may be areally differentiated. For example, the clan territories Brookfield (1963) has identified for the Chimbu in the New Guinea Highlands lie at right-angles to the series of land classes and soil types thus ensuring that each clan has a similar distribution of the different terrain types. In most of the shape measures which have been derived little attempt has been made to consider the internal organization of the area under examination. The distinction between the two types of area is rarely brought out.

In chronological order the most significant reviews of shape measures in geography are provided by Bunge (1962), Blair and Biss (1967), Haggett and Chorley (1969), Boots (1970) and Whittington et al. (1972). Until recently there had been little theoretical work on the understanding of the properties of different sorts of shape measures. This is surprising since there is a large body of theoretical and empirical literature which is concerned with point-patterns, and the method of comparing real-world point-patterns with patterns generated according to probabilistic or deterministic rules is well established. However, when we consider patterns of areas there is a dearth of material. Goodchild (1972b) has noted this fact and in his paper he examined a variety of probabilistic partitioning processes and their statistical properties. The areas under examination can be considered the result of spatial partitioning processes. Pielou (1969) has investigated procedures for describing such patterns which she calls two-phase mosaics. These are maps of the spatial clumping of plant species, and the two phases refer to the presence or absence of the species. Both Goodchild and Pielou draw attention to the fact that the study of the spatial characteristics of distributions is in its early stages. More work is needed before we have a body of knowledge about shape measures which is comparable to that which exists for point patterns.

We will examine measures which are most useful for describing areas under two headings. The first, *shape measures on homogeneous surfaces* does not take into account areal distributions within the boundary. The areas are considered to be homogeneous and it is the spatial configuration of the unit as defined by its boundary which is described. The second, *shape measures on non-homogeneous surfaces* attempts to take into account distributions within the area, and the indices are therefore more usefully applied to units which display a high degree of internal variance.

2   Shape measures on homogeneous surfaces

One of the most interesting findings that the theoretical work offers us concerns the measure called the *contact number* (CN). This is defined as the number of neighbours touching each area. Figure 2.1 illustrates it. We can calculate the CN for each area and also derive a summary statistic, the mean CN, for a set of areas.

Several workers have calculated the mean CN for sets of areas in different parts of the world. Haggett (1965) studies a sample of *municipos* in Brazil. The number of contacts varied from two to fourteen, though approximately 30 out of the sample of 100 had 6 neighbours. The mean was 5·71. Pedersen (1967) extended this work to administrative communes in Jutland and Fyn in Denmark. He examined 553 communes and found the mean CN to be 5·83. Similar work in Southern Ontario, Canada by

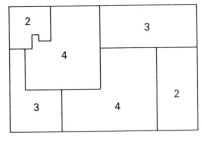

Figure 2.1 The contact number 2, 3, etc., are the CNs for each area, the mean CN is

$$\frac{2 + 3 + 4 + 4 + 2 + 3}{6} = 3$$

Massam (1970) revealed a mean CN of 5·85 for a set of 26 areas used by the Ontario Hydro-electric Power Commission. Boots (1970) provides a table of different types of administrative areas with their respective CNs, part of this is reproduced in table 2.1.

Table 2.1 The contact number of administrative patterns

	Administrative Patterns	Data	Mean CN
1	United States: States	1969	6·00
2	Tennessee: counties	1969	5·57
3	Pennsylvania: counties	1969	5·66
4	Montana: counties	1969	5·50
5	France: departments	1965	5·81
6	France: ecclesiastical parishes	1789	5·60
7	France: ecclesiastical parishes	1802	5·82
8	France: ecclesiastical parishes	1820	5·79
9	France: ecclesiastical parishes	1961	5·76
10	Poland: eastern provinces	1946	5·37
11	India: southern states	1941	5·48
12	New South Wales, Australia: counties	1912	5·35
13	USA: Metropolitan regions	1929	5·39
14	USA: Federal Reserve Districts and branches	1954	5·40
15	Cornwall, England: civil parishes	1961	5·64
16	Gloucestershire, England: civil parishes	1961	5·74
17	Wiltshire, England: civil parishes	1961	6·00
18	Dorset, England: civil parishes	1961	5·28

(*After Boots, 1970*)

Empirical studies suggest a spatial regularity. Proof of this is the fact of that values converge towards a CN of six. This has led to speculation about hexagonal forms for administrative areas; however, the theoretical work of Woldenburg (1970) and Goodchild (1972*b*) shows us 'that irrespective of the generating process, the mean CN must be close to six, provided that the greater number of vertices are formed at the junction of three areas' (Goodchild 1972*b*). This conclusion stems from one of Euler's theorems which relates counts of the number of edges, (E) vertices (V) and areas (A) in the equation $A - E + V = 1$.

Goodchild (1972*b*) has pointed out the major problems concerning

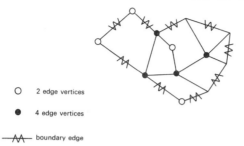

○   2 edge vertices

●   4 edge vertices

—AA— boundary edge

Figure 2.2   Problems in counting edges and vertices (*After Goodchild, 1972b*)

the counting of edges and vertices. These are summarized in figure 2.2. He shows that if four-edge contacts are fairly rare, then as the number of areas increases the mean CN approaches six. This is a topological attribute of the pattern, and it is independent of any particular principles of spatial organization. It is therefore clear that if we are to make use of pattern measures for descriptive purposes then we must first fully understand the properties of the measure we are using.

Compactness is the spatial property that has attracted the greatest attention, and this can be considered intuitively as the spatial distribution of an area around a central point. It can be argued that a circle represents the shape with maximum compactness. It also has the minimum length of boundary enclosing the maximum sized area. Haggett (1965) has proposed a shape index (S) which is calculated from the equation $S = 1.27A/l^2$, where A is the area and l is the length of the long axis. The two parameters are measured in compatible units and in the equation they cancel thus making S a dimensionless number. This is in line with our earlier comment that pattern measures are independent of scale. If $S = 1.0$ the area is a circle and as the shape becomes elongated S tends towards zero; an equilateral triangle is 0.42, a square is 0.64 and a regular hexagon is 0.83. Boots (1970) found that the mean value of S for patterns 15, 16, 17, and 18 in table 2.1 are 0.46, 0.50, 0.43, and 0.49 and the triangular form occurs most frequently. We can also argue that a circular shape for an administrative area has particular advantages, because of its high degree of compactness. Boundary contacts are minimized and thus potential conflict situations may be restricted, but more important it can be shown that a circle represents the shape within which the distance between the centre and a random point or between two random points is smaller than for any other shape. The implication is clear: transportation costs within a circular area are less than within an area of other shape (*ceteris paribus*).

These attempts to provide an objective classification for the form of administrative areas must be seen in historical perspective. The values *per se* tell us little about the generative processes, but they do allow us to classify different areas and later in this chapter we will explain how we attempt to relate shape to the other attributes of an area.

Blair and Biss (1967) were probably the first to develop a sophisticated procedure for calculating the compactness of shapes. They used the formula

$$C = \frac{D}{\sqrt{2\pi \int_A r^2 \, \mathrm{dxdy}}}$$

where C is the coefficient of compactness, D is the area of the shape under examination r is the distance of an infinitely small rectangle of length dx and breadth dy from the centroid (the centre of gravity) of the area. It is virtually impossible to calculate C without the use of a computer, though as Blair and Biss point out if an electronic computer is available the calculation is trivial. The C index takes on a value of 1·000 when the shape is circular, a regular hexagon is 0·996, a square 0·977 and an equilateral triangle 0·909. A rectangular shape with a length 7·5 times the breath has a C value of approximately 0·500. Blair and Biss have classified parishes, the lowest units in the spatial political hierarchy in Britain, in Cheshire, Somerset, Wiltshire and Lincolnshire using the C index. The results are summarized in table 2.2. The shapes of parishes reflect the

Table. 2.2   Classification of selected parishes using C index

Parish classification		C Index		
		max.	min.	mean
Cheshire	Regular and compact	0·961	0·677	0·873
Somerset	Irregular	0·968	0·702	0·859
Wiltshire	Elongated irregular	0·951	0·668	0·775
Lincolnshire	Elongated uncompact	0·815	0·248	0·593

(*After Blair and Biss, 1967*)

interplay of many factors and Mitchell (1954) and Stamp (1964) have drawn attention to the main factors. The quotation from Mitchell (1963, 114–115) is included to add depth to our argument:

> The shapes as well as the sizes of the parishes are illuminating. Where there is little variation in soil the parishes tend to be approximately round or square more or less symmetrically disposed about the village. Most of the parishes of High Norfolk and Suffolk are like this. But where the quality of the land is variable, the parishes boundaries tend to be arranged so that each village has a share of the different soils. Where the structure is a simple tilt or fold and different rocks outcrop in linear bands, the parishes are often a series of long narrow rectangles cutting across the outcrops. The parishes of Lincoln Edge show this arrangement, two great groups meet along the crest. Each parish of the eastern group runs from crest to fenland, including within its boundaries a stretch of downland for pasture, of arable along the dip slope and of fen for meadow in the valley of the Witham; each parish of the western group lies half upon the downland, half in the Trent valley. The villages of both series lie on the spring line halfway along the long axis of the parishes. The parishes

of the chalklands of eastern Cambridgeshire show a similar arrangement. In narrow river valleys the parishes tend to be arranged transversely across the valleys; in the upper and narrower parts running right across the valley, in the lower and wider part in a double series each occupying one side of the valley, the river itself forming a common boundary along one of the short sides of the parish rectangle. This arrangement too gives an economic variety of land; upland pastures and water meadows with well-drained gentle slopes between for arable. In areas where one patch of soil is particularly desirable, the parish boundaries often make peculiar patterns so that each may have a share. On Cambridgeshire chalk five villages share an outlying patch of Fenland particularly valued no doubt for its hay meadows and summer pastures as well as its reeds and rushes, turf, fish and water fowl. Where villagers could not, satisfy their needs in the immediate area, they sometimes acquired rights to pasture beasts, cut wood, evaporate salt, or mine iron, for example, in an outlying area. Sometimes several villages each some distance away parcelled out among them an area that possessed a valuable local resource. The existence until very lately of small areas detached from the rest of the parish mark these old right of common, in nearby, but not ajacent, areas.

With respect to changes of shape over time Massam and Goodchild (1971) have examined the compactness of a set of administrative areas in Ontario over the period 1948 to 1967. It was found that at the aggregate level – that is, using mean values for each year – the degree of spatial compactness has increased over time. A shape measure which was derived from the moment of inertia of a body was used in this study, and it is very similar to the one derived by Blair and Biss. It originated in the field of pure mechanics and serves as a useful measure of dispersion of matter around a point.[4] The moment of inertia (I_x) for any point x in an area is defined as the sum over the area of each minute segment of area multiplied by the square of the distance separating it from the point x. Symbolically we can define this

$$I_x = \int_a r^2 \, da$$

The index I_x allows us to calculate the degree of compactness of an area and also to measure the centrality of a point within the area. For these reasons it is particularly useful when describing spatial units which are homogeneous with respect to the spatial distribution of demand points and which are served by a single depot within the unit. The provision of services in rural districts provides a good example of an administrative pattern which can usefully be examined using this index.

Let us call the shape measure S_I and we can define this as follows,

$$S_I = A^2 / 2\pi I_a$$

where A is area of the unit under examination and I_a is the moment of inertia of the unit around its centre of gravity. Values for S_I vary from $1 \cdot 0$ for a circle with the distribution point at the centre of gravity to values which approach zero as the shape becomes elongated. It should be noted that this type of measure is versatile and it can be applied to areas in which it is assumed that the demand is evenly distributed *or* to areas in which demand is localized at a set of discrete point locations. Where demand is assumed to be homogeneous we calculate I_a by subdividing the area into an exhaustive set of mutually exlusive triangles,[5] using the vertices of the area as the vertices of the triangles. Details for calculating the index are provided in Massam and Goodchild (1971).

The shape index S_I has been calculated for a set of administrative areas in Ontario and values range from 0·50 to 0·95. A later chapter will deal with the detailed empirical findings of this particular study. An independent presentation of this index has been given by Whittington, Beavon and Mabin (1972), and they have used it to evaluate the level of spatial compactness of 38 magisterial districts in South Africa in 1951, 1960 and 1970. They found that in the 1951 South African sample 52 per cent of the coefficients of compactness lie below the value for a triangle. The value for a regular triangle is 0·83.[6] The implementation of the policy of apartheid made separate black and white magisterial districts necessary and Whittington *et al.* (1972, 35) suggest that,

> The use of the coefficient of compactness demonstrates that the South African network of administrative units constituted by the magisterial districts is far from the ideal form associated with the principle of least effort. Furthermore, recent trends in the creation of magisterial districts [due to the apartheid policy] are causing it to move even further from the ideal.

Our definitions of ideal in this section are largely based upon considerations of spatial compactness, political expendiency is not considered, though frequently this is the dominating force in spatial organization.

We will close this section with a brief discussion of two indices presented by Boots (1972) to evaluate the regularity of the shape of cellular nets. He noted that such nets occur widely under a great variety of conditions yet 'All such patterns [froth; liquids: frog's eggs: political units] have one common unifying property; their raison d'être. They all have their origin in processes which involve the sub-division of a finite space.' Boots claims that any cellular net pattern is dependent upon geometric and non-geometric features and thus if we can isolate the influence of geometry then we can possibly evaluate the influence of other forces. This is a relatively unexplored topic.

In order to classify shapes according to regularity Boots derived two indices, the Edge Length Variance (*ELV*) and the Mean Percent Angular Distortion (*MPAD*). They are defined below:

$$ELV = \sum_{i=1}^{n} (x_i - \bar{x})^2/n$$

where n is the number of edges, x_i is the length of the ith edge and $\bar{x}$ is the mean length of the n edges. If the shape is a regular polygon the variance is zero. The second index considers the internal angles of the polygon.

$$MPAD = \sum_{i=1}^{n} \left(\frac{|\theta_n - \theta_i|}{\theta_n} \times 100 \right) / n$$

where n is the number of sides of the polygon, θ_i is the value in degrees of the ith internal angle. θ_n is the value for a regular polygon of n sides where θ_n is given by $(2n - 4)$ right angles. If $MPAD$ is zero the shape is a regular polygon and as the value tends to 100 so the shape approaches a straight line.

3   Shape measures on non-homogeneous surfaces

The indices discussed in the last section were primarily concerned with evaluating the level of compactness of a service district and the space in question was assumed to be homogeneous. Let us now turn to the problem of evaluating the compactness of a piece of space which is non-homogeneous. We can visualize this as a population density map as shown in figure 2.3.

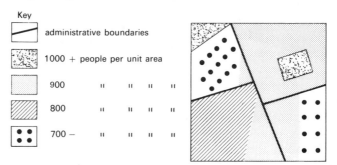

Figure 2.3   Non-homogeneous areas

In order to incorporate the variation in density into our calculations we usually convert the surface into a set of points.[7] These could be regularly distributed over the study area or existing nodes of population concentration can be used. Each point has a unique location and it is weighted according to the value it represents for the part of the surface it summarizes. We are using a spatial sampling procedure. Figure 2.4 illustrates the conversion of non-homogeneous surface into a set of weighted points.

Once we have converted our data to type B in figure 2.3 we can apply a set of procedures for describing the scatter of the points around a reference point in order to evaluate the level of compactness of non-homogeneous surfaces. We can argue that maximum compactness is achieved

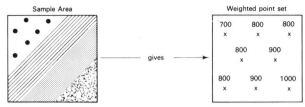

Figure 2.4 Derivation of a set of weighted points

when there is a concentration of values in a single point. Three different point sets are shown in figure 2.5, the two extremes are readily classified, patterns of the B-type require an objective procedure.

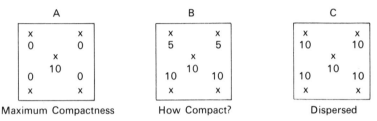

Figure 2.5 Compactness problem

The compactness of a weighted point-set can be calculated as follows:

1 Calculate the centre of gravity of the distribution, this is our reference point. The procedure for calculating the co-ordinates of the centre of gravity of a weighted point set is shown on figure 2.6. We locate the points within a co-ordinate system and measure the distances a, b, etc. The point X_{CG}, Y_{CG} is now marked on the original map.

2 Measure the distance between each weighted point and (X_{CG}, Y_{CG}).

3 Define measure of compactness as $MC = \sum_{i=1}^{n} d_{ij} m_i$ where d_{ij} is the distance between the ith point and j, where j is (X_{CG}, Y_{CG}), m_i is the weight of the ith point and there are n points.

The lower the value of MC the greater the level of compactness of the weighted point set. However, in order to attach more meaning to this index we need to standardize it and use it to measure the spatial efficiency of the scatter of points. This next step assumes that the points are 'serviced' by a central point, we are concerned with evaluating the locational efficiency of this service point vis-à-vis the demand points. We next calculate the centre of gravity of the distribution of points for area B in figure 2.7 using the method already described. The moment of inertia of the points around the centre of gravity (M_G) can be calculated using the same procedure that was used to calculate M_B.

It should be noted that when we calculate M_B or M_G we multiply

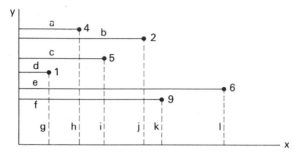

Figure 2.6 Calculation of centre of gravity of a set of points. The *X* co-ordinate of the centre of gravity is given by:

$$X_{CG} = \frac{(4.a) + (2.b) + (5.c) + (1.d) + (6.e) + (9.f)}{4 + 2 + 5 + 1 + 6 + 9}$$

the *Y* co-ordinate is:

and　$$Y_{CG} = \frac{(1.g) + (4.h) + (5.i) + (2.j) + (9.k) + (6.l)}{1 + 4 + 5 + 2 + 9 + 6}$$

the weight of the point by the *square of the distance*, therefore points which are twice as far from the centre carry a weight of four times and those three times as far carry a weight of nine times. We are biasing our measure by weighting very heavily those points which are farthest from the centre. A method has recently been found of calculating the point within the set of points which minimizes the linear distance to all points. This is the point of minimum aggregate travel (*MAT*). The technique for determining this point is complex and until now most students have used the location which minimizes the square of the distance (this is the centre of gravity). The point of *MAT* is found on a trial and error basis. However, the solution which results is also unique though clearly it may be different from the centre of gravity. Mathematical proof that the point of *MAT* is at a unique location is given by Haley (1963) and it is discussed in detail by Eilon *et al.* (1971, 36–110) in their work on choosing depot locations.

Finally we should note that certain spatial configurations of demand the use of the centre of gravity as the location for the service centre will not be a good choice to maximize accessibility. This problem has been examined by Vergin and Rogers (1967) and Watson-Gandy (1972) but further work is needed before we can evaluate the precise disadvantages of using the centre of gravity.

4　Spatial efficiency measures

Using the concept Moment of Inertia (*M*) we can define a measure of spatial efficiency of the location of an administrative centre with respect

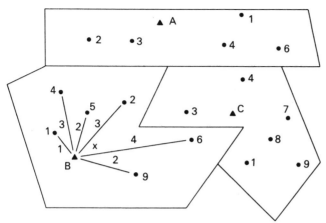

Figure 2.7 A theoretical set of three administrative units:
▲A Administrative centres; ·6 Points represent location and
number of consumers; x Centre of gravity of administrative unit *B*

to the distribution of consumers in the administrative area. Figure 2.7
shows an administrative system with a set of points representing the consumers and the location of the centre. The boundaries are also shown.
For each area we can calculate *M*, the distance are straight-line distances.
Using

$$M = \sum_{i=1}^{n} d_{ij}^2 m_i$$

as the general formula for calculating the Moment of Inertia, we can
apply this to area *B*.

$$M_B = \sum_{i=1}^{6} d_{ij}^2 m_i$$

$$M_B = (1 \times 1^2) + (4 \times 3^2) + (5 \times 2^2) + (2 \times 3^2) + (6 \times 4^2) + (9 \times 2^2)$$

$$M_B = 207 \text{ units}$$

We can now define an index of spatial efficiency (E) as $E = \dfrac{M_G}{M_B}$;
if this is equal to 1·0 then the actual administrative centre is at the centre
of gravity. As the value of *E* becomes smaller the distance between the
actual centre and the theoretically located centre increases. We assume
that the latter centre is at the centre of gravity of the distribution of
consumers.

An empirical study of the spatial efficiency at eight administrative
agencies in Ontario has been undertaken by Massam and Burghardt
(1968) using the *E* index defined above. Each agency divides the province
into administrative units and each unit is served from a regional centre.
Table 2.3 summarizes the efficiency incides for each agency. The mean

value of E for each agency is shown and it appears that the Ontario
Hospital Services Commission has the highest level of spatial efficiency,
and the Ontario Hydro-electric Commission the lowest value. The E
index provides a standard which can be used as a starting-point for further
analysis of the spatial structure of administration. If we examine the
variation of E for each area and each agency we can evaluate the spatial
efficiency values to specific locations and for the Ontario agencies answer
questions such as, what will be the loss in spatial efficiency due to locating
centres away from the US–Canada border, away from Ottawa, the
Federal capital, near major route intersections, or in a small centre which
has lower office rents than the large cities.

Table 2.3 Indices of spatial efficiency – mean E index

1	Department of Economics and Development	0·796
2	Department of Education	0·760
3	Department of Highways	0·719
4	Ontario Hydro-electric Commission	0·679
5	Ontario Hospital Service Commission	0·860
6	Ontario Provincial Police	0·732
7	Department of Public Welfare	0·717
8	Department of Transport	0·776

The E index was calculated using a weighted point-set to describe
the distribution of consumers in Ontario but we can also calculate E
using a homogeneous distribution because the two terms M_G and M_B
can be determined for shapes using the method that was described earlier
in this chapter. This latter procedure has been used to measure the spatial
efficiency of school locations with respect to their catchment areas on the
Island of Montréal. The S_I index was also calculated to evaluate the level
of compactness of each school district. The values for S_I range from 0·23
to 0·96, the mean value is 0·73 and the standard deviation is 0·18. This
suggests that on average the school districts are fairly compact with very
little variation among them. With respect to the E index, the values have
a similar range and the mean is 0·76 again suggesting that the aggregate
spatial efficiency of school locations with respect to school district boundaries is quite high. A further attribute of the spatial structure was calculated for each district, that is the distance between the school and the centre
of gravity in the district. The average distance for the elementary school
system is approximately 0·5 miles (0·8 km), and the comparable value
for the high school system is 0·9 miles (1·44 km). These distances support
the notion that the schools on average are quite well located with respect
to their catchment areas.

Now that we have objective shape measures the next task is to search
for relationships between shape and function. Hampson (1971) has
tackled this problem with respect to the influence of territorial shape
on municipal expenditures for country boroughs in England and Wales.
He attempted to answer the question: does the shape of a city have any

influence on *per capita* municipal expenditures? He argued that his work had relevance for the city planner because, 'the relative importance of city-shape in the mind of the planner depends on the magnitude of the financial savings which circularity could import to the city (with no loss in quality of service).' He used Gibbs' (1970) index of circularity (M_C) to measure the shape of county boroughs. This index is defined below:

$$M_C = 100 \, A/(\pi) \, (D/2)^2$$

where A is the area of the borough and D is the distance between the two most distant points on the boundary of the borough. When $M_C = 100$ the shape is a circle and as M_C tends towards zero the degree of elongation increases. This index is similar to the S measure defined by Haggett and discussed earlier. Data for nine categories of municipal expenditures for 60 county boroughs from the set of 83 which existed in 1961 were used. Table 2.4 summarises the expenditure groups.

Table 2.4 Municipal expenditures

1	Highways, bridges, footpaths	Approximately 6% of municipal expenditures
2	Public health	10%
3	Sewage disposal	2·5%
4	House and trade refuse collection	2·5%
5	Parks, pleasure grounds and open spaces	2·5%
6	Police protection	6·5%
7	Fire protection	2%
8	Education	48%
9	Total expenditures	100%

The eight services account for approximately 80 per cent of total municipal expenditures.

Hampson hypothesized that there should be a negative relationship between circularity and expenditure, with the exception of expenditure on parks, pleasure grounds and open spaces. The empirical results suggested that M_C is only significantly related to municipal expenditure groups 5 and 8. A positive relationship was found in the case of education suggesting that the greater the circularity of the borough the higher the costs, whereas a negative relationship was found for expenditure on parks, pleasure grounds and open spaces. In this work no specific account was taken of the different functions of the cities, though Hampson did draw attention to possible causes for the direction of the relationships, for example, the fact that resort cities tend to have very high park expenditures and have elongated forms. It could also be argued that the older industrial centres tend to be more spatially compact, that environmental conditions are lower than normal and thus expenditure on education is greater. Clearly these sorts of variables need to be incorporated into our tests of the relationship between shape and expenditure patterns before we can make specific recommendations for modifying the form of service districts.

Finally, we should stress that shape and spatial efficiency indices can only be used as a starting-point for the analysis of service districts. To understand spatial organization more completely we have to examine the exchange of the service from the centres to the consumers. Thus for the services such as hospital facilities or school districts, which demand physical movement of people or goods, the spatial form of the unit strongly influences its efficiency. However, where messages are sent by mail or telephone we are operating in spaces which cannot be measured in traditional ways, and the indices so far discussed are often useless. In such services, for example the distribution of welfare cheques, the primary concern is to delimit areas with respect to the number of cheques to be distributed, so that efficiency can be maximized at the administrative centre. Little attention need be paid to the location of the recipients. The problem would be quite different if we were trying to establish in cities welfare centres which offered counselling. In this case we would have to consider the location of clients, we would be searching for locations that minimized their travelling. This problem in its general form is the *Allocation–Location Problem*,[8] and it will be examined in detail in a later chapter.

Notes on further reading

Good reviews of shape measures are given in Bunge (1962), Haggett (1965) and Haggett and Chorley (1969). The papers by Blair and Biss (1967), Whittington (1972) and Massam and Goodchild (1971) provide technical details for calculation of shape indices.

An examination of the processes which generate spatial patterns is well presented by Goodchild (1972b). Boots (1972) also considers this aspect in his PhD thesis, and he tests his idea using parish data from selected areas in Britain. A rigorous treatment of the mathematics of the processes is offered in Pielou (1969).

A useful overview of a wide variety of case studies which used shape measures is provided by Boots (1970).

Notes

1 *Ad hoc* committee (1965, 31).

2 For a discussion of other sorts of geometries see Sawyer (1955, Chapter 6).

3 With respect to connectivity of points in urban areas see Fairthorne (1965) and Smeed (1964).

4 For the background information on moment of inertia and centre of gravity see Ramsay (1959) or Temperley (1953, 30).

5 We could sub-divide the area into other shapes such as squares or rectangles; Whittington *et al.* (1972) outlines a procedure using rectangles.

6 The coefficient of compactness for a regular hexagon is 0·99 and for a square 0·95.

7 A discussion on point sets is given in Haggett and Chorley (1969).

8 There is a large body of literature on this topic. Summaries are provided in Scott (1971a).

3   The size of administrative units

1 Introduction

In the last chapter we concentrated upon the spatial form of administrative units and we noted that the pattern indices we used were independent of the size of the area under examination. However, empirical observation of patterns of areas shows us clearly that there are considerable variations in the size of areas. In this chapter we will discuss this attribute and consider how size affects the functioning of an area. Some of the ideas expressed here will be developed in later chapters, particularly when we discuss optimal administrative units, changes over time and interaction within and between units.

The artificial divisions which we use in this book when examining the major elements of administrative areas should be seen within the total framework of administration. The systemic nature of the subject-matter is self-evident, yet for analytical purposes we usually deal with parts of the total system. The system approach to analysing spatial organization is presented in Eliot-Hurst (1972). The advantages of this procedure consist in the relative ease with which we can measure the variables and determine relationships for a small group of interactions. Its disadvantages however are great. We are examining one part in isolation and if we are to draw conclusions from our partial analysis then we need to know how this section relates to the total system. The problems of partial model-building and holistic model-building are of great concern to social-scientists. They are of interest from a conceptual point of view and also can be used to make practical suggestions for modifying existing organizational structures.[1] We frequently make statements about the relationship within part of an administrative structure between, for example, the size of the organization and the cost per unit output. Much more rarely, if ever, are we able to relate this to the overall efficiency of the organization.

While we should recognize the merit of trying to construct macro-models of human spatial organization we should note that the technique is still in its very early stages. This point is clearly demonstrated in recent attempts to build models of cities.[2] We need to have a clear understanding of the individual relationships between components before we can assemble these components into a large model. This principle applies equally well to administrative systems. In the sections which follow we will stress, therefore, the major factors affecting the size of administrative units without specifically trying to establish the total patterns of interaction among the elements. We will start by looking at the size and spacing of public facilities and follow this with a closer examination of the forces which give rise to current spatial arrangements.

2   The determination of size and spacing of facilities

The location theories which have been developed to explain the size and spacing of activities in the private sector have depended heavily on the analysis of the flows of expenditures to centres.[3] In particular it is claimed that if too few customers patronize an outlet then the firm goes out of business, whereas if an excess of customers is available then the outlet can be increased in size. These two notions have been formalized in spatial terms by the range and the threshold for particular goods.[4] If we consider shopping trips by consumers to centres then for a given spatial distribution of consumers, each with a known purchasing power, we can define the range and the threshold for a particular good in a particular centre. This is shown in figure 3.1. In this case we assume that people travel to the nearest place offering the good. If $T < R$, the centre receives sufficient funds to stay in business and there is room for expansion; if $T = R$, a balance is achieved and the firm stays in business; however, if $T > R$, then the centre will not receive sufficient funds and it cannot continue to survive at this location – it either disappears or moves periodically.[5]

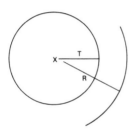

Figure 3.1   Range and threshold for a good. X central facility offering good X (assume customers evenly distributed) ; R range ; T threshold.

There have been very few attempts to determine empirically the range and threshold for public goods. The most comprehensive study is probably that of Kriesel (1971) who attempted to define the thresholds for a set of public services using data from the Greater Detroit Metropolitan Area. He argues that 'the threshold of any public service dispensed extra-territorially [provided to adjacent municipalities] by contract can be taken as the size of the population of the smallest government unit which provides it'. Table 3.1 lists the services and their empirically derived threshold sizes. The column: *per cent of service recipients with population below threshold* clearly shows that the majority of municipalities fit into the classification suggested. Evidence of the hierarchial structure of services and threshold sizes in given by the figures in the column: *number of contract service providers*.

With regard to the provision of health care Eliot-Hurst (1972) claims that: 'In total, [for the USA] the approximate supply of doctors is roughly equivalent to the total medical demand, so that any maldistribution in the system is a function of the distribution of doctors rather than of the number

Table 3.1 Public services provided by service contract in the greater Detroit metropolitan area, threshold population, per cent of service recipients with population below threshold, and number of contract service providers

Public service	Threshold	Per cent of service recipients with population below threshold	Number of contract service providers
Police patrol: emergency	757,000	100·0	1
Police investigation	757,000	100·0	1
Police patrol: regular	190,000	100·0	2
Storm sewerage	190,000	98·2	5
Public health	112,291	94·1	4
Hospitals	110,440	94·1	4
Planning	110,440	100·0	4
Water distribution	24,056	100·0	5
Sanitary sewerage	16,900	97·4	12
Jails	15,600	98·4	12
Street construction and maintenance	15,600	96·4	9
Sanitary sewage treatment and disposal	4,490	95·2	13
Fire protection: emergency	3,460	78·3	9
Library services: part	1,890	95·6	11
Library services: all	1,880	95·6	10
Refuse disposal	1,801	84·6	10
Water supply	1,527	95·9	12
Fire protection: all	990	67·4	26

(*Kriesel, 1970*)

of doctors.' He notes that doctors tend to concentrate in the largest cities and that in numerical terms there are too many doctors in cities over 100,000. People living in small towns and in rural districts are relatively short of doctors. In reply to the question: 'How many people are needed to support a doctor?' Eliot-Hurst relies on Garrison's (1959) empirical findings. Garrison suggested that general practice thresholds range from 800 to 1,500 people. Where specialized skills are involved the figure increases. A pediatrician, for example, needs a population of about 6,000, an obstetrician approximately 7,500 and 40,000, the highest threshold level, is needed for services such as urology and neurology.

Another example of a threshold population is provided by the Canadian Library Association. From practical experience of offering books to rural populations they claim that 50,000 is a necessary population base for a travelling library when population density is low.

Returning to the private sector we can see that the viability of the centre is directly determined by its accessibility to customers and the flows of money. In the case of the public sector we do not have the same kind of controlling mechanism to regulate the viability of facilities. Though the amount of service available at hospitals, schools, fire stations, welfare clinics and police stations depends upon the availability of funds, the supply is not provided directly by consumers as in the private sector. Usually customers do not personally transfer their financial contribution to the point which generates the service. Rather, the controlling mechanism is more diffuse, and usually involves individuals, local governments and adjacent areas, as well as the central government. Harvey (1972) has recently outlined the four major mechanisms which control the allocation of goods and services in the public sector. They are voting, direct bargaining and negotiations, the delegation or reliquishing of decision-making authority to others and the distribution of wealth among municipalities. Essentially the first three are variations on a theme for reaching collective decisions and the latter is related to the potential tax base and the ability of a municipality to be financially independent.

There is a growing body of empirical case studies on decision-making in the public sector and the events which precede the construction of facilities such as schools, highways, police stations or hospitals, but geographers are only just beginning to formalize the processes into analytical frameworks. Wolpert (1972) has led the way in this respect. He has built up an impressive list of case studies of location decisions for public facilities and from these he has tried to outline the elements for analytical models. He argues that public facilities have varying degrees of utility depending upon their location vis-à-vis individuals in space. Fot this reason attempts to locate highways, for example, in heavily populated areas often produce a considerable reaction from those who are likely to be displaced and who have limited financial ability to choose new homes. Thus, at the outset, when the cost of locating a facility is being calculated, it is necessary to judge how great the opposition will be and to add to the cost a sum for overcoming this opposition. This is the side-payment and though it may take the form of a direct bribe it frequently shows itself as either a dislocation grant to the person who is forced to move or as an addition to the facility to make it less noxious to nearby residents. The latter could be soundproofing, decorative architectural styles, or the installation of apparatus to prevent pollution. At the moment we lack objective methods for determining the costs and benefits of public facilities and it is thus extremely difficult to determine the exact amount of compensation that should be paid to individuals. Usually a sum just sufficient to placate disgruntled individuals is paid. The publication of the paper Put People First (1972) suggests that the British government is concerned with providing a just method for compensating individuals who suffer environmental degradation through no fault of their own. For example, those living near an airport or highway should be compensated for the increase in noise and air pollution generated by the facility, The analytical procedures which are being developed to handle these types of decision-making processes are listed in table 3.2. The procedures range from intuitive interpretations of a community's political strength through rigorous mathematical formulations for the calculation of side payments to game-theory models to explain the emergence of 'opposition coalitions, the distribution of political power and side-payments, and the political process by which decisions are made' (Hinman 1970; 1971).

Table 3.2 Procedures for analysing location decisions of noxious facilities

Procedure	Facility (empirical example)	Date/Author	
Scenario	Communities in the US	1972	Wolpert et al.
Questionnaires	64 public and private facilities (schools, power stations, etc.)	1972	Wolpert et al.
Simulation	Incinerator or electricity plant (footloose noxious facility)	1971	Hinman
Game-theory	A general formulation	1970	Hinman
Dynamic programming	Sports stadium	1970	Austin et al.

Let us now consider some of the financial aspects of public services and their effect on the size and spacing of facilities. One of government's major functions is to collect revenues from its constituents and to redistribute it via the provision of public facilities. These facilities are often referred to as merit goods, which suggests that they should be available to all irrespective of the individual's means. Thus in theory all communities should have the same standard of services. While this is frequently the expressed wish of the central government we often notice that because municipalities have control over their revenues the richer communities tend to have higher quality services than the poorer ones. We also find that in many areas because municipalities are close together and because people are mobile the services which are provided and paid for by the residents of one area may be utilized by residents of nearby municipalities. There is a spill-over of the benefits. Spill-overs have been recognized in many services particularly in metropolitan areas which have numerous semi-autonomous political units in a fairly restricted area. As a result of spill-over several strategies have been devised to make the system more equitable and table 3.3 outlines examples taken from the Montréal area.

A hierarchy of strategies emerges. At the lowest level the facility is provided on a unrestricted basis for all to use, as, for example, street lighting and cleaning, and parks. Next we have facilities which are restricted to residents who make a contribution to the upkeep of the facility, for example libraries, recreation facilities and schools. At a slightly higher level we see the implementation of user-changes. In the Montreal area this applies to some libraries, but it is standard practice for transportation facilities in many countries. Finally, there is the attempt to enlarge the administrative unit so that all users are contained within it.

Table 3.3 Strategies to overcome spillovers

Service	Strategy	Municipality
Library	(i) Free to residents of Westmount (ii) Fee ($12.50) for non-residents	Westmount
Tennis courts	Restricted to residents	Westmount
Skating rink	Restricted to residents	Westmount
Parks	Unrestricted	Westmount
Police/Fire protection	Currently an attempt is being made to amalgamate all municipalities into a single spatial unit	Island of Montréal

With respect to the US, Fitch (1964) has drawn attention to the increasing proportion of highway and street expenditures which are covered by revenues derived from users. In 1930, for example, user revenues accounted for approximately 30 per cent of expenditure, but since 1945 the figure has been slightly greater than 100 per cent. User revenues are derived from state gross registration receipts, state net gasoline tax, special city and county taxes including parking meter revenues, bridge, tunnel, ferry and road tolls, and federal excise taxes.

The main sources of revenue for other public services are property taxes and income taxes. I will discuss these in a later section of this chapter. At this point it is sufficient to note that in the UK, local rates provide approximately 40 per cent of expenditures and the other 60 per cent is generated by general taxation which is administered by the central government. This proportion has been increasing steadily over the years. A breakdown of local government expenditures shows that with a rate of between 4 per cent and 6 per cent per year during the 1960s it was one of the fastest growing sectors of the economy. In contrast we find that total rateable values increased by slightly more than 2 per cent during the same period. It seems very likely that the central government will continue to take on an increasing share of expenditure on public services. This pheno-menon is common to most countries, both developed and developing. It is at this point that we must recognize the political aspects of the distri-bution of these services. The government has to mediate and choose between competing demands. Thus the pattern of services which exists represents a balance between these competing demands. We can identify four major sets of factors which will enter into this competition and these will be examined under the heads:

1   Local sentiment and control.
2   Distance-decay and utilization.
3   Economies of scale.
4   Satisfaction, costs and social justice.

3 Local sentiment and control

A man's attachment to his immediate environment has been widely documented under a variety of titles within several disciplines. Haggett (1972), in his discussion on location and spatial organization, draws attention to the work of the biologist Lorenz (1963) and the psychologist Hall (1969) and their conclusion that primates and man himself have a strongly developed sense of territoriality and desire to guard, protect and maintain control over their space. Soja's (1971) work on *de facto* areas has been mentioned in Chapter 1 and it serves to reinforce our notions of local control. A recent study by Clark (1972) of an English-speaking enclave in Gaspé peninsula Quebec gives a further example of the 'us versus them' mentality. The language used to reinforce this viewpoint has been discussed by Hoggart (1957) who draws examples from the UK to suggest that lower socio-economic groups have a greater fear of 'them', the administrators, than the higher socio-economic groups. This view is in line with studies in the US. Sociologists Terrein and Mills (1955) have drawn attention to the anomie which can result from being part of a large-scale organization and they commend complete participation in government decision-making by all the inhabitants of a community. They note that Plato claimed that the optimum size of a community was 5,040 as this was the number that could be accommodated in a Greek forum of his day. Mass participation in local decision-making has been a feature in New England[6] and Switzerland. Only recently have individuals chosen to delegate responsibility to elected representatives. This attachment to the locality manifests itself in individuals' expressed desire to control their surroundings without interference from outside. It is suggested that small locally-controlled social structures are more desirable than large structures because the former encourages a high level of cognizance of the persons in the structure and also, in theory, allows easy access to those who make decisions about the supply of public services to the community. Stemming from this is the notion that smaller organizations are easier to control and greater satisfaction is more likely to follow as the particular needs of small groups are catered for.

Though we have a general feeling for this relationship between the size of an area and the level of control we lack operational definitions. The relationship is portrayed graphically in figure 3.2.

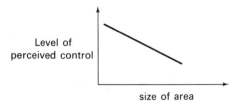

Level of perceived control

size of area

Figure 3.2 Relationship between perceived control and size of area

A distinction should be drawn between the perceived level of control and the actual level of control. It is perceived values which give rise to a certain level of satisfaction, and which must be taken into account when defining units for the provision of services. A further distinction can be drawn between the types of public services and we can postulate an ordinal scale of concern. The ordinal scale only provides a ranking, it does not contain information about the relative position of concern with respect to the services.

Hirsch (1964) offers a two-fold classification of services; those for which political proximity is considered essential, for example, education, police and fire protection, public welfare, libraries and public housing, and those for which political proximity is considered to be less important, such as, air pollution control, sewage disposal, water, public health and hospitals, refuse collection and street maintenance. He argues that if the people are in close contact with the decision-makers malpractice may be prevented. Proximity may also ensure that changes are evolutionary rather than revolutionary. The link provides a useful feedback of information from the consumers to those responsible for providing the service. The level of concern not only varies from service to service: it may also vary from group to group in society. Banfield and Wilson (1963) recognized this in American cities and attempted to formulate an ethos theory. Communities which are characterized by lower socio-economic status tend to generate a 'private regarding' ethos where strong emphasis is placed upon local control, whereas the highest socio-economic status communities with their 'public regarding' ethos favour 'efficient' government. (This ethos theory will be re-examined in Chapter 8.) Communities of high socio-economic status are less concerned with local control than with good government which provides high quality services as efficiently as possible. This dichotomy needs amplification because not infrequently the affluent community also likes to maintain its autonomy and so guarantee high quality services without fear of the influence of neighbouring municipalities. For example, Thompson (1965) claims that, 'it is very hard to believe that the consumer–taxpayer will opt for utilitarian public goods to substitute for or complement his high-style private goods.' In an affluent society municipalities may opt for local provision of expensive services rather than join with their neighbour and have a standard service at a lower cost. The proposal, in 1972, to amalgamate police forces on Montréal Island met strong resistance from Westmount, a small affluent community anxious to preserve its autonomy and control of its own police force. Similar cases have been documented by Williams (1965) among Philadelphia communities, Morando (1968) in Detroit and Massam (1971a) for a group of municipalities in the Hamilton area, Southern Ontario. Whitney (1970) has evidence of a similar phenomenon in China. He notes that when the Republic was founded the attempt by the government to abolish the tsung-tsu ch'ü (areas under the control of Governor Generals) foundered because *de facto* local groups were powerful enough to prevent them simply being abolished by decree. In the UK much evidence was presented to the commissioners who prepared the report on local government reform to support the desire for local control, and in a summary of their main conclusion we note that 'authorities must not be so large in terms of population that organization of their business becomes difficult and the elected representatives cannot keep in touch with the people affected by their policies. This is especially important in the personal services' (Royal Commission 1969, Vol. I, p. 4).

The need for a vigorous local democracy with power to make decisions and take action without being excessively restricted by the financial reins of a central government is reiterated in the report, *Government Proposals for Reorganization* (Feb 1971, 6, par. 8). Boaden (1971, 5) supports this claim when he suggests that increasing the size of areas may produce diseconomies in terms of democracy and participation.

In the US a recent trend in some of the larger urban centres has been to establish 'little city halls' throughout the metropolitan areas. These are more accessible to constituents, and Washin (1971) argues that this pattern is more responsive to local needs than the centralized municipal government. New York has forty-five centres distributed throughout the city to deal with complaints from citizens and special city projects. In contrast Chicago has thirteen centres, located in poor areas, which deal specifically with social welfare. Los Angeles provides a variation in this theme. It has eleven centres distributed throughout the city to deal with all municipal services.

4 Distance-decay and utilization

The relative position of facilities and consumers in space often affects awareness, attractiveness or utilization of the facilities. The intervening space tends to have a strong influence on the services actual pattern of effectiveness. A general distance-decay relationship is a useful starting-point in describing this pattern as it varies over space. This is shown schematically in figure 3.3. From *O* to *A* the effect of the facility is felt with decreasing intensity, after *A* the intensity is zero, and the facility is not available to any demand which occurs here.

If we use this curve in examining a number of different services and consider satisfaction in terms of personal wishes or desires rather than

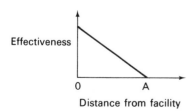

Figure 3.3 Relationship between effectiveness and distance from facilities

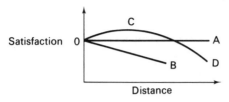

Figure 3.4   Satisfaction and distance

effectiveness in its broadest sense then a family of curves emerges. Basically there are three underlying types. They are shown in figure 3.4. Examples of services and their related curves are provided in table 3.4. The data for this table was derived from a series of studies undertaken at the University of Philadelphia, Pennsylvania, under the direction of Julian Wolpert (1972). Using questionarires, ordinal data were collected for services using the four distance categories: (1) on your block; (2) on a neighbouring block; (3) within rest of neighbourhood; (4) within neighbouring community. A seven-point scale was derived for each service and distance type in an attempt to calibrate a pride–stigma continuum for a group of sixty-three facilities in both the private and the public sector. On the evidence available it is clear that for most public services people compromise between accessibility and noise, congestion and pollution. In general people like to be near facilities, but not too near if the facility is considered 'noxious'. The less noxious the facility attributes the less is the desire to be at a distance from it. The relative strength of the two factors in the compromise varies between services;

Table 3.4   Curve types for a selection of services

Service	Curve types
Hospital	OC
Police station	OC
Museum	OC
Public meeting house or town hall	OC
Church	OC
Day care centre	OC
Post office	OC
Community recreation centre	OC
Urban expressway	OC
Public dump or incinerator	OC
Sewage treatment plant	OC
Public high school	OC
Government bureaus, eg social security	OC
Fire station	OC
Railway station	OC
Sanitorium	OA
Seminary	OA
Public library	OA
Park	OA

(*After Wolpert et al. 1972*)

for example, quiet, non-polluting activities such as seminaries, hospitals and libraries appear to generate spatial indifference, whereas people want public dumps and sewage treatment plants to be at a considerable distance. Fire stations, police stations, train stations, day-care centres and other facilities which generate relatively little local noise, congestion or pollution, tend to occupy an intermediate position on the scale. However, before we can state firmly the shape of the curve for various services we must offer clients sets of alternative combinations of distance-service types. Their choices could be analysed by searching for preference patterns. This type of work is still in its early stages in studies of spatial organization though it seems that it will be a useful improvement over the more traditional classification of questionnaire responses by counting the frequency of values for each type of response without considering the opportunities which are available to different groups. Clearly, all people do not have the same sets of choices and this must be incorporated into analytical procedure for evaluating spatial patterns. Preference analysis is concerned with systematically searching comparisons of alternatives available to an individual and on the basis of the responses; for example, between pairs of alternatives, the underlying structure of the individual's preference is determined. This type of analysis also allows us to determine indifference to sets of alternatives. Indices of the amount of regularity in the choices are usually calculated. Tiebout (1956) suggests that house-buyers demonstrate their preferences for particular combinations of public services when they choose to live in a municipality and reject neighbouring alternatives. Examples of recent contributions by geographers in the area of preference analysis are provided by Rushton (1969), Ewing (1970) and Ross (1972). Tiebout argues that this market action tends to support the most desirable combinations of public services, that the least desirable municipalities are denied house-buyers and thus local tax revenues decline. This controlling mechanism is sluggish and seems to have only a limited ability to bring about a more desirable distribution of public services. Also it could only come about as Tiebout suggests when many contiguous municipalities are available to house-holders and the moves respond freely to full information about the state of all the alternatives. We note the similarity of these assumptions to those of a classical market system under complete competition. In fact central governments usually have to take the initiative by redistributing taxes to ensure a basic level of quality for public facilities.

Empirical evidence has not substantiated a curve of the classical distance-decay form OB in figure 3.4, though intuitively it is felt that if the scale of analysis was increased then curves of this shape would result. Most probably the overall curve would be OCD, with the distance from O to the peak C varying for different services.

Where physical movement is involved and the facility occupies a structure or space which makes it different from neighbouring structures and spaces, satisfaction will vary over space. However, if the service is delivered by mail, telephone, television or radio then location in space is less important, *ceteris paribus*. Receipt of welfare cheques, telephoned help and advice in times of crises and diffusion of educational services all fall into this category. These types of services generate a horizontal line in figure 3.4.

A theoretical relationship between the size of administrative areas and the efficiency with which taxes could be collected at a central city has been undertaken by Whitney (1970) using Chinese data. He argues that an inverse relationship existed in China between the amount of taxes that could be raised and the distance from seats of imperial authority.

> Thus, while the control of increasingly large areas would have brought in higher revenues and would have reduced the number of centres needed to collect and recruit the taxes, this increase in size would also result in either rapidly increasing costs, if all the revenues were to be collected, or in soaring rates of tax delinquency, if enforcement were not effected. The point, therefore, at which marginal administrative costs began to exceed marginal revenues would mark the optimum span of control of any one administrative centre.

Whitney attempts to formalize these ideas in a graph which relates distance to revenues in an attempt to define the ideal size for a tax-collection district. However, in order to make the scheme operational the tax potential of land must be taken into account. Traditionally this tended to vary inversely with the distance from population centres with their supplies of human manure.

An empirical example of the influence of distance on utilization is provided by the work of Wilkinson (1973). He tried to determine the distances people are prepared to travel to urban parks in Toronto. He concluded that approximately 75 per cent of users travel less than a quarter of a mile and approximately 40 per cent travel half this distance. However, in order to establish that this is an empirical regularity in human spatial behaviour we should take account of the configuration of parks and the spatial distribution of demand. What would happen if the nearest park was over a quarter of a mile away for example?

5 Economies of scale

The literature on economies is full of references to economies and diseconomies of scale and it is a subject which has occupied the attention of economists over the years. One of the most recent summaries is provided by Hirsch (1973). However, as Dawson (1972) points out, it is only in the last two or three decades that serious attempts have been made to measure the nature of economies in particular activities, and most of this work has concentrated upon the private sector. More recently attention has been directed towards the public sector and in the last ten years there has been a surge of empirical analyses of organizations which have been concerned with the provision of services such as police and fire protection, health and welfare, education, refuse collection and water supply. (Alesch and Dougharty, 1971*a* and *b*.) Most of these recent studies have attempted to determine the form of the average cost curve for the particular activity. The average cost curve relates the size of the organization to the production cost per unit output. As the size of the organization and the level of output increases there are three possibilities for the systematic trend of the cost per unit curve. These are shown in figure 3.5.

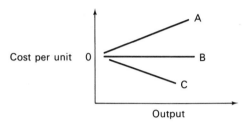

Figure 3.5 Relationships between output and cost per unit

OA represents diseconomies of scale, as the output grows the cost per unit increases; *OB* shows a constant return to scale and *OC* demonstrates economies of scale. In the latter case the larger the organization the lower the per unit production cost. These three curves can be combined in different ways and figure 3.6 illustrates some typical combinations that have been identified using empirical data. Usually we do not have sufficient data to examine the curve over the full range of output levels and so if we identify a curve of the form (*A–B*) in figure 3.6 we conclude that *over the range examined* economies of scale exist. We should not use this curve to extrapolate an optimum level of production.

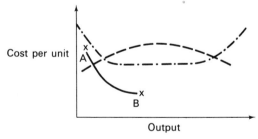

Figure 3.6 Combinations of average cost curves

It is argued that unit production costs vary with the size of the organization for at least three reasons. These reasons are discussed at length in standard economic texts and they are widely treated in geographical literature. We can summarize the reasons under the headings used by Lloyd and Dicken (1972):

1   Specialization of manpower and equipment.
2   Economies of massed reserves.
3   Economies of large-scale purchasing.

These cause unit production costs to vary with the level of output and, more specifically, the greater the level of output the lower the unit costs. It is also suggested that because of the indivisibility of inputs in the production process (eg one teacher, one nurse, one fireman) and the managerial problems that occur in large organizations, the form of the relationship is a *U*-shape curve, economies of scale operate up to a certain size, after the low point on the curve diseconomies set in. If therefore we can determine the precise shape of the average cost curve for a service and if it has the classical *U*-shape, then we can calculate the optimum level of production. Optimum in this case is concerned *only* with cost per unit output, the optimum level of produdtion is that level which is associated with the lowest cost per unit output.

If we superimpose the average cost curves for a group of services then we can determine the form of the total cost curve for the set of services. In this way we may be able to determine an optimal size for a city such that the aggregate cost of providing services is minimized. This is shown schematically in figure 3.7.

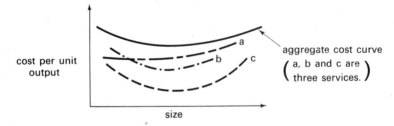

Figure 3.7   Aggregate cost curve for a set of services

The literature on public policy-making contains many references to the concept of economies of scale in the production of public services, and not infrequently it is suggested that administrative units, for a wide variety of services, should be expanded: adjacent areas should be annexed to take advantage of economies of scale and so improve production efficiency. We should note, however, that the advantages to be gained by increasing the size of administrative areas have to be balanced against the inconveniences of large-scale organizations. The points have been well documented by Hirsch (1968) and more recently in the Maud report on local government reform in Britain. The inconveniences tend to be of two main types. First, large organizations tend to generate a feeling of isolation on the part of those who receive the service and access to the decision-makers appears to be more difficult than in a smaller organization. Second, large units suggest fewer units and this has spatial repercussions particularly if clients have to travel to the place where the service is given.

Though we can follow through the debate on trade-offs between economies of scale and other features of a production system it is important to remember that before we can make any definitive statements the precise form of the average cost curve for the service under examination must be established.

Let us turn directly to the question of determining the shape of the average cost. First we must examine the two attributes which have to be measured; cost per unit production and output. Hirsch (1968) has drawn attention to the problems of measuring output levels. He suggests that some services, such as water and refuse, have reasonably well-defined output characteristics, whereas many other services have multidimensional output characteristics.[7] In the case of water the basic output unit could be a cubic foot of water delivered to particular site, and for refuse collection we could use a ton of refuse collected and disposed. Other units of output are shown in table 3.5.

Table 3.5 Output units for public services

Service	Output unit
Street cleaning	mile of street cleaned
Snow removal	mile of street cleaned
Street lighting	mile of street lit
Police protection	frequency of police patrol
Fire protection	a house protected from fire
Hospital service	patient days in hospital
	number of hospital admissions
	rated bed capacity
Education	number of students enrolled
	number of pupils achieving a certain grade
	score on educational test

These output variables do not take explicit account of variations in quality. For example, the number of patient-days and the number of children reaching grade 13 or 'A' level is a crude measuring which may hide considerable variation in the quality of the hospital and educational systems respectively. The task of measurement is made more complex if we examine the output over time. However, this approach should not be overlooked because expenditure patterns over time must be considered when taking into account high investments during the initial development stage or during periods of major overhaul as well as seasonal variations in supply. A cross-sectional study often loses sight of the influence of the age of the facility on the expenditure patterns.

With respect to the cost per unit variable the normal prodecure is to use a *per capita* value with annual operating costs. Investments in plant and other fixed costs which amortize over long periods are usually treated

Table 3.6 Illustrative governmental activities and public services arrayed in terms of the difficulty of applying economies-of-scale analysis to define the relationship between size and the unit costs of production

	Group 1 *Economies-of-scale analysis is relatively simple*	Group 2 *Economies-of-scale analysis is relatively complex*	Group 3 *Economies-of-scale analysis is complex and difficult*
Characteristics of the public service	Routine processes Standardized resources and products	More complex processes Variations in resources and products	Highly complex processes Important variations in resources and products
Governmental activities	Clerical Operations and maintenance Construction Fleets and fleet maintenance Purchasing	Communications Data processing Licenses and permits Land acquisition Audits	Management and administration Research and analysis Planning and budgeting Personnel Legal services
Illustrative public services	Water supply Sewage treatment Refuse collection Solid waste disposal Streets and highways Other transportation facilities Other utilities	Fire protection Housing and renewal Library services Public assistance Regulatory services	Recreation services Education Delivery of health care services Anti-poverty programs Police services

(Alesch and Dougharty 1971, 14, table 1)

separately. As with output levels are problems in defining the quality of the service produced. At the outset normal levels with tolerable deviations should be stated. While this is not so difficult for a service such as water, for its chemical and physical properties are easily defined, it becomes very complex for social services such as health, welfare, education, police and fire protection. Street cleaning and lighting, garbage collection and snow removal are easier to treat and fairly rigid norms can be meaningfully defined. A summary of problems relating to analysis of economics of scale is presented in table 3.6.

Almost thirty years ago Ridley and Simon (1947) drew attention to the problem of measuring public services, and though analytical procedures have advanced rapidly in the intervening period we still lack a definitive methodology. The dearth of academic writing on variations in the quality of social services among administrative units has been commented upon by Davies (1968). He claims that 'few have risked stating value judgements in any detail about how standards should vary, and no one has systematically compared the actual distribution of standards with a concept of optimal distribution which would follow from their value judgements.' Since the mid-sixties when Davies made this claim there have been advances in the UK largely as a result of the work that was undertaken in the preparation of the Research Reports for the Maud commission.[8] Several of these reports dealt with the influence of size on the provision of housing, highways, health services and education. And their primary aim was to search for the shape of the average cost curve for each service. The variety of empirical results is a useful introduction to a large set of empirical studies. Because the services were treated at different scales, county council, county borough, non-county borough, urban-district council and rural district council, and because several variables were used to measure the size of the output only a selection of the empirical findings is presented here. For education a horizontal cost curve was identified. This agrees with the findings of Hirsch (1968), Kiesling (1966) and Dawson (1972). Using data from Ontario, Canada, Dawson identified a 'lazy S' ($\sim$) curve with a low point of approximately 6,000–7,000 population. Conflicting empirical results have been presented by Hanson (1966) and Riew (1966). They identified U-shape curves. The lowest optimal level was suggested by Riew: 1,700 pupils in the district, that is approximately 6,000 people. Kahn-Gaumintz suggest an optimum size district should contain between 10,000 and 25,000, while Hanson presents empirical data for a sample of ten states in the US and argues for 50,000. This figure coincides with the optimum-size area for health care that was identified in Research Report No. 3. The particular service referred to is ambulance services in County Boroughs. A U-shape curve was identified and as all the County Boroughs in the study area have a population greater than the optimal level of 50,000 it is concluded that significant diseconomies of scale obtain. Hirsch identified the classical U-shape curve for fire protection and school administration. In the former case the low point occurred with a population of 110,000 and in the latter 44,000.

The most common type of cost curve appears to be the horizontal one. Three empirical studies of education services with this form have been cited above and to these we can add police protection (Hirsch in Perloff and Wingo (eds.) 1958, 508) and (Schmandt-Stevens, *ibid.*, p. 508). garbage collection (Hirsch, 1965), municipal expenditures (Scott and Feder, 1957), and electricity servicing in urban areas (Massam, 1971*b*, 402–406). Only a couple of services demonstrate declining cost curves of the form *A–B* on Figure 6: they are water supplies and sewage plants (Cook in Feldman and Goldrick, 1969, 93). Finally, we should note that there are empirical examples of inverted *U*-shaped curves for housing and highway, both are reported in Research Report No. 3. For housing, diseconomies operate up to a level of approximately 60,000 when costs are maximum, after this point it is suggested that the curve may be asymptotic. In the case of highways, using expenditures per mile at the County Borough level, it was found that diseconomies operate up to a level of about 104,000. As the population increases costs decrease, and as the mean population size of County Boroughs is approximately 186,000 they enjoy some economies of scale. Theoretically they could increase this by becoming larger.

In summary we concur with Cook (1969) in her claim that:

> Evidence that services other than sewer and water would attain further economies of scale by consolidating, federating or amalgamating local units is scanty. . . . The main potential advantages of a rationalization of political structure in metropolitan areas lies in the distribution of the cost of providing public services more in accordance with the benefits received from them and in pcssible increased co-ordination of facilities leading to increased quality of service.

This leads us directly into a discussion of costs and the quality of service provided.

6 Satisfaction, justice and costs

The examination of the spatial patterns of justice, satisfaction and costs has attracted the attention of workers in several fields including public finance, social welfare and geography. Most recent statements in geography have come from Harvey (1972) and Wolpert (1972) both of whom have presented theoretical, philosphical and empirical evidence in this area. Harvey talks of a 'just distribution justly arived at' as a normative goal for social and spatial organization. This concept is similar to Davies' (1968) notion of spatial justice which he defines as follows: 'to each area according to the needs of the population of that area'. Wolpert has examined the sequence of steps in the decision-making process which locates public facilities and he notes that the facilities have mixed costs and benefits that vary over space and in their effect on different social groups. Wolpert's concern is with the amount of power and influence groups can bring to bear on the decision-making process. He is primarily concerned with empirical examples whereas Harvey takes a more philosophical view. Clearly there is a trend in contemporary human geography, and the social sciences at large, to focus attention on social sissues. Buttimer (1972) dramatically summarizes the situation thus: 'many social scientists in this country [US] have turned their attention to social issues and have not hesitated to draft blue-prints for social reform. The metaphorical language used to describe this exodus from the Ivory Tower is also interesting: for some it's a "plunge", for others an "expedition" and for others still a "surge", depending on one's disciplinary background and ideological orientation.' Another geographer, Brown (1972), puts the matter on a firm basis when he suggests that terms such as spatial injustice, because of its evocative nature, conjures up images of hungry children, suffering ladies and rat-infested alleys that occur in some places and not in others'. He goes on to say that 'I am piqued by this imagery because it is important that geographers become concerned with the application of their skills to real world problems, and imagery of this sort really diverts our efforts.' It seems to Brown that 'talk in this area often suffers by being naïve in the specification of problems, specifying problems that are really nonproblems by being either too vague, intractable or better left to philosophers'.

Practical problems concerning the provision of public services were examined in a recent edition of Antipode (1971). The articles in this edition concentrated upon the efficiency with which a particular distribution of facilities satisfies the needs of society. The emphasis is upon accessibility both in a spatial context and a social setting. Some people find a public service inefficient because they have to travel a long way to use it, while others are deprived of services because they lack the information necessary to claim their supply. The geographer has traditionally been concerned with spatial access but it is clear that utilization is also related to awareness and familiarity with the procedures for obtaining services. These points deserve closer attention. The work of Earickson (1971) and Lankford (1971) on the low accessibility to public services of blacks, native Hawaiians, part-Hawaiians and dark-skinned Orientals in the US suggests that much needs to be done to improve public facilities and that the problems are not only spatial. DeVise (1971), using his work in Chicago, takes up the argument that size and economies of scale should not dominate the planning of the supply of health services. This point has been developed by Davies (1968) in the UK and he has argued that to raise the quality of service utilization in deprived areas it is often necessary to oversupply- the facility and so ensure that low awareness will not prevent a minimum standard being achieved.

Examples of inequality and differences between the services which are available to blacks and whites in the US have been vividly portrayed by W. L. Taylor (1971). For example, he claims that police protection is lowest in non-white districts and that non-whites are almost twice as likely to be the victims of burglary. Response time for police calls is also lower in these districts. With respect to health care using data for the mid-sixties he found that life expectancy for whites was 71 years compared with 64 years for non-whites, and that almost 60 per cent more non-white than white babies die during the first month of life. The ratio of doctors to residents in ghettos tends to be one-fifth to one-half of the average for the city. And it was reported during a US Commission on Civil Rights in 1966 that in Cleveland the only public hospital for prenatal care was on the west side of the city, over three miles from the major Negro district which is in the east side. It takes approximately one and a half hours by bus to reach the hospital from the east side. If we examine education then Taylor suggests that in the late sixties in over thirty-five metropolitan areas the average expenditures by the central city school districts was $449 per pupil compared with an average suburban expenditure rate of $573. Though this suggests that the quality of education is lower in the inner city than in the suburbs it is unlikely that the performance of the inner city schools will be radically improved simply by adding money. Findings reported by the Coleman (1966) study on educational opportunity suggest that educational achievement is not strictly related to investments in expensive physical plant. The complex of social environmental variables are involved.

Let us now move from specific examples and look at some general principles. With respect to the spatial extent of the influence of an administrative or service centre we may find that a very large area with a centrally located facility offers poor services to clients at the periphery. However, if we redistribute the investment in the single central facility and create a set of smaller facilities which are readily accessible to all clients, then we usually have to reduce the amount of service and possibly the quality of the service which is available. We illustrate this diagrammatically in figure 3.8. With a fixed budget we could have one large facility, such as a hospital with good equipment, or we could have five small clinics.

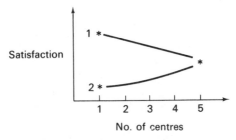

Figure 3.8 Relationship between satisfaction and the number of centres in an area.

1 * People living near large hospital
2 * People living far from hospital

Figure 3.8 suggests that with five centres the satisfaction of all people has reached the same level. However, in order to use this as a procedure for evaluating spatial justice we should take into account the number of people within different social groups who have different levels of demand, and their position in space.

Those people who are near the single facility will prefer this as it offers accessibility to high quality of services, whereas those located on the edge of the area will have low satisfaction with this arrangement. Their satisfaction level will increase as the small clinics are located near them. It is highly likely that their satisfaction should increase if the facilities of these clinics improved or accessibility to the large facility was improved. Here we have a good example of a pay-off problem in which the decision-maker has to choose an equitable distribution of services given a fixed budget.

The inefficiency that results from only locating one facility may have high social costs, particularly with respect to health care. This point has been stressed by Abler, Adams and Gould (1971, 532–4) in their discussion on optimization under conflicting goals. They offer two conceptual diagrams to clarify the conflicting goals. In summary, as the number of centres increases there is an increase in costs, assuming all offer the same quality of service, and at the same time the social costs due to insufficiency of facilities decreases.

If we take these points one stage further and consider the relationship between the costs of setting up many centres and thus producing small areas and the satisfaction of customers we can suggest a curve of the form shown in figure 3.9.

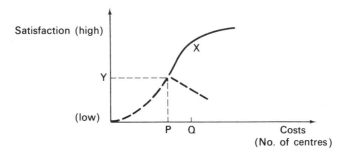

Figure 3.9 Relationship between satisfaction and costs

We can conceive of this curve taking the form of a classical production function, namely as the inputs increase, in this case number of centres, then the outputs, here the satisfaction of the customers, increases. We should notice that diminishing returns set in at approximately X on the curve. In this instance we consider that the costs are not borne by the customers. If they were then it is likely that the shape of the curve would be of the form shown by the dotted line(- - - -) in figure 3.8. Y is the maximum level of satisfaction that their budget will yield and this gives us P centres. Any increase in the number of centres will incur an increase in the costs for the customers and this will give rise to a decrease in satisfaction.

The general problem of finding the best combination of centres in order to maximize overall satisfaction has not been solved. Abler, Adams and Gould point out the three major components of the problem. They are first, the number of centres to be located second, the size of centre each and third, the position of each centre in space. In the next chapter we will address this location problem and give example of partial solutions.

In a broader context which involves consumers making decisions to support the allocation of funds to public services we can argue that the individual consumer balances his consumption of public and private goods and this places a constraint on the financial resources available to the central government which it uses to construct public facilities. Williams (1966), has examined the theoretical basis of this balancing process with respect to municipalities given that spill-overs can occur between adjacent units. He has attempted to determine the optimal provision of public goods among a set of local governments. It is suggested that the government units are fixed in spatial extent and boundaries should not be treated as variable, rather the emphasis should rest on examining the flows between units. Williams concludes that no foreseeable boundary reorganization is likely to reduce inter-community spill overs very substantially, so that the analysis of flows between units and the search for the optimal level is likely to persist as a topic worthy of closer examination. Chapter 6 will take up the topic of interaction between administrative units.

In terms of social justice we might argue that in figure 3.9 if P is the level of service which the local budget can support and Q is some level defined as a necessary minimum to satisfy certain objectives, then funds from outside the area must be brought in to make up the deficiency. This is the normal case whereby the central government takes on the role of income redistributor via transfer payments. The main purpose of these transfer payments is to equalise the quality of service among a set of areas. Sacks and Harris (1964) have examined the flow of funds into municipalities in the US and they note a rapid increase since 1960. Previously *per capita* expenditures for public services could largely be explained by the three variables, per capita income, population density and per cent urban. More recently it is necessary to consider the flow of state aid to localities and federal aid to state and local governments, particularly when we examine the expenditure patterns for education, health, welfare and highways. Local taxes, largely produced from property taxes, fall far short of providing sufficient funds to guarantee required levels of services. In Britain grants are made from the central government to support local rates and as Godley and Rhodes (no date) have pointed out, 'this grant is so large, nearly £3,000 million in 1972–3, that changes in its overall size and the way it is distributed between individual Local Authorities are decisions of great national and regional importance.' They suggest that in economic and financial circles insufficient attention is given to these problems. Basically this lack of attention stems from the fact that the Rate Support Grant does not appear in the annual White Papers on public expenditure. And further results from rules for distributing the grants that are obscure. They argue for a rational equitable system but suggest that this will only come about if a spirit of change is first introduced.

A further solution to the problem of narrowing the gap between P and Q is suggested. This solution depends upon increasing the size of the area so that sufficient funds can be found within it to provide a satisfactory level of services.

In North America there are several examples of metropolitan governments being reorganized with this end in view. One of the earliest was in Toronto, where in 1954 the 241 square mile (622 km²) Municipality of Metropolitan Toronto was established. Other large metro reform examples include Nashville, Tennessee (1962), and Jacksonville, Florida (1968). In both these cases a single metropolitan government was established. In several places area-wide jurisdictions were established but the level of consolidation was less rigid. Thus, Miami, Baton Rouge, Seattle, Portland and Indianapolis. The last example is noteworthy because the city-county amalgamation between Indianapolis and Marion county which occurred on 1 January 1969 creating an area of 402 square miles (1,041 km²) with a population of 780,000 was brought about without popular referendum. This was the first time this had taken place in the northern US since New York City was created by the amalgamation of five counties in 1898.

Some of the most recent examples of local government reform are in Florida where in 1970 the legislature made three proposals for consolidating local government. First, the adoption of a home-rule charter for Volusia County providing for a council-manager form of county government. Second, county-municipality consolidations of Hillsborough County with Tampa and Escambia County with Persacola, and finally a joint resolution was passed to create a 10-member committee to consider whether one regional government should be established in south-east Florida. In the same year, 1970, Wisconsin enacted an executive order to consolidate and reorganize state government administrative districts into eight uniform districts, and in the state of Utah the metropolitan area around Salt Lake City is being organized into a new federal structure. In Canada a similar concern with government reorganization has been expressed and we see evidence of this in the form of new metropolitan governments in Winnipeg and Montreal. The Ontario Provincial government is continuing in its stated aim of reorganizing municipal government and it is hoped that a set of detailed studies will help decide whether a single or a two-tier structure will be created. It has been argued that the minimum population size should be between 8,000 and 10,000.

Reforms of local government structures are influenced by the financial wealth of the municipalities involved. In Canada Plunkett's report (1972) suggests that public finance deserves much closer attention from

analysts than it has previously received. And when we talk about funds
for the provision of services we have to consider the contribution that is
made by property taxes within the service area. We have already
mentioned the fact that local taxes are virtually synonymous with property
taxes. In North America, however, we frequently have a local sales tax.
In passing we should note that in Delaware in 1970, legislation was passed
giving cities with a population of over 50,000 the power to levy a municipal
user tax on wages and salaries earned by residents and/or persons who work
within the municipal area. However, generally speaking municipal income
taxes are very rare. The comments presented below will concentrate upon
the major local tax source, namely property taxes. If at a point in time
we could define an area on the basis that it enclosed a sufficiently large
taxbase to support a satisfactory level of service, then after a short period,
possibly one year, this equilibrium position would have shifted. There are
at least two reasons for this. First, the rate of increase of property taxes
tends to be less than the rate of increases of costs for public services.
These services tend to be labour intensive and wages and salaries are a
major factor in operating expenditure. Second, relocation of tax-bearing
activities such as industries can boost the revenue base of a municipality
above the minimum necessary to satisfy local demands for services.
Thus if a factory closed or new plant was installed in a community the
revenue of a small district could be severely affected. Clearly, the larger
and more varied the municipality the less liable it is to sudden changes
in its tax base. There is another problem relating to property tax and this
concerns standards for evaluating the value of properties. According to
Netzer (1966) assessment practices and levels vary considerably from
area to area, and in order to achieve overall improvement and standardization in procedures he makes specific recommendations for the optimal
size of assessment districts. He claims that good property tax administration should use approximately 1·5 per cent of the taxes collected. This
figure is based upon comparative studies and experiental notions. Further
the assessment function should be handled by a professional full-time
staff and thus it is likely that even small jurisdictions will incur costs
of between $60,000 and $70,000. From this it follows that only in jurisdictions which yield about $4 million will the costs be less than 1·5 per
cent, since per capita property tax revenue is approximately $100.
The implication is that a population base of 40,000–50,000 is the required
size for an assessment district.

Netzer goes on to point out that in the US in the late 1960s there were
more than 18,000 assessment districts with populations of about 10,000.
The county has been suggested as an appropriate unit, but only one-fifth
have populations greater than 50,000 and of these many yield less than
$4 million in tax revenues. The argument against consolidating assess-
ment districts has been based on the notion that larger units are more
impersonal and are not in touch with the people. It should be noted that
in England and Wales valuation is conducted through a central agency,

the Inland Revenue Department, and it is argued that this does not infringe upon local control and autonomy. An attempt to define a standard of excellence in assessment has been suggested by Bird (1960), and he suggests that a margin of 20 per cent between assessed value and sales value for a property is the upper limit of tolerance.

The general property tax is reviewed by Clover (1966) who attempts to evaluate the degree of uniformity and the relationship between the amount of taxes paid and the ability to pay taxes as measured by personal income and the value of the taxed property. He is concerned with justice and taxation. Clover argues that we now have sufficient data about the operation of property tax among and within states in the US to examine its uniformity. Non farm single-family dwellings bear a large proportion of the property tax, and because homes are of such great socio-economic significance questions of justice and fairness of treatment are of considerable importance. Excessive variation is shown in ratios between assessed values and sales values of taxed property and he claims that a difference of 10 per cent in the ratio should not be exceeded. This contrasts with Netzer's figure of 20 per cent which was derived from Bird's study. In summary, state-wide control of tax assessment is necessary. Property tax is also essentially a regressive tax, the higher market-value properties carry a smaller proportion of tax than the cheaper houses, '. . . this tax [property tax] remains the most regressive and haphazardly nonuniform or unequal of all major taxes'. Clover's quotation can be added to Seligman's (1925) comment made in the mid-twenties: "Practically, the general property tax as administered is beyond all doubt one of the worst taxes known in the civilised world.'

Clearly then property tax could and should be more fairly assessed, particularly as this tax is still recognized as the basic source of local revenue for the provision of public services.

Notes on further reading

Standard references on central place theory should be consulted for details of the concepts of range, threshold and periodic markets, for example, Berry (1967) or Berry and Pred (1965).

With respect to defining the threshold for public goods see Kriesel (1971).

A useful introduction to the mechanisms for allocating public goods and services is provided in Harvey (1972).

The economist's view point, including comments on economies of scale, measurement problems of productivity, and definitions of input and output are given in Hirsch (1964, 1968, 1973).

The topic of social justice has recently entered geographical literature via Harvey (1973). The subject is well introduced in Davies (1968).

Notes

1 A good summary of different approaches to model building and the contrasts between partial and holistic models is provided in Harris (in Perloff and Wingo (eds.) (1968).

2 There are several articles which develop this point: Colenutt in Board *et al.* (eds.) (1970); Taylor in Board *et al.* (eds.) (1971); Massam (1972*a*, 279–292).

3 The basic principles of the theory developed by Christaller to explain the size and spacing of activities occurs in Berry and Pred (1965).

4 For a full definition of these terms see Berry and Garrison (1958, 304–311).

5 There is a large body of literature in the field of periodic market systems. A good summary is provided in Berry (1967, 93–105).

6 This point is discussed in detail in Committee for Economic Development (1968).

7 Other problems relating to the measurement of public services will be discussed in Chapter 8.

8 The full list of Research Studies occurs in: Royal Commission (1969, 390 Annex 9).

4 Allocation-location models in the public sector

1 Introduction

The distribution of public services is determined by the interplay of many factors as has been shown in earlier chapters. However, basically we can recognize two procedures which determine the location of facilities and the supply structure. The first, and the most common, incorporates trial and errors tests in the real world. For example, public facilities such as hospitals, schools, fire stations and police stations are not relocated every time there is a slight shift in demand, rather occasional modifications are made if the quality of the service declines. Changes tend to be of an *ad hoc* nature usually by additions in capacity at the original site. However, from time to time major adjustments are made and new sites are chosen. *Ad hoc* adjustments can also be made to the boundaries of service districts as well as to collection or delivery routes. Intuitively this seems to be a logical procedure but not a perfectly efficient one because we confine ourselves to an evaluation of additions to existing facilities as a means of improving service levels. The second approach is concerned explicitly with examining a large set of alternatives, even if they do not really exist, and choosing the one which in some sense is best.

This second strategy is used in both the public and the private sectors. Industrialists and retailing concerns often refer to management consultants for advice on choosing the best location for their activities.[1] Similarly, in the public sector many governments[2] use the same kind of approaches to tackle the problem of locating facilities to satisfy the consumers. In this case, however, the primary object is not to maximize profits or returns on investments, as in the private sector, but rather to find the most efficient way to provide a given quality of service. This basic distinction between public and private location models was discussed in the last chapter and with respect to allocation–location models it has been examined by Revelle *et al.* (1970). The methods for determining the optimal arrangement of activities are most highly developed with regard to the location of facilities and the flow of goods between centres and customers. In this chapter we will examine some of these procedures and will attempt to draw together a large body of literature which focuses upon the determination of the optimal arrangement for services under different sets of conditions. Cooper and Steinberg (1970) summarize the problem of defining optimization in symbolic terms. This is a necessary first step as most of the procedures required to solve these problems involve manipulating symbolic relationships. These relationships, however, are summary statements of problems which can be expressed neatly in ordinary language. The general class of problem we will address is the allocation–location problem and it has been defined by Abler, Adams and Gould (1971) in the following way. How shall we allocate one set of facilities to serve a second set of people? This is shown diagrammatically in figure 4.1. Clearly this problem is very common in the real world when we realize that:

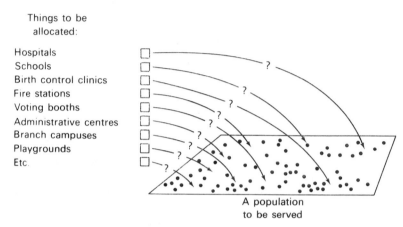

Figure 4.1   A set of facilities to be assigned to serve a population (*After Abler, Adams, and Gould, 1971*)

Hospitals must be located in geographic space to serve the people with complete medical care, and we must build schools close to the children who have to learn. Fire stations must be located to give rapid access to potential conflagrations, and voting booth must be placed so that people can cast their ballots without expending unreasonable amounts of time, effort or money to reach the polling stations (Abler *et al*).

Because we cannot solve this problem in its most general form we have to limit it to specific sorts of problems. In the following sections we will look at the most important aspects of these problems and particular solutions to specific topics. However, before we do this let us digress for a moment and develop the argument for trying to solve an allocation–location problem. There are two reasons other than the intellectual satisfaction which stems from the solution of difficult problems. The first is so to determine the location for facilities in our everyday world that they operate as efficiently as possible and that the influence of space on efficiency is fully accounted for. This may mean that we want so to locate schools that the average distance travelled by pupils is as short as possible, or that we want to determine the smallest number of fire stations necessary and locate them so that all parts of the area under surveillence can be reached within a fixed time limit, say five minutes. In most practical cases we try to find sites which will minimize travel time, cost or effort in moving to or from a set of facilities. If we can determine ideal or normative locations then we are in a position to examine the differences between these normative locations and actual locations, and thus we can evaluate costs which will be incurred in extra travelling effort to facilities which are not ideally located. This is the second reason for tackling the allocation–location problem, and it stems directly from the first. We briefly touched on these reasons in Chapter 2 when we constructed indices of spatial efficiency for a depot or service centre with respect to a set of customers.

In a general way it is easy to state the allocation–location problem, but when we try to apply it to specific services, for example, schools, hospitals, clinics, fire stations, or day-care centres, under conditions which exist in particular places such as small municipalities, large metropolitan areas, or agricultural regions, both for the developed and developing world, then the general problem has to be restated to take local factors into account. These may be related to the transportation system, to financial constraints on the timing of investments in the construction of central facilities or to constraints on the set of alternatives which are available for use for public facilities.[3] As well as local factors which have to be considered there are several technical problems which relate to the procedures used for solving allocation–location problems. Basically, if we are concerned with five stations and we have to choose the best set of three sites out of five possible ones then it is not difficult to develop a method for evaluating all possible locations and we choose the best three. Best in this instance is defined as the set of three which is most accessible to all potential conflagrations. However, for non-trivial problems the number of combinations to be examined is frequently astronomical and even with modern computers it is often impossible to evaluate all possible sites in a reasonable amount of time.

Several workers have drawn attention to this aspect of the problem. Schneider (1971) considers the task of choosing 5 ambulance depots from a possible set of 77 sites; there are over 19 million possibilities. Dee (1970) faced the problem of selecting 17 playgrounds of 3 different types from a set of 20 available sites to serve 198 population origins. He claims there are $3^{17} \binom{20}{17}$ feasible solutions. In a slightly different context Scott (1971) has evaluated the number of different ways six cities can be connected; there are over 32,000 different ways. Finally Gould's recent summary (1971) of combinatorial problems notes that if we wish to locate 4 facilities to serve a population which is located in 1,000 cells there are $9 \cdot 94 \times 10^{11}$ possibilities. In Gould's words 'the problem is brutal.' It is clear that we have to restrict the size of the problem to one which can be handled with the equipment which is currently available. At the same time we should consider the effects of simplifying the problem so that it can be solved, especially we should examine the utility of our results in the light of the efforts and costs which are involved in solving the problem.

In this chapter we will examine the major aspects of solving allocation-location problems and we will begin by considering the underlying principles of the procedures. Some of these points have been introduced in a cursory fashion in the first chapter. Explicit attention to temporal aspects of allocation–location problems will be reserved for a later chapter. The models we treat here are static.

2   Objectives, constraints, and assumptions

Though each problem often has to be posed in slightly different terms and variations can be introduced by the nature of the mode of distribution and the type of service under examination there are certain common traits to all problems. These will be treated in this section. We will start with the objectives. At the outset the usual practice is to state an objective function for each problem, let us call this Z. For example, we may be interested in moving children to schools thus we can write Z in the following way

$$Z = \sum_{j=1}^{2} \sum_{i=1}^{6} m_{ij} d_{ij}$$

this is a symbolic way of expressing the situation shown on figure 2; there are six locations for the children and two schools, the distance between each location and each school is d_{ij}, at each of the six locations there are a group of children as shown in table 4.1.

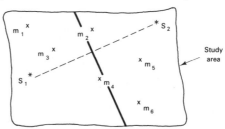

Figure 4.2   Schools and children: × m_1–m_6 Location of children;
* S_1 and S_2 school locations

Table 4.1   Number of children

m_1	4
m_2	20
m_3	9
m_4	10
m_5	5
m_6	16

$$\sum_{i=1}^{6} m_i = 64$$

The objective function is a description of the spatial arrangement and it refers to the degree of spatial efficiency with which it operates. Single objective functions are normal, for example, one of the following variables is generally used; distance, cost, or time, together with a measure of quantity to be moved, for example, the number of children, clients or customers. Not infrequently it is assumed that there is a direct relationship between these accessibility measures, so if we minimize distance travelled we also minimize time and cost, from this it is inferred that we minimize inconvenience and thus maximize social welfare.

If we wish to reduce travel distances for all children then we send each child to the nearest school. We have minimized Z and this is our best solution. If we draw the school district boundaries on this allocation pattern we would produce shapes called Theissen polygons.[4] Within a Theissen polygon all points are closest to their centre (school) than to any other centre. The general problem of locating boundaries for service districts around a set of central facilities is discussed by Keeney (1972). Theissen polygons can be constructed geometrically as in figure 4.2. For three centres the construction of the polygons is shown in figure 4.3.

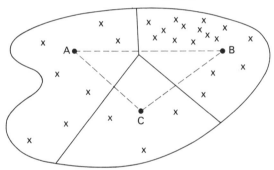

Figure 4.3   Construction of Theissen polygons

Let us now calculate how many children attend each school; S_1 has $(m_1 + m_2 + m_3 + m_4)$ 43 children and S_2 has $(m_5 + m_6)$ 21 children. From this we can see clearly that a geometrical solution while minimizing the objective function will *not* necessarily ensure an equal allocation of origins (pupils) to destinations (schools). This leads directly to statements about constraints. In this problem we may wish each school to receive 32 pupils and thus we place a constraint on the capacity of the destination. We have now transferred the problem from a geometrical one into an origin–destination problem. This type of problem is usually referred to as the Transportation Problem and it can be stated in the form of a matrix as shown in figure 4.4.

The objective function remains the same, however. In order to solve this problem we need one more piece of information; the distances between the origins and the destinations. There are several types of distance

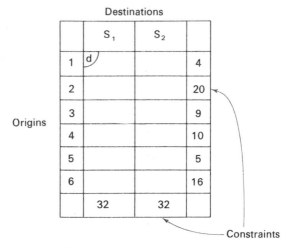

Figure 4.4   Transportation problem matrix

measures which could be used. Many studies use straight-line distances because they can be readily calculated from co-ordinates of the origins and destinations and further they correlate quite highly with real-world distances. In cities with grid transportation patterns it is often appropriate to use the Manhattan distance measure This is shown in figure 4.5.

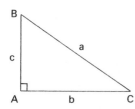

Figure 4.5   Manhattan distance measure
Manhattan distance between B and $C = c + b$;
Pythagoras distance between B and $C =$
$\sqrt{c^2 + b^2}$

This is always larger than the straight-line distance. An interesting exercise is to construct Theissen polygons under the rectangular travel system. This is shown in Carter *et al.* (1971). In areas with non-linear, horizontal or stepped cost functions as in figure 4.6, it is often better to incorporate real-world values. In the matrix in figure 4.6 we should add a distance value in the corner of each cell. The next task is to find the allocation of origins to destinations, to satisfy the capacity constraint and to minimize the total distance travelled. We then have the optimal solution and a normative model. We determine the optimal allocation using one of several logarithms which have been developed within the field of linear programming. Good non-technical reviews of the procedures for tackling the transportation problem are provided by Cox (1965) and Yeates (1968). It is sufficient for our purposes to know that in order to solve non-trivial problems we need a computer, and that fairly large matrices

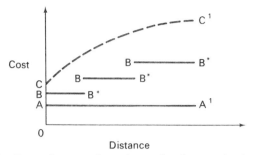

Figure 4.6   Cost–distance functions. A—A^1 standard rate; B—$B*$ step functions; C/C^1 haulage charges decrease with increasing distance

of origins and destination can be solved in reasonable time. If we add a further constraint to our problem, that the groups of children cannot be split because they all travel in the same car or school-bus, then this could mean that a perfect allocation cannot be found and thus the capacity conditions may have to be relaxed slightly. This occurs most frequently with a small number of origins and destinations. The general practice is to combine manual methods with computer solutions to make adjustments to the capacities of the destinations.

In this simple example of schools we have outlined the basic ideas and associated difficulties of the allocation problem. Let us now turn to the location problem. This time we begin with a spatial distribution of origins and our task is to find the best location for one or more destinations. Again we start with an objective function and the purpose of the exercise is to minimize this under certain conditions. In a recent paper Palmer (1973) attempted to derive theoretical relationship between the density of centres and the population density so that the mean travel distance is as low as possible. He suggests that the density of centres should be proportional to the two-thirds power of the population density. As he points out in his study this general approach must be modified before it can be applied to a specific region with its particular characteristics.

Let us now consider a location problem in which we have six origins and we wish to locate one destination in such a way that the distance travelled from the origins is minimum. The problem is shown graphically in figure 4.7.

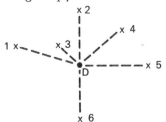

Figure 4.7   The location problem. D is 'destination'

The objective function can be expressed as

$$\sum_{i=1}^{6} m_i d_{ij}.$$

At origin i there are m_i people, and the distance between this and the destination is d_{ij}. We are trying to find the position of D such that the aggregate distance travelled is minimum. This is the most accessible point for collection or distribution. It should be noted that in this location problem we assume that D can be located anywhere, the transportation system is a planar surface. While this may be a reasonable assumption prior to the opening-up of an area to human settlement, it is not a realistic assumption when we consider existing transportation links and a network of connections. Thus in most cases we have to modify the location problem so that it can be applied to a network. A summary of where feasible locations are to be found is shown in figure 4.8, and a discussion is pro-

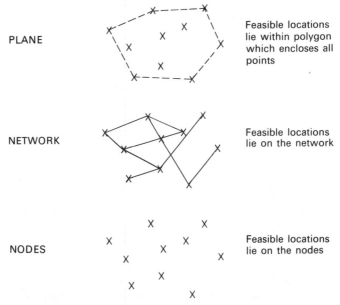

Figure 4.8 Feasible locations for destinations: solution – spaces

vided by Roberts (1971). In the case of a set of points on a plane the solution lies in the space defined by the perimeter. However, for a network the solution lies somewhere along the links between the modes. It has been shown in this second case that if we are trying to minimize transportation costs to a set of destinations, and costs are a linear function of distance along the network then the optimal locations for destinations can be at the nodes.[5] Thus the solution space is effectively narrowed to a set of points.

With these basic points in mind let us move on to examine the procedures for handling allocation-location problem. Later we will consider specific case studies.

3 Procedures

We can identify a spectrum of technical procedures which range from physical analogue models of the distribution system under examination to abstract mathematical models. The components of this spectrum may be summarized as follows:

1   Mechanical.
2   Geometrical.
3   Heuristic.
4   Numeric–analytical.
5   Simulation.
6   Intuition.

There is a developing body of literature on all these procedures. Advances are rapid. Particular progress has been made by those working on the last four, in the size of the problems that can be handled and the accuracy of the solution. It follows that the relative importance of the different methods for solving real-world problems is likely to change as technical and analytical procedures improve. Advances are usually reported in journals of operations research.[6] In this section we will focus attention on the first four in the list. Mechanical and geometrical approaches are included primarily for historical reasons, contemporary problems are solved heuristically or analytically. Simulation and intuition are basically variations on heuristics; the former uses a mechanical device such as a computer to examine alternate solutions, each new solution is a development of the prior step, and the search for the optimal is via a code learning process. Intuition represents a human skill, the eye and the brain interact to arrive at what is considered the best solution. A specific evaluation of alternative solutions is not normally part of intuition, whereas in simulation it is a vital part.

Mechanical analogues
The mechanical approach is shown in figure 4.9 and discussions are presented by Eilon *et al.* (1971), Abler *et al.* (1971) and Burstall, Leaver and Sussams (1962), Shea (1966) and Wesolowsky (1973). The single advantage of this approach according to Eilon, quoting Shea, is that it arouses people's interest in the problem. Alternative locations for the single destination are not evaluated, thus we have no means of measuring the degree of sub-optimality of a location choice. Friction can prevent a unique solution being determined for one destination, and if we wish to locate more than one destination then predetermined allocations of origins to destinations are needed. These are the strings. This predeter-

Mechanical Analogue

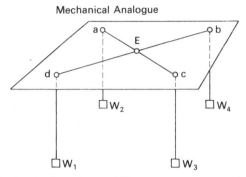

Figure 4.9 Mechanical analogue. Ws represent the number of people at a specific location *a*, *b*, *c*, and *d*

mination influences the outcome and we have no way of knowing which is the best allocation. When the system is in equilibrium E is the most accessible point to *a*, *b*, *c*, and *d*, the weight determines the pull of a place. It is clear that the number of people at each place influences the position of the destination and while this is an explicit component of the mechanical approach it was not incorporated into the early geometrical models.

Geometrical

Some three hundred years ago, Cavalieri tackled the problem of determining a single location with maximum accessibility to a set of other points. He considered the problem of finding the point that minimized the sum of the distances to three given points. An historical review of methods is presented by Wesolowsky (1973). Cooper (1963) notes that other mathematicians, Heinen, Fagnano and Tedenat approached similar problems in an attempt to discover how this general problem could be solved. Three years after Heinen, Steiner proved that for *n* points the necessary and sufficient conditions for the destination are that 'the sum of the cosines of the angles between any arbitrary line in the plane and the set of lines connecting the given points with the minimum point [destination] must equal zero'. It should be stressed that only one destination was being located and that as regards the number of customers all points were assumed to have equal importance. As with the mechanical solution we are not able to evaluate the proximity of a site to the optimal

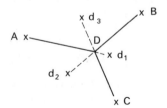

Figure 4.10 The location of a depot: *A*, *B*, *C* origins; *D* destination; d_1, d_2, d_3 alternate sites. Which is the best? If $A = B = C$ and $d_{1D} < d_{2D} < d_{3D}$ then d_1 is closes to optimal location

location in cost terms. We may be able to plot alternative sites on the same plan as the optimal, but we cannot always apply geometry to find the best of the alternatives. This is shown diagrammatically in figure 4.10. However, if $A \neq B \neq C$, then we cannot use geometry and the simple measurement of distance or angles. We must weight the origins and this leads us directly into heuristic and numeric-analytical prodecures.

Heuristic

Scott (1971) claims that, 'heuristic programming is less a rigidly defined mathematical procedure than a very general problem-solving philosophy'. Basically we define an objective function for the situation such that it captures the property we are particularly interested in, for example, in the case of a school and a set of children we are attempting to find the most accessible location, thus the objective function $Z = \sum_{i=1}^{n} m_i d_{ij}$, can be used. This is exactly the same as the one referred to earlier. The procedure normally adopted for this type of location problem using the heuristic approach is shown below as a sequence of steps.

1   Define solution space – see figure 4.8.
2   Choose an arbitrary point that looks reasonable p_1.
3   Calculate

$$\sum_{i=1}^{n} m_i d_{ip_1}, \text{ call this } Z_1.$$

4   Choose another point p_2; a short distance from p_1.
5   Calculate

$$\sum_{i=1}^{n} m_i d_{ip_2}, \text{ call this } Z_2.$$

6   Continue to search the space around p_1 until the lowest value of Z is found.

Conceptually we can describe the procedure as searching over a cost surface which has at least one hollow, the lowest part represents the least cost solution. If the surface has only one hollow, then this heuristic procedure will find the overall best solution. This is called the *global* optimum. However, if there are several hollows on the surface then we may only find a *local* optimum. No matter in which direction we move from the *local* optimum values for Z increase, we therefore never move out of this hollow. In order to test the utility of the heuristic procedure, and to see if a global optimum exists, several different starting points are usually used. If we always converge on the same final position for the lowest Z value, then we can be reasonably confident that this is the global optimum, though we cannot be certain.

Several workers have stressed that the great merit of the heuristic approach is that it allows us to tackle systematically large problems of the type mentioned earlier in this chapter. Simulation procedures are very similar for they too can be applied to allocation-location problems which are too large or complicated to treat by the method of examining all alternatives. A useful description of simulation procedures and introductions to the subject are provided by Ward (1964) and Moore (1968). The latter argues that because many organizations are large and complex 'operational policies are usually established by intuition, judgement, and simulation rather than by direct experimentation.' While this is indeed common practice in the day-to-day organization of an enterprise, there are researchers who contrive to search for procedures to determine the optimum allocation–location pattern. This work falls into the numeric-analytical cagegory.

Numeric–analytical

Within this category there are a sequence of procedures. The first is concerned with the identification of the problem and its statement in a symbolic form. This can be compared to the objective function which we have already discussed earlier. Second, an attempt is made to prove that an optimum allocation–location pattern exists using this objective function and any extra constraints such as capacity of destinations, maximum distance to be travelled or a budget for the total investment in destinations. Third, we wish to know if this optimum is unique. A normal strategy to achieve these goals is to apply differential calculus and examine the form of the function by establishing whether it is concave or convex. The former suggests an optimum exists at the lowest point on the concave curve. In some cases it cannot be proved that the function is either convex or concave and thus we have no analytical way of showing the form of the function and we have to depend upon the results of empirical trial and error to interpret the shape of the function. Next try to identify the conditions which are necessary and/or sufficient to tell us when we have located the optimum. The steps outlined above fall into the domain of pure mathematics and it is sufficient at this stage for us to recognize that these procedures exist. However, we should know something about the state of the art and the progress that has been made thus far. One of the most recent contributions to this field comes from Katz and Cooper (1973). They have developed a method of discovering the point which minimizes $\sum d_{ij}$'s when the d_{ij}'s are generated from a probability distribution for the x and y co-ordinates. They show analytically that their algorithm will find the point and it is unique. Further, the method is globally convergent, and convergence on the optimum is monotonic and linear.

For a relatively simple relationship of the type $Z = \sum m_i d_{ij}$, Haley (1963) has proved that this is a convex function. Therefore a unique location exists where Z takes on its minimum value. There is a single best location for the school. However, to locate this solution we have to proceed via a searching algorithm and we can be fairly confident that if we always converge on the same point irrespective of our starting position we have found the global optimum. If we had defined a slightly different objective function of the form

$$Z = \sum_{i=1}^{n} m_i d_{ij}^2$$

which suggests that we are concerned with finding the destination which minimizes the sum of the distance *squared* then we have a simple procedure for determining the exact position of this point. This is the centre of gravity of the distribution and the method for finding this unique location was discussed in detail in Chapter 2. However, we should note that even though we have a set procedure for determining the exact solution and we know that the answer is unique, as we use d^2 in the objective function we are giving disproportionally greater pull to the places which are located on the periphery of the area, *ceteris paribus*.

In order to tackle the problem of choosing the best *set* of destinations then the normal strategy is to use an heuristic approach as outlined as a series of steps below.

1   Choose arbitrary centres as destinations.
2   Allocate origins to destinations
     (i) using transportation problem approach or
     (ii) Theissen polygon approach, ie nearest unconstrained.
3   Evaluate the cost of the allocation pattern using the objective function.
4   Relocate the destinations.
5   Reallocate origins to destinations.
6   Evaluate new pattern, if cheaper than previous one (3) then go to step 4 and continue, if more expensive than previous one, then stop and 3 is cheapest allocation–location pattern.

Eilon *et al.* (1971) have argued that the objective function is convergent and should yield a unique optimal solution to this multi-destination problem. However, using empirical data it has been shown that the starting-point for the initial location of destinations influences the outcome of the procedure, and it is clear that at this time we do not have a method that will provide an exact solution to this problem of locating a set of destinations. Further research is needed in this field.

Let us now consider a similar problem concerning a network joining population centres. The problem is to select a set of destinations such that aggregate accessible is maximized. A method for tackling this problem has been applied by Maranzana (1964), and essentially it is the same as the one outlined in the steps above. He suggests that as an analytical solution does not at present exist it is necessary to use an iterative procedure, and 'judicious selection of alternate starting values will assure a good, if not optimal, solution'.

4   Exact versus intuitive solutions

Thus far in this chapter we have stressed systematic procedures for solving allocation–location problems. In some cases the procedures will give use an exact answer, in others, because of the size or nature of the problem, we only have an approximation, though by experimentation we feel that our approximate answer is close to the very best or exact solution. However, there remains another approach which does not depend directly on computing the costs of alternate allocations in a rigorous fashion but rather depends upon an individual ability to treat the problem visually. This intuitive approach has attracted attention in the last few years, particularly since we can now compare intuitive answers to exact ones, and thus evaluate the utility of the intuitive approach. Until this stage was reached we based our confidence on faith. We now have a firmer base for our confidence. We can also, evaluate the attributes of individuals relation to their intuitive skill in solving allocation–location problems. This is vital if we hope to train people to make better intuitive decisions in this field. We can also evaluate the severity of problems which can be handled with reasonable accuracy. Some of these points have been taken up by Schneider, Eilon et al., and Rushton.[7] Rushton is currently working in this field and in particular is concentrating on locating facilities in rural districts in developing countries. He is using data for south India and he is concerned with the accuracy with which 1, 5 or 10 centres can be located to serve a dispersed population in an area with centres of different size and several transportation modes. The study area Talala Taluka, Junagadh District is approximately 200 square miles (518 km^2) in extent and has a fairly compact spatial form.

In 1971 Scott reported that on limited kinds of combinatorial problems random sampling will produce solutions with high probability which are within 10 to 20 per cent of optimal. More rigorous work has been reported by Eilon et al. (1971) and they compare solutions which start with a random choice of locations with solutions derived from estimates made by students. They conducted an experiment for 50 origins and 2, 3, 4 and 5 destinations. Their findings suggest that there is no advantage to be gained for the 2 and 3 destination problems, the intuitive starting

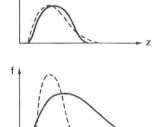

Figure 4.11   Comparison of frequency–cost distributions: 2 and 3 destinations (above), 4 and 5 destinations (below): with random starting points (continuous line) and with intuitive starting points (dashed line)

points and random starting-points yield similar frequency–cost distributions. This is shown diagrammatically in figure 4.11. However, they claim that for 4 and 5 destinations the random starting-points give a wider spread of cost values compared with the intuitive starting positions (see figure 4.11).

We should note, however, that the best solution appear to be the same irrespective of the value of the starting position. In summary it seems that it makes little difference which method is used for determining the starting position in the iterative algorithms. It would be useful, however, if a comparison of costs was available; there may be savings here as the intuitive solution may be nearer the optimal and therefore less computing time may be required.

Schneider conducted a slighly different type of experiment. He asked his subject to choose final locations for emergency facilities in a hypothetical city. Seventy-seven possible locations were available for five ambulance dispatch centres. The transport system and a dot distribution of likely accidents was given together with the constraint that the maximum time lapse to reach an accident is ten minutes. It was assumed that average speed on the rectangular road system was 20 miles per hour (32 km/hr) compared to 40 miles per hour (64 km/hr) on five arterial roads that cut through the city. It is rather difficult to support Schneider's conclusions fully because he chose a computer algorithm which selected possible sites on a random basis. The frequency-cost distribution therefore approached a normal bell-shaped curve whereas the student's solutions tend to cluster at the low-cost end. This is shown in figure 4.12.

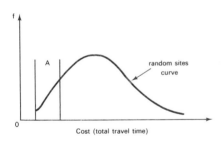

Figure 4.12 Comparison of random sites with intuitive choices. *A* is zone of intuitive choices. (See Chapter 5, Section 8, for another example of the intuitive approach.)

We would, however, concur with the suggestion examining only the intuitive sites is likely to yield as good an optimal selection as randomly searching a large number of possibilities: the former strategy is possibly less costly in computing expenses. Finally, this branch of allocation-location studies demands closer attention before definitive claims on the pros and cons of intuitive versus computer procedures can be made. At this stage it would seem that an interface system is most appropriate. Intuition could possibly be used to define a solution space, the computer could then search within this for the best site.

5 Empirical examples

In this section we will turn our attention to a selection of empirical studies which have applied the allocation–location problem. A wide variety of public services are considered and the studies have been chosen because they represent an almost complete coverage of the different forms of the problem. A summary is provided in table 4.2.

Table 4.2 Summary of empirical studies*

Author	Date	Public service	Area
Yeates	1963	School districts	Wisconsin, Grant County, USA
Gould and Leinbach	1966	Hospitals	W. Gautemala
Mills	1967	Voting districts	Bristol, UK
Hogg	1968	Fire stations	Bristol, UK
Goodchild and Massam	1969	Administrative area electricity service	S. Ontario, Canada
Coyle and Martin	1969	Refuse collection	A northern industrial city of 150,000 UK
Dee	1970	Urban playgrounds	Baltimore City, USA
Mercer, O'Neil and Shepherd	1970	Churches	Preston, UK
Whitacker	1971	Hospitals	British Columbia, Canada
Holmes, Williams and Brown	1972	Daycare centres	Columbus, Ohio, USA

*See also Markland *et al.* (1972) police: Hess and Samuels (1971) sales districts using legislative apportionment algorithm, and Drake *et al.* (1972) emergency services in cities.

Yeates's paper (1963) has been widely cited in geographical literature as one of the first examples of the application of an objective allocation procedure to a real-world spatial problem. His particular task was to evaluate the savings in transport costs that could be made by redrawing school district boundaries in Grant County, Wisconsin. Thirteen schools were involved and each had a given capacity. For the purposes of the allocation it was assumed that all the children could be described by a set of 754 points. This was the weighted point set. Obvious proximal allocations were made manually and the origin set was reduced to 293. A standard trasportation problem was set up with 13 destinations (schools) and 293 origins with the capacities as currently existing. The optimal allocation, that is the one which minimised aggregate distance travelled, was calculated and new school district maps drawn. Visually there are no great differences between the actual boundary locations and the theoretical set of boundaries. However, in terms of transportation savings it is suggested that between $3,000 and $4,000 could be saved each year by using the revised boundaries. This study is characterized by fixed capacities for the destinations unlike the work by Gould and Leinbach (1966) in which adjustments to the size of the destinations (hospitals) were made as part of the allocation–location procedure. Their task was to choose three hospital sites from a set of five, then allocate population to these sites so that no cross-flows occurred. They collapsed the population surface of Western Guatemala into eighteen points; these served as origins. Next they found the best three sites by examining the possible combinations. They defined 'best' as the set of sites which gave the lowest total mileage travelled. They started by assuming that each hospital was the same size. This generated a set of cross-flows. Changes to the size of the hospitals were introduced on two successive runs of the procedure and the final allocation was considered to be optimal. The allocation procedure used was a modification of the transportation problem. It could be argued that as the capacities of the destinations were unconstrained the easiest procedure would have been to allocate people to their nearest hospital once a set of three had been selected.

Turning to a much smaller scale problem and to another field of spatial organization we will examine Mills' (1967) paper. He was concerned with developing an objective procedure to overcome gerrymandering in urban areas and the particular aspect which attracted his attention was the problem of defining voting districts with equal populations. This subject has been tackled by several workers including Kaiser (1966), Silva (1965), Weaver and Hess (1963). Mills generated optimal patterns for voting districts in Bristol, UK, using data for 1954 and 1965. He was able to evaluate the utility of his procedure by comparing his model with the real-world situation. At the outset it was stated that by combining indivisible polling units the method should produce spatially compact districts with equal populations. The sequence of steps defined below outlines the procedure, and it should be noticed that it is an iterative procedure, using manual skill and computer aid:

1   Choose arbitrary set of voting district centres. These are the destinations. The polling units are the origins and a single central point is used to describe each one.

2   Allocate origins to destinations, using the transportation algorithm and assuming equal capacity for each destination.

3   Combine split districts manually.

4   Compute a new set of destinations using centre of gravity of the district.

5   Use these new centres to reallocate the polling units.

6   If any of the new centres are different from the old go back to 2, if not stop and this is the optimal allocation.

Because the area is divided by river Avon the procedure was modified so that districts would not be split by this natural feature. The outcome of the algorithm was a set of voting districts which were fairly similar in population size and more spatially compact than those previously used. In 1954 the greatest difference in population size among the 28 voting units was approximately 4,000, and in 1965 almost three times this amount. The computer model reduced these to less than 3,000 both times. The variation in size between the voting districts produced by Mills was due to the fact that the basic units, polling units, were considered indivisible. It was also felt that continuous districts were necessary.

Another spatial allocation problem was tackled in Bristol, UK, at about the same time. Hogg (1968) examined the location of fire stations in the area. This work was a specific application of the general problem of choosing r stations from n sites, where n is greater than r, to satisfy specific goals. Just after the second world war fire protection standards were defined in the UK and they persist to this day, with only slight modifications being made in the late 'fifties. In urban areas with high risk it was suggested that 3 or 4 pumps should be available and the first should arrive within 5 minutes of the alarm. In rural areas one pump should arrive within 20 minutes. This defines a quality level for the service. In the Bristol area there are nineteen possible fire station sites and currently six are used. The spatial pattern of fire incidence over several years is also available. With these basic data Hogg divided the area into fifteen sub-areas. She used intuition and attempted to define boundaries in low fire risk areas and to take note of the location of barriers such as rivers, canals and railways. One or more of the nineteen sites were associated with each area. The number of fires per km^2yr^{-1} were also plotted. This varied from approximately 100 in the centre to less than nine over the major part of the region. For each area a reference point was defined. This was the centre of gravity. The junction of roads nearest to this was taken as the point to summarize the area. Time distances from these fifteen reference points to the nineteen possible sites were calculated empirically. By systemmatically examining the cost in time of serving the points with a varying number of fire stations utility curves were prepared. The basic form of the curve is shown in figure 4.13.

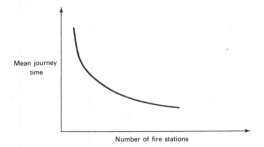

Figure 4.13   Utility curve for fire protection

From this curve it can be shown that with about five or six fire stations all areas can be serviced in approximately 3 minutes and by adding two or three to this set the savings in time are very small. With only three stations the average time is 4 minutes but as the curve is very steep here it is suggested that significant improvement would follow by increasing the number to five or six.

Finally, a table of site selections was prepared. A hypothetical example is given in table 4.3.

Table 4.3 Optimal site selection table

No. of sites	Site codes
1	a
2	a, c
3	c, b, d
.	.
.	.
.	.

It should be noted that the choice of site depends upon the number to be chosen, the sequence is not necessarily additive. In the example shown in table 4.3, if only one site is needed then site *a* is selected. However, if we choose three sites *a* is not included and we use sites *c*, *b* and *d*. This kind of information can help us make objective rational choices to solve fire station location problems. However, before suggestions can be made for the optimal number of stations, we must have data on construction and maintenance costs as well as estimates of fire damage losses.

In 1969 Goodchild and Massam presented their findings on an application of the allocation–location problem to electrical service areas in Southern Ontario, Canada. They attempted to find the best location for eight service centres and to draw service area boundaries around these centres so that each served a particular work load. The work loads for the centres were unequal yet consistent with the variation which currently exists. If an equal work load constraint is added then because of the high population density near Toronto, the areal extent of this service area is very small. At the time of the study the capacity of the destinations (service centres) was as shown in table 4.4.

Table 4.4 Capacity of destinations

	population served Per cent
Toronto	50
London	15
Ottawa	12
Hamilton	12
Chatham	5
Kingston	2
Peterborough	2
Barrie	2

The population of Southern Ontario was assigned to a set of 504 township centres. These served as the origins in the transportation problem, together with the eight destinations and the capacity constraints. Airline distances were used and the objective function was to minimize the total distance travelled. While it is not possible to solve the allocation and the location parts of the problem at the same time, by tackling them in sequence a good final solution emerges. The procedure is outlined as a series of steps:

1   Using eight actual centres, allocate origins to destinations solving the transportation problem.
2   Draw boundaries around the origins and their associated destination.
3   Within each service area which was defined in Step 2, find the point of minimum aggregate travel with respect to the origins.
4   If these new centres are different from the ones used in Step 1, go to Step 1 and repeat Steps 2, 3 and 4 until there are no changes in the location of the centres.

This sequence was applied to the Ontario data set and the savings in distance travelled are shown in table 4.5.

Table 4.5   Distance travelled in Ontario

Models	Average distance travelled
1 Actual system existing	52 miles (83·2 km)
2 Proximal – Theissen polygon model, *the* most efficient, but has no capacity constraints	19 miles (30·5 km)
3 Optimal model with capacity constraints	20 miles (32 km)

It can clearly be seen that even with capacity constraints the new pattern is considerably better than the real-world situation. However, to achieve this it is necessary to relocate centres. If the centres were not relocated and only the boundaries redefined on the basis of allocating origins to their nearest destination then Theissen polygons would result and the average distance would decline to 19 miles (10·5 km). Possibly this represents the best policy recommendation.

A further example of an application of the allocation problem to aid in making policy decisions is provided by the work of Coyle and Martin (1969). Using empirical data on the times of refuse collection and distances in a city in the north of England they showed how savings could be made by reorganizing the spatial pattern of collection routes. For the city under examination, which had a population of 150,000, they demonstrated that approximately £10,000 per year could be saved. The city was divided into 190 sections, each containing about 250 houses. A series of empirical assumptions were defined, for example: each collection team should not work more than 8 hours per day for 5 days per week; collection should be once a week; individual refuse collectors should collect *and* empty the container as it was demonstrated that it is less efficient to use two teams, one collecting containers and one loading the vehicle. The characteristics which affect the timing of refuse collection in each housing section were also evaluated.

An allocation procedure was defined to assign men to vehicles and vehicles to rounds so that total collection costs were minimized. To begin with a section was chosen arbitrarily, then other sections were added if they were contiguous. In order to choose the additional section when two or more were adjacent the moment of inertia fo each was calculated. The one with the lowest value was added. This procedure attempted to produce spatially compact units and is comparable to Mills' method which we have already discussed. The centroid for the set of sections recalculated and the sequence continued until the constraints were satisfied. Alternate patterns were evaluated and the least cost solution was considered to be optimal, the authors claim that this may not be the global optimum, but it is likely to be very close.

In all the allocation–location problems treated thus far it is implicit that decisions are made according to distance or cost criteria and capacity constraints. However, there are specific types of problem which explicity involve 'yes-no' types of decisions. They refer specifically to the location of facilities to a specific site. For example, we cannot locate half or one-quarter of a hospital to a site, but we can choose between one hospital or no hospital at a particular location. These types of integer decision problems depend upon a technique which is a modification of the usual linear programming procedure used to solve the normal transportation problem. The new technique is integer programming and a good summary is provided by Scott (1971). Dee's study (1970) provides us with an empirical application. His work was concerned with choosing the best combination of three alternative types of recreation facilities for a small number of sites given that a larger number of possible locations are available. Empirical work in the study area showed that attendance at a recreation facility was related to proximity to residences, and particularly the number of street crossings which separated the park from the home. The three types of facilities are:

1   Open spaces, 'asphalt jungles', with few slides and swings.
2   Open space with facilities for arts and crafts room for films and a basketball area.
3   Type 2 with a swimming pool.

Expected daily attendance varied from 20 in type one, 40 in the second type to 110 in type three. The demand for recreational facilities was localized into a set of 198 population centres. These served as the origins. The object of this allocation–location problem was to maximize attendance at recreation facilities. The problem was set up as follows:

1   Each population centre could be assigned to only one park.
2   At each site only one type of park is possible.

3   A budget constraint, which is determined outside the procedure,
     is given. This is the number of parks of each type.
4   The formula which described the level of attendance at a park
     as a function of distance was derived empirically.

The procedure was tested for an area of almost 4,000 acres (1,618·7
hectares) and 767 city blocks in the City of Baltimore. Twenty potential
sites were available and eleven parks had to be located. The current
attendance figures are slightly greater than 80,000. However, by reallocat-
ing the three types among the eleven current sites it is possible to increase
attendance by over 30,000. If we chose the best set of eleven locations
from the set of twenty and allocated the three types among these to maximize the objective function then attendance could reach over 130,000.
Clearly improvements to the current arrangement could be made. The
advantages of the new system are not direct savings in time or cost as
in most of the earlier empirical examples but rather improvements to
public welfare.

A further example which touches on public welfare is the study by
Mercer et al. (1970), which examines the spatial organization of urban
parishes. They claim that Preston is 'over-churched', and the situation
is being aggravated because families are moving into the suburbs and
away from the strong concentration of churches in the central city.
On the basis of a series of interviews and church surveys the relationships
between distance and levels of attendance were determined. Using these
as inputs into a general allocation model it was suggested that if up to
5 churches were closed the drop in attendance would likely be about
1 per cent and a financial saving of over £3,000 per year would be
achieved. If the five sites were also sold the financial gains would be
considerable. In this paper a strict objective function was not defined,
rather a series of possible curves were produced relating attendance levels
to the number of churches much in the same way as the study by Hogg
generated curves for fire services in Bristol. However, in the former
instance at best we can only say something about attendance levels and
from these infer welfare, whereas in the latter example an attempt could
be made to keep the whole problem on a strictly financial basis. Often
for analytical purposes we refer to objective measures and not infrequently we use these as surrogates for social satisfaction and to measure
the quality of the service offered.[8]

The majority of the case studies examined deal with allocations or
locations on planar surfaces and the solution spaces are frequently areas
as shown in figure 4.8 earlier in this chapter. We will now turn to a study
which focused attention on a network problem. The solution is confined
to nodes located on a transportation network. The study is by Whitacker
(1971) and the service he examined was hospitals in a selected area of
south-east British Columbia. The size of the study area is approximately
500 by 250 miles (804 by 402 km) and the road network which serves

the area has 171 nodes. Of these, 52 have a population greater than 1,000 and these were treated as potential hospital sites. Currently 33 hospitals are used. Whitacker set up a location problem to find the optimum location for 33 hospitals such that accessibility was maximized. Capacity constraints for the hospital sites were defined and it was concluded that for the three types of health services examined, medical, surgical and maternity, savings of at least 10 per cent on the distances patients travelled could be achieved by relocating the hospitals to the optimum sites. Given that construction and maintenance of hospitals represents a substantial proportion of expenditures in a health service programme it is essential that the funds be wisely used and that decisions regarding the choice of sites should take into account the spatial distribution of potential demand. Whitacker's work could be used to this end.

The final study by Holmes *et al.* (1972) is an application of an integer programming problem with distance constraints between the clients and the facilities. The objective was to maximize the number of people who have access to a set of day-care facilities by choosing the optimal locations for facilities under the constraint that there is a threshold distance beyond which people are not prepared to travel. The study area was part of Columbus, Ohio. Threshold distances of $\frac{1}{4}$, $\frac{1}{2}$ and 1 mile (0·4, 0·8, 1·6 km) were used. Currently 8 centres are used and the authors argue that of these 4 are not ideally located with regard to maximum accessibility. The threshold level in this instance was $\frac{1}{2}$ mile (0·8 km).

Further work was undertaken with a wide variety of numbers of centres ranging from 10 to 45, using intervals of five. A half-mile threshold was used. The eight centres which exist at this time were explicitly contained within the set selected. This simulation study showed that only a marginal increase (approximately 1,000) in the number of people served resulted from increasing the number of centres from 10 to 45.

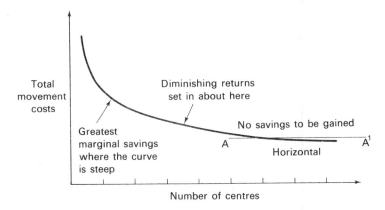

Figure 4.14   Relationship between movement costs and the number of centres

The largest increase occurred when the number shifted from 15 to 20. However, the extra five centres only opened up the area to about 600 people. In terms of movement costs the marginal savings continues at about the same rate until there are 35 centres, after this number the curve becomes flatter and diminishing returns set in. This is shown in figure 4.14.

6   Conclusions

Before we move on to Chapter 5 which will deal with some of the dynamic aspects of interaction within administrative areas let us summarize the main faetures of the allocation–location models treated in this chapter:

1   The models are partial, one service is treated at a time.
2   The models are static, we do not consider investments over time or movement patterns as they vary from day to day. Queues and congestion do not enter into the transportation problem discussed in this chapter.
3   Good data are needed to solve the models and we usually depend upon computers to evaluate the costs of alternate spatial configurations.
4   Large problems frequently have to be modified so that the alternate patterns can be examined in a reasonable amount of time.
5   Intuition may be useful to solve allocation–location problems and probably it can be used most effectively in conjunction with a computer algorithm.
6   An understanding of the principles underlying the formulation of allocation–location problems may help in more objective policy-making with respect to the location of public facilities.
7   There is a growing interest in the application of these models to aid in policy-making in the Third World, both to solve specific problems and to teach planners some of the principles of physical planning (Elshaffi, 1972).

Notes on further reading

An excellent summary of the location–allocation problem is provided in Abler, Adams and Gould (1971).

A useful non-technical review of the methods used for solving combinatorial problems, of the allocation–location type, is given in Scott (1971b).

For details on the rigorous statement of the problem see Cooper (1963) and Eilon et al. (1971). Both references also discuss methods for solving the problem.

The utility of using intuition to solve the problem is discussed in Schneider (1971). A variety of case studies are listed in table 2.

Notes

1 See, for example, the elementary text by Sussams (1969) or the very complex treatment by Serck-Hanssen (1970).

2 Ward 1964). This is a non-technical overview of the topic.

3 A general review of the interplay of investments, returns and timing with respect to retailing is provided in Applebaum (1970).

4 A discussion on Theissen polygons is provided in: Haggett and Chorley (1969, 236ff).

5 This is discussed in Sussams (1969, 8–21).

6 See, for example: Operations Research; Operational Research Quarterly; Management Science; Geographical Analysis.

7 Private correspondence with Dr G. Rushton, University of Iowa, Iowa City (1973).

8 Those interested in church location problems should consult Cole and King (1968, 491).

5　Interaction within administrative districts

1　Introduction

The models and procedures which were examined in Chapter 4 depend upon the assumptions that demand and supply are fixed at specific locations and that the efficiency of the distribution system is influenced directly by the relative position of these points. It was shown that manipulation of the relative positions in space of supply and demand, under a set of constraints, could produce distribution systems of different degrees of spatial efficiency. The aim of the allocation–location models was to find the spatial configuration which produced maximum spatial efficiency. Clearly, these models are restrictive in the real-world as they do not take into account variations in supply and demand over time; also they do not consider the varying quality of the transportation links over time. These variations can be of two distinct types. First, those which occur at regular intervals within a day, week, month or year, and second, those events which occur at random. Thus if we are to evaluate the functional efficiency of a system for providing services then the procedure used should take note of these types of occurrences. This point will be developed later when we discuss a method for incorporating cyclic and random fluctuations into the basic models discussed earlier.

The allocation–location models presented in Chapter 4 are characterized by apparent elegance and sophistication, and even though several of them cannot be solved by rigorous analytical procedures it is claimed that they capture the essential ingredients of a distribution system. Therefore if we can find the arrangement of flows which maximizes the specific objective function then the level of efficiency of the system is very high. However, before we can accept this claim the temporal variations mentioned above must be taken into account and we should evaluate the efficiency of a particular arrangement over a specific period of time. The models discussed so far only consider efficiency at a single point in time. Possibly they represent a good approximation of a longer period, and thus an optimum arrangement at a single point in time is as good as the optimum arrangement derived by evaluating the system over time. We can only be sure of this by considering both possibilities. Eilon *et al*, (1971, 88) have considered the influence of variable demand on local delivery costs from depots, and they suggest that though it is unlikely to influence bulk deliveries from factories to depots, at the local level it is 'a problem that needs to be examined'. This chapter aims to introduce the influence of time into the models for distributing public goods and services.

At the outset we can recognize a range of time influences, from the small-scale variations, hourly, daily, weekly, or seasonal, which occur within a basic organization structure, to large-scale changes which occur over a period of years. The large-scale changes will be considered in Chapter 8. The basic structure refers to the location and quantity of customers, depots, service personnel and the transportation links and modes of conveyance. In this chapter we are not concerned with the consequences of opening up a new road, of an increase in consumers because of the construction of a new suburb or with the results of closing supply points. Also we assume that the nature of the service provided remains fairly constant over short periods of time. If we examine a service system over several years then it is very likely that events of these types will have occurred and any statements about long-run efficiency should take them into account. With these points in mind we can define three distinct levels which provide a temporal framework within which we can evaluate the efficiency of a distribution system. These are summarized below:

1   Static (allocation–location models of the type considered in Chapter 4).
2   Dynamic, within a constrained structure of supply, demand, personnel, service type and transportation.
3   Dynamic, with no constraints on supply, etc (see Chapter 8).

Within the second group there are a set of procedures which can be used to evaluate distributions systems for public goods, and though most of these procedures have been developed outside the discipline of geography, it is appropriate that geographers take note of such work as the subject-matter is essentially spatial. In the rest of the chapter we will examine some of this work, and we will begin by focusing attention on queuing theory and simulation, in a later section we will examine the concept of expected distance. This concept appears to have considerable potential for the analysis of interaction within service districts. In this chapter we consider that the service district is an autonomous unit but later, in Chapter 6, we will examine interaction between districts.

2   An overview of queuing problems

When a customer arrives at a service centre the length of time he has to wait for the service influences his impression of the efficiency of the system. Similarly if a demand for service which is distributed from a depot is not satisfied within a reasonable time then the client may question the utility of the service. Examples of the first case include hospitals, clinics, public offices and doctors' surgeries and in the second category we could include fire, police and emergency ambulance calls. In certain cases there is a diminishing utility for the service as the waiting time increases, this usually applies to emergency calls. This diminishing utility is shown diagrammatically for fire services in figure 5.1.

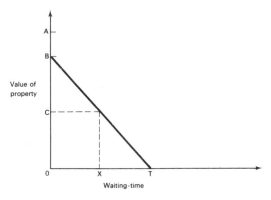

Figure 5.1   Utility of fire service with respect to waiting-time

If a fire appliance arrives the instant a fire alarm is made, a time equal to zero, then the fire damage is likely to be limited. This is *A–B* in figure 5.1. However, after *X* minutes the damage has increased to *AC* and after *T* minutes the fire has completely destroyed the property. If the appliance arrives after *T* minutes it is therefore of no utility. However, for most services waiting is an inconvenience that has to be endured and the disutility of waiting-time is assumed to be of low consequence compared with the utility of the service which is provided. This is no excuse, of course, for not trying to improve the organization of the supply so that the waiting-time can be kept as low as possible. As in many public facility decisions a compromise has to be achieved between a very expensive system which has low waiting-time and a less expensive arrangement where waiting-times are longer.

In this section we will examine some of the problems of queuing and their effect on the efficiency of a service. As a starting-point we should note that if a client uses the supply centre which minimizes his travel time, this does not guarantee that the total amount of time spent obtaining the service is minimized. Carter *et al.* (1971) have examined this situation and they offer a method for determining the location of a single service district boundary within an area which is characterized by two levels of demand for service. Under the assumptions that:

1   the area is autonomous and services do not cross the boundary,
2   the area is characterized by a high demand region and a low demand region,
3   only one unit serves each incident,
4   total service time (including travel) is independent of the incident and the unit which serves it,
5   the transport network is rectangular.

they offer a method of calculating the position of the boundary to minimize the average travel time. If we consider the area shown in figure 5.2 then intuitively we would locate the boundary towards 2 if we wished to equalize the balance of work-loads for the two centres. By moving the boundary towards the side which has the higher demand it is also possible to reduce the average travel time. The problem is to find the precise location for the boundary and hence achieve the lowest average response time. Carter *et al.* (1971) show that the distance $O-K$ which satisfies this is defined by a fairly complex equation which incorporates the demand rates for services, the service times and the average response times. However, we cannot immediately apply this procedure to the real world simply because we can solve this trivial problem. Much more work is needed to incorporate complex spatial demand surfaces and irregularly shaped service districts.

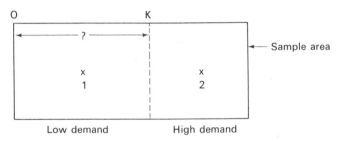

Figure 5.2 A boundary location problem: 1 and 2: Service depots

In an area of varying demand it may be more profitable, in a time sense, for a client to travel to a centre in a low-demand region because service at such a centre is provided very rapidly. We assume that centres do not have rigidly defined service areas, rather several centres serve a single district, and there is no interaction across this boundary. The actual patterns of patronage of centres are frequently influenced by cultural factors. For example, the nearest hospital may not be suitable for a patient for religious or ethnic reasons or because the patient's doctor has an arrangement with another hospital. Morrill and Earickson (1969) have noted these influences on hospital usage in Chicago, but in this section our concern is primarily with waiting-time, and we will hold the cultural aspects constant for the moment. Stidham (1971) has drawn attention to the need to incorporate congestion and waiting-time into models for locating public facilities. He notes that several models for dealing with varying levels of demand and service over time have been developed primarily in the private sector and he claims that only Hillier's work (1963) takes the customer's travel-time *and* waiting-time into account. More recently, the geographer Monroe (1972) has considered the problem of travel-time and service-time for a public service. He was concerned with evaluating the efficiency, in terms of time, of an emergency ambulance service in Madison, Wisconsin. Details of his study will be given in a later section.

One of the major problems in analysing queues is to evaluate waiting costs. This is much more difficult than determining direct costs, such as rent, salaries and equipment associated with a service. Waiting costs are related to the time wasted, the inconvenience and the alternate opportunities available for using this time. Further, perception of the length of time a client has to wait may influence the decision whether to come to the centre (Jackson and Adelson, 1962, 19). This decision will also depend upon the need which will be satisfied by the receipt of the service. These considerations should be appreciated when service areas are defined and centres are staffed. For example, if we wish to locate welfare centres or health clinics in an urban area, then to help us determine how large the centres must be and how many centres are to be located we need to know the frequency with which clients are likely to visit a centre and the importance that potential clients place on time. Is it reasonable to assume that people who need public medical attention or welfare services should be asked to wait several hours? In the private sector perhaps more attention is given to this aspect particularly when it manifests itself as a decline in returns to the entrepreneur. Stidham (1971) has attempted to construct a theoretical model in which waiting-time is minimized subject to constraints on service costs. This is a continuation of his earlier work (1970) in which he introduced the notion of optimality into queuing systems. He was concerned with the number of servers and the rate at which each serves, also the total cost of operating the system over a defined period of time. Previous studies in queuing theory have largely concentrated upon the behaviour of queues without explicitly mentioning an optimality criterion or objective. The studies have been largely descriptive and aspatial with minimal formal attention to optimization.

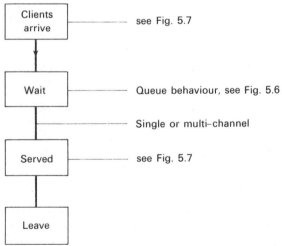

Figure 5.3 Dynamic service system

Let us now examine queues in more detail, and start by dividing the service process into four stages. These are shown in figure 5.3. In general customers arrive at varying time intervals, and as the time to serve clients also tends to vary, so a queue may be generated. The length of the queue should determine the size of the waiting facilities and it will probably influence the customer's decision to wait. Further it will influence the client's impression of the efficiency of the organization. If there are no clients waiting then the server at the centre will not be serving and this reflects on efficiency and the use of manpower and investments. Though we can describe the basic stages of the process in subjective terms, for a rigorous treatment of the relationships we must turn to a branch of operations research and to the field of queuing theory.

3   Graphical and statistical approaches to queuing

Panico (1969) and Newell (1971) provide good recent statements on the subject of queuing theory. The former clarifies his comments on the theory by a detailed case study of a hospital, which includes an evaluation of the handling of admissions, the emergency room, laboratories, obstetric and surgical cases. However, no mention is made of the location of the hospital with respect to the demand for the different types of services or the spatial distribution of patients. It is implicit in Panico's work that the quality of the health care facility is evaluated once the patient arrives at the hospital. Travel-time is not incorporated into the statements on quality of health care. However, there are several geographers who have focused on this element without considering the waiting-time at the destination (Morrill and Earickson, 1969; Schneider, 1967). Eliot-Hurst (1972) has also noted that people are generally prepared to travel long distances for health services and because they attach great utility to the service the inconvenience of the journey is reduced. We should note, however, that we lack a clear statement on the relative weightings of utility of the service and the disutility of travelling and waiting. Panico (1969, 96) claims that:

Entering the hospital as a patient is an emotional experience, and anything not functioning perfectly is usually regarded with exaggerated concern. . . . A five-minute delay to such persons seems an eternity. . . . A hospital can be characterized as a whole series of waiting lines because every station in the complex has the potential of forming queues.

Newell (1971, vii) draws attention to the vast literature on queuing theory and suggests that, 'despite this tremendous activity, queuing theory, as a tool for the analysis of practical problems, remains in a primitive state.' Further, in many cases the queues that exist in the real world have characteristics which prohibit elegant analysis, and he argues that methods which use approximations should not be overlooked. These apply particularly to rush hour situations in which large queues may build up because the rate of arrival temporarily exceeds the rate of service.

He offers a graphical interpretation of queuing using data for the arrival-time and service-time of each customer. Under the assumption that there is a single server and customers are served on the principle of first come first served we can use a graph to calculate how long the queue is at different points in time and to gain a visual impression of the amount of time spent waiting. A sample graph is shown on figure 5.4, and we notice that at time t, there are three customers waiting, customer 4 waits x minutes to be served and between times A and B, during y minutes, the server is idle.

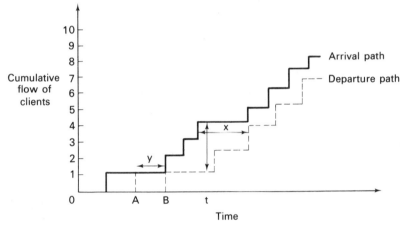

Figure 5.4   Graphical presentation of a queuing situation (*After Newell, 1971*, 8)

When analysing a queue we rarely have the time or resources to observe time paths for individual customers and the normal procedure is to examine a small number of characteristics of the queue, for example, the *average* rate of arrival and the *average* service time. These data are then used to derive descriptive measures of the average conditions of the queue, such as the average length of a queue or the average time spent waiting. With these indices we can make statements about the relative efficiency of queues. Initially these efficiency statements expressed in terms of time units, and only if we have information on the service costs of the system and the opportunity costs of the clients can we transpose them into monetary terms. We should note that the theory which allows us to calculate the average length of a queue or the average waiting-time applies only to queues which have specific properties for the arrival and service rates. Also we assume that many customers pass through the system. It is necessary for this to occur before the indices settle down to

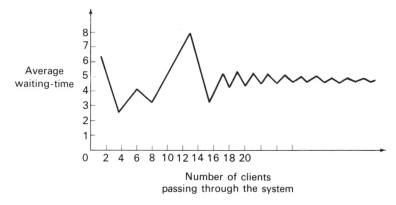

Figure 5.5 Average waiting time

an average figure. For example, in figure 5.5 we can see clearly that with respect to waiting-time with only four customers the average waiting-time is two and a half minutes and with twelve customers it is seven minutes. However, as the number of customers increases to about twenty[1] the average waiting-time settles to approximately four and a half minutes. In some practical problems a queue may not have the chance to settle down to average conditions because the facility has restricted opening hours. This may apply to facilities which operate like retail stores, for example, clinics, welfare centres, doctors' surgeries and post offices. Bailey (1954) has drawn attention to this problem with regard to clinics which involve only about 25 to 30 patients and it is suggested that in such cases queuing theory may not be appropriate as the system has not settled down to a steady state.

Figure 5.6 Types of queue behaviour

Type of queue behaviour	*Facility examples*
First come, first served	Post office, welfare office
Scheduled visits, eg one customer arrives every 10 minutes – appointment system operates	Medical services, social services
Certain customers move to the front of the queue (emergency cases)	Out-patients' clinics

Facilities which are open all the time can probably be handled more readily using average figures, though these facilities frequently encounter cyclic demands. For example, most accidents tend to occur in the mid-afternoon period between 1 pm and 4 pm (Monroe, 1972, 19) and according to Chaiken and Larson (1971, 8) most fire calls (in New York) occur around 8 pm. Steimetz (1972) has suggested that the peak period for visits to out-patient clinics in Montreal is between 8 am and 12 noon. We should also note that access in urban areas is often restricted in the morning and evening rush hours. Further complications are added by different forms of queue discipline and by changing the number of servers. A summary of these variations is given in figure 5.6.

4 Average waiting-time and traffic intensity

One of the more interesting properties of queues is the relationship between the average waiting-time and service and arrival rates. The latter two rates can be combined into a single index is usually called the traffic intensity ϱ.

$$\varrho = \text{average service time/average inter-arrival time}$$

The general form of the relationship between ϱ and the average waiting-time can be determined under specific conditions. These conditions are:

1   Random arrival and service time distributions (this is shown in figure 5.7).
2   A single channel.
3   First come first served queue discipline.

In a simple service system with the necessary conditions, such as a doctor's office with only one doctor on duty, a value of ϱ less than 1·0 indicates an absence of a queue *if the service times and arrival times are constant*. However, in most cases these times fluctuate and if we know the distribution of arrival-times and service-times then we can calculate the *average*

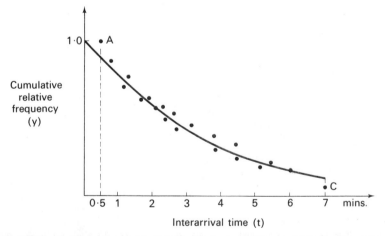

Figure 5.7 A typical arrival distribution curve. An empirical determination of a curve of this form is presented by Monroe (1972, 17) using inter-arrival times of 200 emergencies selected at random for Madison, Wisconsin.

waiting-time (this includes the time being served). A typical curve of an arrival distribution is given in figure 5.7. Using empirical data we can determine the shape of the distribution. On this graph we can see that the shortest inter-arrival time is 0·5 minutes (point *A*) and all other inter-arrival times are equal to or greater than this. Point *C* indicates the largest inter-arrival time, this is seven minutes and there are two customers which fit into this category.

On the scatter diagram a smooth curve has been drawn and this closely approximates the distribution. The general equation of this line is $y = e^{-at}$ where y is the cumulative relative frequency, t is the inter-arrival time, e is a constant (2·7182) and a is a coefficient which gives a particular form to the curve. This type of distribution is known as the *negative exponential* and it is quite common in queuing situations to find an equation of this form that describes the arrival- and service-time distributions.

Turning back to the traffic intensity, if ϱ has a value of 0·88, then a slight increase in the average service-time has the effect of sharply increasing the average waiting-time. Consider the case with an average service-time of 4·6 minutes and an average inter-arrival time of 5·2 minutes. If the service-time is increased to 5 minutes the average waiting-time increases by four minutes, but if the service-time increases to 6 minutes, this moves the average waiting-time to over 50 minutes. The general relationship between traffic intensity and mean waiting time is shown in figure 8. We should note that the waiting-time here *excludes*

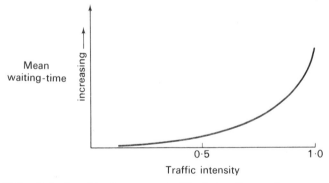

Figure 5.8 Relationship between traffic intensity and mean waiting-time

the time spent receiving the service. In general, as the traffic intensity approaches 0·7 the sensitivity of the mean waiting-time rapidly increases as is shown in the example above. The waiting-time and travel-time aspects of facility location problems have been brought together in Chaiken and Larson's work (1971) with respect to the provision of emergency services in urban areas. They claim that 'should a situation arise where nearly all calls must be placed in a queue for 20 or 30 minutes, then the precise geographical distribution of the units (designed to keep travel-time down to a few minutes) is largely irrelevant.' Clearly, only with an infinitely large supply of vehicles could this situation be consistently prevented. Thus, the objective in using a queuing analysis is 'to assure that the probability of an important call encountering a queue is below some specified threshold . . . that the average time to wait in queue is below specified limit (such as one minute)' (Chaiken and Larson, 1971, 17).

In summary we should note that the efficiency of a facility's location is not only dependent upon the accessibility to customers, but also on the time spent waiting for the service and in certain cases the overall efficiency in terms of travelling and waiting-time may be insensitive to the location of the supply point. Further, the dynamic elements of public facility location problems are important and they should be incorporated into models which analyse the current arrangement or which are used for making policy decisions. Finally, queuing theory can provide a framework for handling some of the dynamic elements, but the relationships used for deriving average conditions depend upon assumptions which cannot always be satisfied. It is for this reason that we will turn to the much more versatile procedure of simulation and in so doing note the comment of Jackson and Adelson (1962) that: 'Simulation seems to have provided the only usable solutions to . . . involved [servicing allocation] problems.[1]

5   The use of simulation procedures

Simulation can be used to evaluate the efficiency of a particular organization for the provision of services by taking into account temporal fluctuations in demand and supply and variations in accessibility.[2] These features make simulation a powerful tool for aiding the decision-maker in choosing between several alternative methods for providing a service without trying out each one in the real world. General introductions to the use of simulation as applied to policy-making in the public sector are provided by Ward (1964) and Eilon (1972) and though they suggest that this procedure has great utility there have not been very many real-world applications in the public sector. It is interesting to note that Savas' work (1969) represented the first use of simulation for solving a practical problem in the public sector in New York.[3] He was concerned with the ambulance services which were available in a district in Brooklyn and he used simulation to analyse proposed changes in the number and location of ambulance depots. An attempt was made to evaluate the cost effectiveness of alternate arrangements of depots. The costs included the capital and operating expenditures of ambulances and depots and the effectiveness of the ambulance service is related 'in a complex way' (Savas, 1969, B–612) to:

1   Spatial distribution of demand – this is represented by the emergency calls.
2   Frequency of calls.
3   Number of ambulances.
4   Location of hospitals which receive emergencies brought by ambulance.
5   Locations of ambulances – these may be hospitals or depots not attached to hospitals.

For the purpose of simulation it is necessary to break down the complex relationship referred to by Savas into a general flow diagram. This flow diagram describes the sequence of steps in the service model. Savas (1969) and Monroe (1972) offer detailed flow diagrams for emergency abmulance problems. A simplified diagram is provided in figure 5.9.

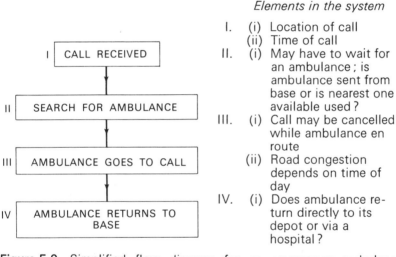

Elements in the system

I.   (i) Location of call
     (ii) Time of call
II. (i) May have to wait for an ambulance ; is ambulance sent from base or is nearest one available used ?
III. (i) Call may be cancelled while ambulance en route
     (ii) Road congestion depends on time of day
IV. (i) Does ambulance return directly to its depot or via a hospital ?

I   CALL RECEIVED

II   SEARCH FOR AMBULANCE

III AMBULANCE GOES TO CALL

IV   AMBULANCE RETURNS TO BASE

Figure 5.9 Simplified flow diagram for an emergency ambulance service

Because the four components of the system are linked by relationships which vary from time to time we cannot use simple mathematics to find the best location of depots and allocations of ambulances. These problems with probabilistic relationship linking the components contrast sharply with those with deterministic relationships of the type examined in Chapter 4. Sussams (1969, 16) has also noted that mathematics is rarely capable of handling complex simultaneous relationships of the kind frequently experienced in servicing problems. He suggests that for most practical purposes it is necessary to solve the problem by breaking it down into a series of steps. This is a necessary part of simulation.

In the Brooklyn study approximately 175,000 calls were generated (there are normally about 44,000 per year in the study area) and an inter-arrival time of 7·28 minutes was used. A single hospital, a single depot in the area of high demand and a set of seven ambulances were used. The results suggest that if all ambulances are located at the depot the overall reponse time is minimized, whereas the maximum value occurs when the ambulances are located at the hospital. It should be noted that in absolute terms the savings in time only amount to about two minutes a call. If the number of ambulances is increased to ten we find that slight improvements (approximately one half minute) in response-time result, but above this number it is clear that no savings occur. If ten ambulances are available the best combination is to place six at the depot and four at the hospital and in these circumstances the response-time improves not only for the area immediately adjacent to the depot, but for outlying areas which are on the periphery of the area served by the hospital. Several other simulations were run using a dispersed pattern of ambulances and it appears that for the problem under examination an improvement of about 30 per cent (compared with ambulances at the hospital) in response-time occurs if all the ambulances are dispersed throughout the district. There is also a considerable improvement in the percentage of calls that are answered in less than 20 minutes. This is the upper threshold level of efficiency referred to earlier. The final part of Savas' paper examines the costs of the alternate arrangements and he suggests that eight ambulances dispersed over the area are as effective as ten ambulances in a depot and using the debatable assumption that costs are zero at the dispersed street locations, this arrangement is far more economic than the single depots pattern which incurs fixed and running costs.

Other workers who have used simulation to evaluate modifications to ambulance services include Gordon and Zelin (1968) and Monroe (1972). This latter work, as yet unpublished, deals with the supply of ambulances in Madison, Wisconsin. One of the particularly interesting aspects of this study is the test of the simulation model against the real-world pattern the process is describing. Using a sample of data for three parts of the city the model was used to generate response-times, service-times and distances travelled. The simulated values were compared with real values and Monroe notes that approximately 70 per cent of the simulations give results which are within 10 per cent of the real values. This vital step in contructing a simulation model should always be included. Having constructed the simulation model of the ambulance system in 1970 Monroe proceeded to evaluate the consequences of an increase in arrival rates. It the arrival rate tripled from the 1970 level the average response-time for the system would only increase by a few seconds per call.

If we turn to the location side of the problem we find that of the ten available sites, three are used by five ambulances. The second part of Monroe's work was to evaluate the efficiency of alternate allocations of ambulances to sites and to find the set which minimized average response-

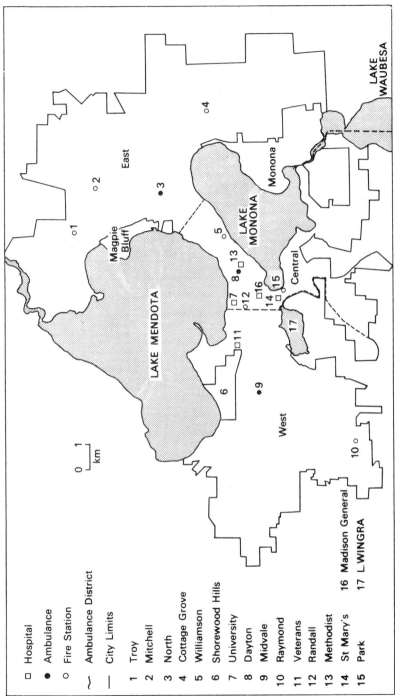

Figure 5.10 Reference map for the Madison ambulance system (*After Monroe, 1972*)

Legend:

□ Hospital
● Ambulance
○ Fire Station
︵ Ambulance District
— City Limits

1 Troy
2 Mitchell
3 North
4 Cottage Grove
5 Williamson
6 Shorewood Hills
7 University
8 Dayton
9 Midvale
10 Raymond
11 Veterans
12 Randall
13 Methodist
14 St Mary's
15 Park
16 Madison General
17 L. WINGRA

LAKE MENDOTA
LAKE MONONA
LAKE WAUBESA

Magpie Bluff
East
West
Central
Monona

0   1
km

time. If all ten sites were evaluated for the five ambulances then we have quite a large number of alternatives to examine. In fact there are

$$\frac{10!}{5!\,(10-2)!} = 252$$

alternatives. Monroe narrowed this set of feasible locations by considering that the three sites currently used each receive one ambulance, thus he was left with seven sites and two ambulances. For this smaller problem there are only

$$\frac{7!}{2!\,(7-2)!} = 21$$

alternatives. Each of the twenty-one alternative location pairs was evaluated using a simulation model of the type shown on figure 5.9 and the pair which generated the lowest average response-time was found. The difference in average time between the best pair and the worst was only of the order of half a minute per call. If this is converted to savings in distance travelled per year we notice a saving of about 600 miles (960 km).

The set of possible ambulance sites is shown in figure 6.10 together with

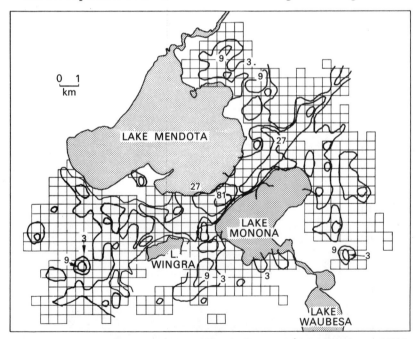

Figure 5.11 Spatial distribution of ambulance calls in Madison, 1970. Represented by a geometric progression of isolines. (*After Monroe, 1972*)

the locations of the hospitals, and in figure 5.11 we have a map of the spatial distribution of emergency calls for 1970. Using the simulation model Monroe identified Williamson and Park as the best pair of locations. In order to evaluate the intuitive approach to this problem a simple experiment was conducted. A group of 20 students were given figures 5.10 and 5.11, the general problem was explained, and they were asked to choose the best pair of locations. Over 50 per cent of the group selected the optimum pair, a frequency distribution of their responses is given in figure 5.12.

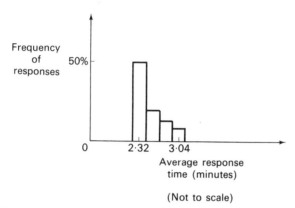

(Not to scale)

Figure 5.12   Intuitive solutions to Monroe's problem

In this example we could argue that intuition serves as a useful method for solving the location problem. However, we should note Monroe's conclusion that 'the performance of an ambulance system is insentive to various facility locations', Thus intuition is hardly under examination as we could possibly achieve good results by chosing locations at random. The general problem of sensitivity in location problems has been examined by Larson and Stevenson (1971) and Goodchild (1972a). Savas' empirical results (1969) give weight to the notion that within cities the savings in average response-time due to relocation of emergency service centres are very small, and judicious use of a manual procedure for choosing sites is likely to be fairly close to the optimum defined by a complex simulation model.

6   Résumé

In the earlier sections of this chapter we examined procedures for evaluating the performance of service systems over time. In particular, we attempted to look at the effectiveness of various spatial arrangements over a short-run period. It is clear that in order to draw definitive conclusions about the relative merits of alternate locations for service centres and district boundaries a considerable body of information is needed on the spatial distribution of demand as it varies through time, the state of the transportation links under various conditions and the reliability of the supply. Rarely, if ever, are all these data available and so we have to base analysis and policy decisions upon restricted information and assumptions. In Chapter 4 we assumed that supply and demand could be localized at specific points in space and the linkages were conducted over routes which had constant properties. This last assumption was stated more formally thus: the cost of transportation is directly related to distance. Under these types of assumptions alternative supply configurations were evaluated and the arrangement which minimized transportation costs was considered to be the best. At least two questions come to mind after this kind of analysis. First, is the best solution under the restricted set of conditions the same as the best solution under more realistic dynamic assumptions? Second, do the results justify the considerable effort in data collection and analysis? Simplistic answers to these questions would not do justice to the work which has been undertaken in this field; however, it is significant to notice that recently there have been attempts to search for alternate methods of handling problems of this type. One of these, the use of intuition, has already been discussed in Chapter 4 and will be discussed further in section 8 of this chapter. However, the major emphasis in this section will be upon a second method which we can consider under the heading *expected distance*.

7 The concept of expected distance

It is almost impossible to find explicit references to this concept in the standard geographical literature, though the basic ideas have been discussed by Bunge (1962, 90) and Taylor (1970). However, within the fields of business management, operations research, and traffic engineering the concept is more widely used.[4] Let us first examine the fundamentals of this concept and then evaluate their utility in solving servicing problems.

If within any enclosed surface – for example, a circle – we choose points at random and measure the distance between pairs of points, then we can draw a frequency distribution which will have the general form shown in figure 5.13. The maximum distance is OA; this represents the diameter of the circle, or the long axis of any shape. Using figure 5.13 we notice that distances of about this magnitude occur very infrequently. However as the distance between points decreases to OB, we find that this combination occurs most frequently. In figures 5.13 distance OB occurs fifty times, whereas distances OC and OD occur only ten times. From this general relationship we can conclude that the expected distance between random points is OB. The expected distance is the distance which occurs most frequently, given that many pairs of points are chosen. For a practical example we could consider a circular police district in which a police car is continually travelling through the

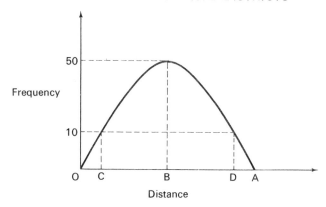

Figure 5.13   General frequency distribution of distance between pairs of random points on an enclosed surface

area and emergency calls occur randomly within the district. The car represents the supply and the call is the demand. At any point in time the location of these two points can be considered to be random points. The average distance travelled by the car under a uniform spatial demand assumption is therefore the expected distance.

Fairthorne (1965) has shown that if the area of a district is constant the minimum expected distance occurs within a circular shape.[5] As the shape becomes elongated the expected distance increases. This reinforces the ideas expressed in Chapter 2 regarding the spatial efficiency of shapes. A circular district has maximum compactness, minimum boundary length, and minimum expected distance properties. Thus it is ideal for many servicing situations.

The expected distances defined above have assumed that the random points are joined by a straight line, that is, transportation is possible in all directions. Let us now consider the influence of different routing configurations on the values for the expected distances. Intuitively we know that the straight line distance is the shortest and if we consider the findings of Fairthorne (1965) we can see the costs of alternate routing patterns. In a circular district the expected distance, $E(d)$, between random points is 0·905 r, where r is the radius of the circle. If a rectangular routing system is used $E(d)$ increases to 1·153 r. This is the same value as for a hexagonal routing network. Values of 0·998 r and 0·994 r result from triangular and polar routing patterns. The latter assumes transportation links run parallel to the circumference with radial intersections. Perhaps the most significant result at this stage is that expected distances increase by about 30 per cent when we change the straight line linkage to the rectangular pattern, and so models of distribution systems which assume straight-line linkages tend to underestimate the total distance travelled and this could range up to 30 per cent error if the actual road linkages were rectangular.

In the simple example of a police district mentioned above we assumed that the supply and the demand points occurred at random. Clearly in the majority of distribution systems this is unrealistic, the supply point has a fixed location and it is only the demand point which may occur at random. Let us now turn to this situation. Eilon *et al.* (1971) have calculated expected distances for distribution systems of this type. With respect to a circular district with the supply point at the centre and straight-line transportation links, the $E(d) = 0.667\ r$; if the supply point is moved to the circumference the $E(d)$ increases to approximately $1.132\ r$. If the district is rectangular with sides of length a and b, then for a district with $a = b$ and the supply point at the centre, and a straight-line linkage assumption, the $E(d)$ is approximately $0.383\ a$. If the supply point is moved to a corner then the $E(d)$ doubles. The effect of the shape of the area on the expected distance has also been explored by Eilon *et al.* (1971). They defined a measure of the shape of a district as the ratio (b/a), the supply point is located at a distance R from the centre of the district. It is assumed that the area of the district is constant, only a and b change. Four shapes were considered, a circle, a square, and two rectangles, the first with $a/b = \frac{1}{2}$ and the second with $a/b = 2$. For each shape the expected distance was calculated with the supply point at different distances from the centre. In the cases of the rectangular shapes the supply was located at different points on the axis of the district which passes through the centre of the area and is parallel to the longest side. The axis is shown in figure 5.14.

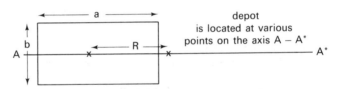

Figure 5.14   Reference axis of a rectangular district

When the supply is located near the centre of the district the values of $E(d)$ are influenced by the variation in shapes. However, as R increases the variations for $E(d)$ among the different shapes become insignificant. The expected distance is insensitive to changes in the form of the district when the supply point is a long way from the geometrical centre. This situation was discussed in a practical context by Savas (1969) in his evaluation of Kings County hospital in Brooklyn, New York. The hospital has a peripheral location with respect to its demand area, and therefore changes in the location of ambulance depots in the district will not have very significant effects on the average distance travelled bringing emergencies to the hospital. The minor improvements in time that were generated by shifting the locations of the ambulance depots were discussed in section 7. If we wish to improve the overall spatial efficiency of emergency ambulance services then it is necessary to look at the total set of hospitals and their service areas. As Savas points out, relatively minor improvements result from partial analysis of individual hospital service areas. A large-scale view is vital if significant improvements are to be made to emergency response-times.

If we incorporate rectangular transportation links into the fixed supply model then the following expected distance values can be derived. For a circular district $E(d)$ is approximately equal to $A + 0.423\ r$, where A is the distance of the supply from the centre of the circle and r is the radius of the district. This relationship only applies when A is greater than or equal to the radius of the area. Thus it can be used in calculating the expected distance for supply points of the form shown in figure 5.15.

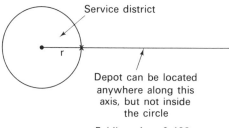

E (d) ≈ A + 0·423 r

Figure 5.15   External supply points – expected distance

When the supply is located within the district another relationship has to be used. Eilon *et al.* (1971, 162–163) show that if the fixed point is at the centre of the circular district $E(d) = 0.846\ r$, this compares with a value of approximately $1.153\ r$ for random supply and demand points. Thus, potentially, we could make savings of about 40 per cent on average distance travelled by choosing a central location over a random location for a depot – under the assumption that the demand for the service was randomly distributed throughout the area. If we can determine the magnitude of potential improvements for a perfectly located supply point over a randomly located supply point, then we can possibly make an argument for developing strict procedures for finding the perfect location. However, if the difference in expected distance between the two possible arrangements – random and perfect – is very small, we can be reasonably sure that any random choice of location for the supply point is quite good and an expensive search for the perfect location will not yield significant savings. This notion has been recently discussed by Larson and Stevenson (1971) in one of a series of studies on location problems of public facilities in urban areas which has been prepared by the Rand Corporation in New York (Carter *et al.* 1971; Chaiken and Larson, 1971).[6] They suggest that if the demand for a service is evenly and randomly distributed over space and the routing system is a rectangular road grid, then savings of about 25 per cent could be gained by choosing the perfect location for the supply as opposed to choosing a point at random. Thus if we assume that our intuition is somewhat better than a random guess, we could argue that the difference between the perfect location and our intuitive guess is, say, 15 per cent, and in terms of average travel time (or distance) this may only be about 4 or 5 minutes. Thus we could argue that a search for the perfect location may be of limited utility. Obviously each case should be treated on its own merits and desirable levels for the quality of service may vary from place to place, but this does not change the basic ideas expressed here. Whenever possible, we should attempt to evaluate the utility of our search for the perfect location before embarking on extensive data collection and analysis. The concepts of expected distance may help in this task. In another paper Larson (1971) has examined the influence of barriers, discrete streets, and one-way streets in service areas on the average response-time for emergency units such as police or ambulance services. He assumes that calls are generated uniformly and independently within the district and that the service is provided by a roving response unit. If a barrier is introduced into the area, for example a limited access highway or a railway with restricted crossing points, then the average response-time to an emergency call increases. But Larson claims that the increase is only of the order of 10 per cent, even when the barrier is significant. Further, if the barrier completely divides the district and a single crossing-point is provided the position of the crossing-point does not have a great influence on the average response-time. The difference between the best location and the worst location for the crossing-point is of the order of 8 per cent. If, therefore, we chose a crossing-point at random and the average response-time was 20 minutes within the service district, we could only reduce this time to about 18 minutes by searching for the optimal location.

With respect to a rectangular grid road system Larson (1971) suggests that an increase of about $\frac{1}{3}$ block (1 block = approx. 1/10 mile) is added to the average response-time calculated on a continuous surface. If the streets have a one-way configuration the extra distance over the continuous surface is about 2 blocks. However, about 6 per cent of responses have to travel an extra 6 blocks. This work suggests that general solutions to location problems under the assumption of a continuous transportation surface are not very far from perfect solutions on surfaces which have rectangular forms of transportation links. We should note, however, that these relationships and conclusions are based upon regular-shaped districts which contain a homogeneous demand. Even though these results have to be treated cautiously we should take careful note of the basic conclusion of the Rand studies: we could possibly use simple analytical models, which incorporate the concept of expected distance and time, to derive solutions to location problems which are close to the optimal solutions we derive with complex algorithms of the type discussed in Chapter 4 and in the earlier sections of this chapter.

8 Comparison of delivery systems using expected distance concepts

Traditionally, geographers have used the sum of distances between origins and destinations as a measure of the cost of a particular location pattern. Measures of spatial efficiency have been defined in these terms (see Chapter 2) and the optimal location for servicing facilities has been defined as that point which minimizes the sum of the distances to the set of destinations. However, we should note that allocation of commodities from origins to destinations is frequently undertaken by a transportation mode which serves more than one customer per trip. It is therefore useful to know the relationship between the actual route distances and the sum of the straight-line distances and so to evaluate the validity of the assumption which underlies the earlier method for determining the cost of an allocation system. Christofides and Eilon (1969) have examined this problem and their results are summarized below. They show that if N customers are uniformly and randomly distributed in a square with the supply at the centre, the expected sum of the straight line distance, $E(D_s) = 0.383\,Na$, where a is the length of the side of the square. Now if we consider a region of area A into which $N + 1$ points (N destinations and 1 origin) are uniformly and randomly distributed, it can be shown that the expected length of the optimal travelling salesman route $E(D_t)$ through all points is given by $E(D_t) = k\sqrt{A}\,\sqrt{N+1}$, where k is a constant; when N is reasonably large, $N + 1$ can be replaced by N. This equation has been verified experimentally and the value of k determined to be 0.75. The dependence of (D_t) on the shape of the area has also been examined experimentally using a circle, a square and an equilaterial triangle, and the effect of the shape of the area is seen to be very small. We should note that there is a well-defined relationship between (D_t) and (D_s) and C, where C is the maximum number of destinations which can be supplied on one route. The relationship is given by

$$D_t = \frac{A/D_s}{C} + B\sqrt{a}\,\sqrt{D_s},$$

where A and B are constants, and a is the length of the side of the square in which the customers lie. The quantity D_t can be expressed as a function of the sum of the straight line distances, but for reasonably small values of C (ie $C < 5$), of for large values of D_s (ie a large number of customers in an area) the graph approximates to a straight line, and therefore under these conditions the origin which is located to minimize D_t would be approximately the same as the location that would result by minimizing the quantity D_s. This again leads us to believe that solutions to the relatively simple problem of determining the most accessible point to all destinations will yield a good location for a supply depot. Under the circumstances discussed above this location is close to the point which minimizes the distance from the supply through a set of destinations and returns to the supply. The procedure for solving this latter problem is complex.

Conclusions

In conclusion it is suggested that we should not at this point reject the more traditional allocation–location models or the queuing and simulation types. Rather we should use them in conjunction with the expected distance–time variety in an attempt to find the most appropriate combination in terms of data requirements, computational expertise, and accuracy and utility of solutions.[7] At the moment the expected distance concepts have only been applied to districts with homogeneous demand, and therefore the results have restricted utility in the real world where demand often exhibits considerable spatial variation. The simulation models of the type used by Savas (1969) and Monroe (1972) are able to take into account this type of spatial variation as well as fluctuations over time. Thus it would seem that simulation appears to be a most useful tool for handling practical location problems, if the necessary data can be collected.

Notes on further reading

A good review of methods for locating emergency services in cities is provided in Drake *et al.* (1972), in the Rand studies of Carter *et al.* (1971) and of Chaiken and Larson (1971).

A rigorous treatment of queuing theory requires a good background in mathematics, especially probability theory. The books by Panico (1969) and Newell (1971) offer good introductions to the subject.

The use of simulation to solve a location problem is clearly illustrated by Savas (1969).

An excellent summary of the use of expected distance in distribution management is presented in Eilon *et al.* (1971).

The topic of sensitivity analysis, as applied to location–allocation problems, is nicely summarized in Larson and Stevenson (1971).

Notes

1 This value varies from problem to problem.

2 Definitions of efficiency in such problems usually refer to average response times with a threshold upper value.

3 Savas (1971; 1972) has been involved in applying district algorithms to improve the efficiency of New York's voting areas.

4 One of the most recent commentaries is provided by Snyder (1971).

5 See also the work by Smeed (1962; 1963; 1964).

6 Other studies will be given at the end of the chapter. Carter *et al.* (1971), Chaiken and Larson (1971).

7 The merging of a location algorithm and a simulation model to solve a fire station location problem is discussed by Toregas and ReVelle (1972).

6 Interaction among administrative units

1 Introduction

In this Chapter we will broaden the focus of attention from individual service districts to sets of districts which are spatially contiguous. These districts may be either *de jure* or *de facto*; the distinction between these two types of units was discussed in Chapter 1 and we should note that for the purposes of this chapter we will concentrate on interactions between *de jure* districts. Each district may be the spatial service area for a single function such as health, education, garbage collection or pollution control, or it may handle a wide range of services. Traditionally small politically autonomous units such as townships, parishes and municipalities offered a wide range of services to their inhabitants. However, as the demand for high-quality expensive specialized services developed so we notice that larger spatial service districts are often defined and several of the first-level units find themselves within a single jurisdiction:

> In those days, [one-hundred years ago in Canada] social security was unknown, pollution control was unheard of, and water supply was a matter of individual concern. Towns and villages drew their boundaries in places that made a lot of sense in those days but have no relevance to the problems of the late 20th Century. Those pioneer local governments were never intended to carry out Community planning, to pass and enforce zoning by-laws, to negotiate and repay huge capital loans, to finance, build and maintain roads, to operate welfare systems, to own and operate parks and recreational buildings, or to administer a dozen and one other modern community needs (*Urban Focus*, 1973).

The creation of larger jurisdictions, the cooperation of smaller political units and the transfer of responsibility has rarely been achieved without a struggle to protect interests. Currently (1973) in Montréal, we are witnessing such a struggle between some of the smaller municipalities who wish to maintain their autonomy, and the newly created Montréal Urban Community authority which is trying to encourage amalgamation of the municipalities on the Island of Montréal. On a larger scale, and also in the Province of Québec, there has been a struggle between the Provincial Minister of Municipal Affairs, Maurice Tessier, and the mayors of the many small rural communities. The latter wish to retain their autonomy whereas the Provincial government wishes to amalgamate the units into larger jurisdictions. As of February 1973 the mayors have won the first round and Tessier has been shifted to a new position in the Provincial Government. The basic elements which enter this type

103

of struggle were introduced in Chapter 3; they are local sentiment and control, economies of scale, distance decay and utilization, satisfaction, justice and costs. The mixture cannot be readily determined though we are led to believe that the two major components are concerned with the quality of services offered and the rising costs of providing public services. These two elements tend to suggest that small units are preferable to large units because the former allow greater citizen participation in guaranteeing quality and meeting individual needs. Also, the larger the unit the more likely is the chance that it will be financially viable. The definition of the exact configuration of the district has to be resolved through the political process. This process may involve the use of a referendum to the constituents, administered by the government, or action by groups of individuals who are directly affected. Though the latter may be outside the 'normal' decision-making forum, the actions of such a group can precipitate a reversal of a decision by fighting the issue in the courts and acquiring a legitimate decision. The role of *ad hoc* groups in the decision-making process has frequently been overlooked by social scientists. The interplay between 'normal' and *ad hoc* forms of public decision-making is highly complex, the latter usually comes to the fore when sufficient highly-motivated people feel that the normal procedure for delegating their authority to a higher level has in some way failed. The subject of local conflicts and public decision-making is fascinating, but in this chapter space prohibits a lengthy excursion into the many types of case studies and the background to them. Rather we will attempt to focus on some central themes within the context of inter-municipal or inter-district cooperation. It would be pretentious to claim that we have theories to explain the current arrangements and policies of interactions, but perhaps it is less unreasonable to suggest that there are some striking similarities between places and situations. It is the identification of these regularities which might one day allow us to advance from a typology or classification of inter-municipal arrangements to a deeper understanding of the processes which give rise to particular types of policies. However, because the environment in which policy-making takes place changes so rapidly one wonders if we shall ever be able to predict over periods greater than a few months or years.

Within the urban context, Curran (1963) suggests that the problems of governmental organization are of such significance that if solutions could be found, then the more frequently stated urban problems such as municipal taxation, housing, transportation, provision of public services and environmental degradation (Lithwick 1970) would be easier to solve. Chinitz (1964, 46) argued that the generic problem of the metropolitan area is related to intergovernmental relations. These manifest themselves in the US as annexations, city–county consolidations, county amalgamations and municipal federations. Soja (1971, 45) has examined the territorial organization of government in metropolitan areas in the United States and he claims that:

There is no doubt that the maze of counties, cities, townships, and special districts, many tending to pursue narrow local interests at the expense of the large functional community, both directly and indirectly exacerbate some of the major problems facing a predominantly urban America.

He draws attention to the core–city–suburban conflict of northern cities in the US and suggests that the predominantly white and wealthy autonomous suburbs are advantageously located to the services, facilities and jobs of the core city while they contribute a disproportionately small financial share to the upkeep of the central city. 'The result has been widespread racial polarization, central city deterioration, zoning and planning based on greed or fear, and the visual pollution of the urban and rural landscape' (p. 46). Basically there are two strategies for solving 'the metropolitan problem'. The first advocates integrating municipalities into a city-wide government system while the second argues for the establishment of cooperative schemes among the municipalities in the area. The latter is generally found to be more acceptable by the constituent municipalities. The elements which define the character and the link with the policy will be examined in the next section under the heading of make-or-buy decisions.

2   Make-or-buy decisions

Local political jurisdictions such as municipalities, each have a range of services which it may choose to provide for itself, within its boundaries. This can be called the option *to make*. However, the jurisdiction can often obtain the service from an outside source and we refer to this as the option *to buy*. Assuming the decision is economically rational, it will be related to a comparison of the costs and benefits of each option. Such costs and benefits are not easy to determine, for though they can primarily be expressed in financial terms, as soon as they reach the decision-making arena they often gain values which are less readily definable. Mowitz (1965) has drawn a distinction between *efficiency values* and *boundary values*. He associates the former with an economic analysis of the comparative costs involved in the make-or-buy alternatives. The latter are determined by answering the question: do the efficiency values warrant giving up the political decision-making discretion associated with retaining the total operation within the boundary of a single jurisdiction? The boundary values, therefore, are those associated with the doctrine of local autonomy. If it is decided that services should be provided within the jurisdiction regardless of the economies of buying outside, then boundary values are greater than efficiency values.

Metropolitan complexes and contiguous jurisdictions, together with the financial problems which face small municipalities in the mid-twentieth century have encouraged make-or-buy decisions to become a common feature of contemporary urban politics. One of the most recent summaries of this topic is presented by Cox (1973). Wheaton

(1964) has noted that despite the apparently chaotic pattern of political communities in American metropolitan areas, and given the lack of substantive evidence on scale economies, coordinated efforts between political communities are not uncommon. He offers a set of propositions explaining inter- and intra-community cooperation in terms of networks of influence. Such networks develop from convergence of interests within and across political boundaries. Morando (1968) has examined inter-municipal cooperation in the Detroit Metropolitan Area, and his study shows that though communities cooperate, and services are transferred across municipal boundaries, this has not led to loss of political autonomy within each municipal area. The communities he examined appear to enjoy the best of both the political and economic worlds.

It appears that in many cases within the North American context boundary values are considerably stronger than efficiency values, and this applies particularly to the social services which evoke strong personal sentiments. This also applies to the provision of services in the United Kingdom.

3   Inter-municipal cooperation

Inter-municipal cooperation can cover a wide range of activities in metropolitan areas. For example, at one extreme we can identify informal, verbal exchanges of information, and at the other we find formal agreements between jurisdictions to integrate and operate as one government. Usually the term is applied in a narrower sense to refer to voluntary, formal, written agreements concerning public service provision, and mechanisms for joint discussion and solution of problems which are felt to be common to more than any one jurisdictional unit. Service agreements have been made for virtually every type of service offered by municipalities and the form of agreement varies considerably. We find, for example, contracts between municipalities to build and operate a major facility (eg, a sewage treatment plant) and contracts under which a large municipality, such as the central city, sells services to smaller communities. Or, there may be agreements by which municipalities offer services to each other in cases of emergency (eg, fire or police protection). Mechanisms for joint action on large-scale problems usually take the form of metropolitan councils of governments, and these can be merely a forum for discussion and consultation, or they can set up regional planning agencies and operate regional services and facilities.

Inter-municipal cooperation is present in one form or other in most North American metropolitan areas. An indication of its growing popularity is that since 1954 when the first metropolitan area council was established in Detroit, the number had grown to ten active councils in the US, by 1966, and only one year later had increased to fifty. At the same time, since the mid-forties when local government reforms began to gain importance very few single government cities have emerged. Some explanation of the popularity of cooperation over integration can be derived from a comparison of the two as strategies to overcome the 'metropolitan problem'.

The 'metropolitan problem,' as referred to earlier, can be viewed as one of adapting government organization to the changing needs of urban growth. Increasing population density increases both the scope and the quantity of public services required, and the outward sprawl of urbanization accentuates the need for new services and coordinated planning. Martin (1967) suggests that a pragmatic approach to the problem is to pose the question: Given the present structure of government in metropolitan areas, what devices are available for making the system operate more effectively? He identifies sixteen such devices ranging from informal cooperation to metropolitan governments, and distinguishes between 'procedural' methods of adaptation and 'structural' methods of adaptation. Thus, forms of cooperation are procedural since they can be achieved without significant effect upon the structure of local government, whereas integration is structural in that it involves radical governmental reorganization.

The traditional arguments for structural reform as mentioned earlier are based on grounds of efficiency and coordination; in a fragmented city, it is claimed, small municipalities cannot reach an efficient level of service provision because they cannot take advantage of economies of scale, and municipal governments tend to put their own local interests before those of the city as a whole thus preventing solution of area-wide problems. However, a number of factors have tended to work against structural reform. To begin with, such reform involves changes in which there are losses of autonomy and shifts in power: thus many reform proposals are obstructed by governments and citizens. Secondly, for many public services there are insignificant economies of scale, and for some a more important consideration is citizen participation. Thus some services benefit from local rather than area-wide control. Finally, activities in many metropolitan areas have demonstrated that efficiency and coordination can be obtained in a fragmented system through service contracts and area councils. Such cooperation is not only capable of achieving desired levels of efficiency and coordination, but also has a number of distinct advantages over integration. Because of its respect for local autonomy, because it maintains governments 'close to the people', and because it adheres to the principle of voluntary action, inter-municipal cooperation is more acceptable to politicians and citizens – it is therefore easier to instigate. Furthermore, the cooperative approach allows greater flexibility for the future: agreements can be changed and partners can be added or dropped to meet changing needs and requirements.

It would seem, at least for the present, that attempts at procedural reform stand a better chance of success than attempts at structural reform. The latter is extremely difficult to initiate and from experience in Ontario in the 1970s it has been suggested (*Urban Focus*, 1973) that the virtues attributed to regional governments are probably more imaginary than real, and the government reforms proposed in Ontario 'have not yet moved beyond the stage of rhetorical recognition of the problem'.

4   Patterns of inter-municipal cooperation

In an attempt to determine the underlying dimensions of the patterns of cooperation some recent work has focused upon analysing the relationship between attributes of municipalities and the make-or-buy policies. Statistical tests have been used to search for regularities and though we find that the results support our intuitive notions about the communities which choose to cooperate and those which choose to guard their autonomy, we should note that we lack studies of the decision-making process *per se*. The conclusions we draw are usually based upon aggregated data. Clearly, future work should look in detail at the sequence of steps which leads to a policy statement.

The pioneering work in the analytical field of inter-municipal cooperation was done by Williams *et al.* (1963*a* and *b*; 1965) using data for the area around Philadelphia for services which had different impacts on the communities. He focused particular attention upon sewage disposal, schools and police radio systems. Schools require large investments[1] and have considerable social significance whereas police radio systems are relatively cheap and have restricted social significance. By contrast, sewage disposal requires considerable capital investment and has limited social significance. It is suggested that inter-municipal cooperation is inversely related to differences in socio-economic status between communities. Williams and his colleagues examined social and fiscal levels of contiguous pairs of municipalities and the evidence supported this hypothesis with respect to education and sewage disposal. Police radio agreements appear not to be influenced by socio-economic differences among communities. It was also suggested that when a cooperating municipality was selected the prime consideration appears to rest on similarity of social status, though we could probably argue that social and economic status are closely linked. Toscano (1964) has examined the pattern of agreements among municipalities and he used an index, originally devised by Deutsch, to compare the actual number of agreements with an expected number. This latter is considered to be the number of agreements that could occur by chance. Using data for the five county area in and around Philadelphia and three pairs of agreements: police radio and sewer: police radio and school consolidation: school consolidation and sewer (the same services that Williams examined), Toscano found that the first, police radio and sewer, was the easiest to achieve whereas the actual number of school consolidation–sewer agreements was less than may have occurred by chance, and thus clearly the most difficult to achieve. We can note Toscano's explanation and the influence of social rank on the patterns of agreements: on the sewer–school agreements which occur at significantly lower levels than would be expected by chance, the pairs of communities which do in fact have agreements are much closer to each other in Social Rank scores than those pairs of communities having 'easier' agreements.

In order to throw more light on the patterns of voluntary cooperation among municipalities in metropolitan areas Morando (1968) conducted detailed research on this topic in Detroit. He used data on the 1964 patterns of inter-local cooperation for fifty-eight Michigan municipalities in the three Detroit metropolitan counties of Wayne, Oakland and Macomb. He found that the socio-economic status of a municipality was similar to the mean of the status for the municipalities with which it cooperated. Cooperation in this instance refers to services with social implications, for example, parks, recreation and hospitals. However, of the sixty types of services which were shared only eleven had social implications. Each municipality maintained control of the services such as zoning, planning, housing, and urban renewal which have considerable potential influence on life-styles. Analysis of *per capita* assessed valuation leads to the conclusion that cooperation will not serve to redistribute wealth among municipalities.

Capital intensive services (for example, water-treatment plants and sewage disposal) are handled on a contractual basis. Morando also examined the influence of the form of local government on the patterns of cooperation. The municipalities with a council city-manager form of government tend to cooperate more frequently than those with the more traditional mayor and city council form. Finally we should note that the patterns of cooperation in the study are tend to support the social and economic *status quo* and cooperation has allowed the smaller municipalities to survive and provide services for their residents. Single government units have not emerged and cooperation in fact has allowed small corporate entities to continue.

5 Two case studies

To add depth to some of the arguments that have been presented in earlier sections we will examine two case studies of inter-municipal cooperation. The first (see figure 6.1) considers the provision of police services for a set of four municipalities in Ontario. We will examine the socio-economic characteristics of the communities and try to relate these to the make-or-buy policies. The second study is an analysis of attitudes towards inter-municipal cooperation within a large metropolitan area, Montréal.

At this point we will add Wheaton's comments (1964) to earlier remarks on patterns of cooperation. Wheaton has suggested that communities which are significantly different in social and economic character will be reluctant to transfer services, and more particularly the higher the socio-economic status of the community the greater will be the desire to guard its autonomy. It is argued that interests are more likely to converge when the communities have similar socio-economic status.

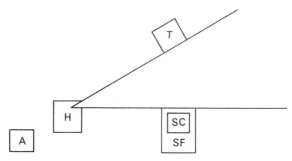

Figure 6.1   Location map of sample communites : S. Ontario (Diagrammatic, not to scale) : *T* Toronto ; *H* Hamilton City Limits ; *A* Ancaster village ; *SF* Saltfleet township limits ; *SC* Stoney Creek town limits

A study of newspaper files in Hamilton, Ontario, over the last twenty years provides basic historical data on the conditions leading up to the policies for providing police protection in the communities. From 1955 to the present day, with the exception of a period during 1960, police services in Ancaster have been provided by the village. However, since the formation of the Board of Police Commission for Ancaster village, in 1958, there have been several attempts to investigate and assess the possibility of buying the service from Hamilton the nearby large industrial city. These attempts have been *ad hoc* and were made at times when the force was suffering a crisis. These crises have taken the form of resignation of police officers, suspension of police and refusal by the council to accept the proposed police budget. Attempts to investigate the costs of buying policing from Hamilton have been hindered by subjective statements from officials in Ancaster. They claim, for example, 'that the costs would be astronomical'. However, an objective report by Lintack and Dawson (1964) did not support this view. This document was prepared primarily to examine the costs for Stoney Creek and Saltfleet, though it contained information on costs for many other Ontario communities. The report was not mentioned at the Ancaster council meetings, though it was prepared in 1964, one year before the above statements were made. During the debates in the village council meetings, references were made to boundary values. It was stated, for example, that 'it was not the proper thing for Ancaster to go to the city for police protection', and that, 'our own department is doing a good job, and is close to the people'. Clearly this represents a myopic view in the light of the actual record of the department. Explicit statements made in the meetings and reported in the press claim that if police services were bought from Hamilton, then Ancaster's higher status would decline, control of the service would be lost, and further, changes in the organization may not be in accord with the wishes of the people of Ancaster. The latter have different values and demands for police services from the people of Hamilton.

With respect to Stoney Creek and Saltfleet, Lintack and Dawson's amalgamation study (1964), recommended that the police forces of the two communities be united. This was supported by the Ontario Police Commission on the grounds of improving efficiency and it was further added that the cost to the ratepayer would be reduced. However, the Stoney Creek council rejected the recommendations. Reports in the press and interviews with local police chiefs and members of the council led to the conclusion that boundary values dominated the decision-making process. Stoney Creek was not willing to surrender control of its police as this would represent some loss in autonomy and a strengthening in the position of Saltfleet in the long-term take-over of the smaller enclave of Stoney Creek.

To test Wheaton's assertion – that the socio-economic characteristics of the communities influences the policy decision – a set of variables used in social area analysis will be examined. The selection is based upon Michaelson's suggestions (1966), and closely follows those used in recent urban factorial ecological studies and those used by Wolfinger and Field (1966) in their studies of local government. The theoretical basis of the social area typology was outlined by Shevky and Bell (1955). The set of variables shown in table 6.1 will be used and for the purposes of statistical

Table 6.1 Socio-economic variables

	Variables to describe socio-economic characteristics	Hamilton	Ancaster	Stoney Creek	Saltfleet
1	Average income per annum (male)	$3,999	$5,507	$5,315	$4,258
2	(female)	$2,081	$2,184	$2,412	$1,807
3	Wages and salary income per head	$4,319	$6,063	$5,779	$4,653
4	Wages and salary income per family	$5,198	$6,765	$6,680	$5,354
	Occupational divisions				
5	Managerial	7·7%	16·4%	4·9%	2·3%
6	Professional and technical	5·9%	13·0%	3·7%	1·3%
7	Craftsmen, production process and related workers	44·3%	less than 1%	10·2%	12·5%
8	Households in need of repair	2·9%	4·0%	0	2·89%
9	Median value of households	$13,402	$16,696	$17,250	$13,089
10	Crowded dwellings	11·0%	7·6%	0	6·4%
11	Persons per room	0·7	0·6	0·6	0·8
12	Owner-occupied households	69%	89%	83%	84%
13	Children per family	1·5	1·8	1·6	1·9
14	Percentage born in Canada	68·8%	84·6%	80·9%	75·9%

(*Census of Canada, 1961*)

Table 6.2 A classification of the communities on the basis of selected socio-economic variables

Variable number (from table 6.1)	Hamilton	Ancaster	Stoney Creek	Saltfleet
1	—	+	+	—
2	—	+	+	—
3	—	+	+	—
4	—	+	+	—
5	—	+	+	—
6	—	+	+	—
7	—	+	+	—
8	+	—	+	—
9	—	+	+	—
10	—	+	—	+
11	—	+	+	—
12	—	+	—	+
13	—	+	—	+
14	—	+	+	—

analysis we will convert the values to signs. These are shown in table 6.2 and the basis of the classification is that the positive signs indicate a higher socio–economic level. The variable 'children per family' has been included to represent the familistic nature of each community. Following Wood (1958), it is argued that the more familistic the community, the stronger will be the feeling towards local autonomy. In the context of this study it is suggested that the higher value for Ancaster supports the decision to provide its own service. In the case of Saltfleet, this community is in the position of selling the service, and thus local autonomy may be extended to include Stoney Creek. The variable 'percentage born in Canada' is included to reflect the notion that newcomers into a social system are less conservative and less inclined to maintain the *status quo* of a current pattern of organization. Positive signs have been assigned to the communities which this variable suggests would wish to guard their autonomy .

The non-parametric chi-square test was used to analyse these data. The first hypothesis is that Ancaster and Hamilton are not significantly different in terms of the socio-economic variables used in this study. If the two communities are not significantly different, then it is argued that the plus and minus signs should be approximately equally divided. In the sample there are thirteen plus signs for Ancaster and one for Hamilton. The statistical test allows us to reject this hypothesis. For the data from Saltfleet and Stoney Creek the same procedure was followed, and it appears that Stoney Creek has a statistically significant higher socio-economic status than Saltfleet. We can conclude that the higher socio-economic status of Ancaster and Stoney Creek, vis-à-vis Hamilton and Saltfleet, supports a political ethos which militates against any move to slacken local control of policing.[2]

A more recent expression of the desire to maintain local control is provided in a report by Le Centre de Recherches sur l'Opinion Publique (CROP 1973), Montréal. On the basis of a series of telephone interviews they claim that 'the vast majority of residents of Cote St Luc, Hampstead, Montréal West, Outremont, Town of Mount Royal and Westmount are in favour of maintaining the sovereignty of their municipal governments' (*The Suburban*, Feb. 28, 1973). The spatial relationships of these municipalities are shown diagrammatically in figure 6.2, and the details on population and size are given in table 6.3.

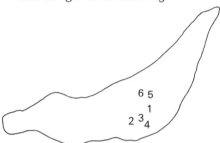

Figure 6.2   Communities peripheral to Montréal (Diagrammatic – not to scale) : 1 City of Montréal ; 2 Cote St Luc ; 3 Hampstead ; 4 Montréal West ; 5 Outremont ; 6 Town of Mount Royal (See figure 7.9 for accurate configuration)

Table 6.3   Municipalities peripheral to Montréal (1973)

Name	Population (approx.)	Size acres (approx.)
Cote St Luc	24,000	1,700 (687·94 hectares)
Hampstead	7,000	500 (202·3 hectares)
Montréal West	6,000	350 (141·7 hectares)
Outremont	30,000	1,000 (404·7 hectares)
Town of Mount Royal	20,000	1,800 (728·41 hectares)
Westmount	25,000	1,000 (404·7 hectares)
City of Montréal	1,200,000	43,000 (19,202·1 hectares)

The CROP study had two objectives. First, to gauge the sentiments of constituents regarding municipal reorganization, and second, to examine the perceived level of satisfaction with municipal services (police; fire; garbage; snow removal; road and park maintenance; recreation and library services). An attempt was also made to evaluate the perceived levels of competence of each municipality's administration. A sample of residents from each of the six municipalities was interviewed and the responses suggest that the preference for maintaining the *status quo* may rest on three factors. First, the 'distinct character' of each municipality; second, the fear that the quality of services will decline; and third, the fear that taxes will rise if municipalities are reorganized.

Almost 90 per cent of the respondents considered that it was very important to preserve the 'distinct character' of their community. The distinctive
character was seen in terms such as 'nice', 'clean', 'happy', 'quiet'.
Over 70 per cent feared loss of this character if their municipality joined
the city of Montréal, whereas 50 per cent had this fear if the six municipalities formed a single unit.

With regard to the quality of services, the majority of people are
currently satisfied whereas approximately 15 per cent feel that the quality
of services would rise if the municipalities were either amalgamated or
joined with the city. However, 42 per cent feared their services would
decline in quality if the six municipalities were amalgamated and
64 per cent feared decline if their municipality joined the city of
Montréal.[3] Taxation trends follow the same pattern, but in this case
30 per cent suggest taxes will increase if each municipality maintains its
autonomy. A regrouping with the city generated a 68 per cent response
for increases, whereas amalgamation of the six communities gave a figure
of 50 per cent

Table 6.4   Level of satisfaction: selected services (from CROP text,
p. 24)

Service	Very satisfied (%)
Police	82
Fire protection	79
Garbage removal	85
Snow removal	74
Road maintenance	79
Parks maintenance	80
Recreation and library	69*
Competence of administration	66 very competent
	26 fairly competent

(*CROP text, p. 24*)

   *This reflects generally very low quality of library services in Quebec, vis-à-vis
Canadian norms.

In summary, both anglophones and francophones follow the general
pattern in favouring the *status quo*. One aspect of perception which was
not evaluated in this study concerns the awareness of those who make
decisions for each municipality. This topic has been examined by Hawley
(1971) using data for Flint, Michigan, and we will close this section by
noting the major findings of this work. Hawley claims that efforts to
unify metropolitan communities have met with almost uniform failure
and he attempts to evaluate the attitudes of residents in peripheral areas
to this phenomenon. He suggests that 'resistance to governmental unification rests largely in ignorance of government and what to expect of it.'
Further, the evidence from the Flint study contradicts the widely-held

notion that township or small-scale government is 'closer' to the people than sity government. Rarely do people know the names of their local administrators in townships, whereas central city residents demonstrate more knowledge and participation in local government, and there is a higher turnout to vote in the city elections than in township elections. Questionnaires and interviews were used to provide the data on which these conclusions were based. It would seem that improvements to city governments are best brought about if all participants are made to feel equally important. The predominant attitude is fear of a take-over by the core city. Hawley concludes that 'the only promise of success would appear to rest in a process of education in the meaning and processes of government.'

So far we have concentrated attention on local aspects of inter-municipal cooperation. However, if we view the process at the national level then certain patterns emerge. Some recent studies have examined patterns of annexations of municipalities on a national scale in an attempt to determine the underlying forces which generate either a strong local sentiment for autonomy, or given rise to expansion of municipal units by annexation. In the next section we will examine these patterns in the US and draw general conclusions about this topic.

6 Patterns of municipal annexations

Glasgow (1971) has attempted to identify regularities in the pattern of municipal annexations in the US using data for 124 urban areas as defined by the US Census Bureau over the period 1950–1960. Specifically he examined three kinds of territory around urban areas:

1   Principal municipality (the most populous municipality in the region).
2   Secondary municipalities (any municipalities in the region other than 1).
3   Non-municipal territory.

The sample excluded approximately sixteen urbanized areas in New England, but fortunately annexations and incorporations were very rare in this region in the decade prior to 1960. Glasgow notes Schmandt's (1961) finding that between 1950 and 1960, of the 1,976 municipal incorporations which occurred in the US only three took place in New England. In order to limit data collection the urbanized areas with a population of over one million in 1960 were excluded because they contained numerous secondary municipalities. Chicago, for example, has over 240 municipalities, and St Louis more than 150. Further, as Bollens and Schmandt (1965, 415) have noted 'ten of the twelve most populous cities of 1950 annexed little or no land during the same decade.' It is widely reported that the period 1950 to 1960 was an era of considerable activity in terms of annexations and Glasgow has suggested that for

the two centuries following 1752 the average was about fifteen incorporations per year, whereas in the study period this rose to over fifty. Zimmerman (1970) also presents evidence to support the claim that interest in
structural reforms in local government in the US reached a peak in the
1950s. He also suggests that the continued existence of autonomous
political units can be attributed to inertia, strong opposition and the
central governments' failure to promote more rational schemes. Further,
grants-in-aid from federal and state governments have allowed the smaller
units to survive and he forecasts that 'barring a dramatic reversal of federal policy, it is unlikely that the 1970s will be a decade of metropolitan
reform' (p. 542).

A theoretical configuration for an urbanized area is shown in figure 6.3.
In passing it should be noted that *urbanized areas* were defined in the US
for the first time in 1950. They contain at least one city of 50,000 together
with a set of contiguous areas, and though these areas are specifically
defined,[4] for our purposes we will note that they contain the more densely
populated places which are near to the major city.

boundary of urbanized area

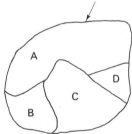

Figure 6.3 Theoretical urbanized
area: *A* city: population over 50,000;
B incorporated place with over 2,500
inhabitants; *C* incorporated place,
less than 2,500 inhabitants, but closely
settled; *D* enumeration districts in
unincorporated space with population
density of over 1,000 per square mile

Using population data for the units within the urbanized area a series
of indices were calculated. First, a non-municipal growth factor (g) was
defined by Glasgow (p. 15) as 'that portion of total urbanized area
population change which occurred during the study period in areas
available for annexation and incorporation.' Following the calculation of
g four other indices were derived:

1   Centralization rate (P)

$$P = 100 \ (a_p/g)$$

where a_p is the 1960 population of any areas annexed to the principal
municipality

2   Suburbanization rate (S)

$$S = 100 \ (a_s + i)/g$$

where a_s is the 1960 population of any areas which had been annexed
to secondary municipalities, and i is the 1960 population of all
municipalities incorporated between 1950 and 1960

3 Municipalization rate (M)

$$M = P + S$$

4 Concentration rate (C)

$$C = P - S$$

Indices 1, 2 and 3 indicate the extent to which growth of non-municipal territories within an urbanized area 'was absorbed by the expansion of the principal municipality through annexation (P), the proliferation and expansion of secondary municipalities by incorporation and annexation (S) and by a combination of all these processes (M)' (p. 18). The fourth index 'measures the degree to which principal municipality expansion exceeded, or was exceeded by, secondary municipality proliferation and expansion as a factor in absorbing non-municipal growth' (p. 18).

By examining the frequency distributions of values for the four indices it was concluded that the patterns did not fit a simple general model of population growth of principal municipalities and a take-over of peripheral areas. It was therefore decided to sub-divide the urban areas into four classes on the bases of the values for the indices. These are shown on table 6.5.

Table 6.5 Classes of urbanized areas in the United States

Class	No. of Areas	Indices	Characteristics
A	41	$M > 40: C > 40$ $S \approx 0$	Principal municipality annexation dominant
B	28	$M > 40: 40 > C > -40$	Centralization *and* suburbanization active
C	7	$C < -40$	High suburbanization rates
D	48	$M < 40$	All indices ≈ 0. Little change occurred

The four class types were mapped (see figure 6.4) and an attempt was made to search for distinct regions.

Only two regions stand out fairly clearly. Firstly, the region Glasgow calls Delmaneo which includes New York, Pennsylvania, New Jersey and Delaware and north-eastern Ohio. The twenty urbanized areas in this region fall into the D Class. Second, a Central Plains region comprised Texas, Oklahoma, Kansas, Nebraska and Colorado. This region also contains twenty urbanized areas, thirteen of which are type A, five are B and the rest C. In an effort to explain the spatial distribution of the patterns of annexations the final part of the study attempted to search for relationships between the index values and a set of independent variables. Three types of independent variables were used; physical terrain, legal structure and population. An hypothesis concerning the influence of terrain was inferred from the, empirical data shown in figure 6.4. Specifically the level terrain of the Central Plains appears to be more conducive to higher

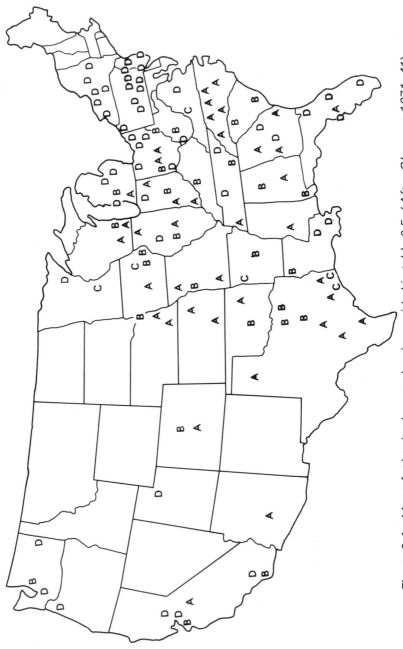

Figure 6.4 Map of urbanized areas: key is provided in table 6.5. (*After Glasgow, 1971, 41*)

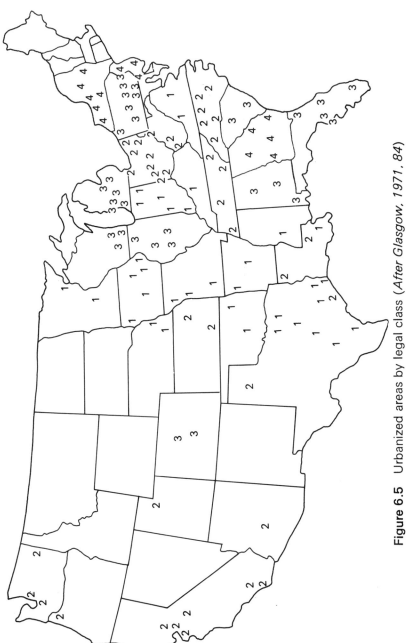

Figure 6.5 Urbanized areas by legal class (*After Glasgow, 1971, 84*)

rates of municipalization and concentration than the rougher terrain of Delmaneo, *ceteris paribus*. In order to relax this latter assumption the two other groups of variables were included. Schmandt (1961), quoted in Glasgow (1971, 48), has suggested that the incidence of incorporation and annexation is closely related to the permissiveness of the incorporation laws which hold in each state, and Wheeler (1965) has classified states on a six-point scale according to the legal requirements for municipal annexation of the principal city in an urbanized area. Glasgow collapsed this scale into four classes and these are shown in figure 6.5 for the set of 124 urbanized area. Class four represents the most restrictive legal requirements and this applies to New Jersey and New York. Within each of the four classes Glasgow considered three attributes of population and the terrain variable. The three attributes were population size and density, and the degree of concentration.

It appears both from the maps and a statistical analysis that the spatial pattern of annexations is not a purely random occurrence. However, the correlation coefficients are generally low and because terrain variable is dichotomized its full effect is not evaluated. This variable is classed as 0 for the plains, 88 cases, and 1 for all other urbanized areas. It is therefore very difficult to determine precisely the combination of terrain, legal and population characteristics which fully explain the patterns. Perhaps more emphasis should be placed upon building up a body of knowledge from many case studies, and searching later for regularities on the large scale. The case study approach is well demonstrated by the work of Bergman (1971) for Minneapolis–St Paul in Minnesota.

Between 1950 and 1960 within the five-county area of Minneapolis–St Paul forty-five municipalities incorporated. Twenty-two contained less than 1,000 people and one had a population of forty-three. The state legislature established a Commission on Municipal Annexation and Consolidation in 1957 to consider the administrative problems that would arise and over the next few years reports were produced noting the political chaos and the need for a rational policy. In 1961 the Minnesota legislature gave to the Minnesota Municipal Commission 'power to eliminate referenda for incorporation or consolidation of a municipality within a township, power to later boundaries, and power to initiate consolidations and annexations' (Bergman 1971, 36). This legislation format has been adopted by several other states. After a decade of public debate, several crises of water pollution, and cases of competition for investment among municipalities there emerged in 1966 a Report of the St Paul Chamber of Commerce, (1966) which stated two fundamental principles:

1   'There are services in the metropolitan area which should . . . be rendered on an area-wide basis . . . as the area grows in population and complexity the list of such metropolitan services can be expected to increase.'

2   'Most municipalities . . . want to maintain their identity and indivi-
duality' (Bergman, p. 84).

The communications media opened the debate to the public and it
seemed they were generally in favour of metropolitan government.
However, there were three foci of opposition. First, county officials,
second, a suburban alliance, AMPLE[5] and third the suburban press.
But as Bergman notes, 'none was completely blind to the need for some
new form of metropolitan coordination' (p. 105). The opposition feared
loss of local control but their efforts were 'only a weak reaction to the
forceful demand for an area government' (p. 105).

In 1967 a metropolitan area government was created. A referendum
was not held and judging from a newspaper survey of the same year
approximately 35 per cent were in favour of a metropolitan government,
only 25 per cent against, and the balance of 40 per cent undecided.
The results of a later survey reported in 1970 suggested that different
opinions were generated according to the service. This is in line with
comments made earlier in this chapter and it was suggested that for
services such as education, law enforcement and street repairs control
should be at the local level, whereas sewage, water, mass transit, highways
and air pollution control should be under metropolitan control. Further,
most people (almost 90 per cent) supported the claim that metropolitan
government would become more important over the next thirty years.

Bergman claims that six general factors which encourage metropolitan
government emerge from this case study of the twin cities of Minneapolis
and St Paul:

1   Federal encouragement.
2   Prior recognition that some problems were area-wide.
3   An infrastructure of intergovernmental cooperation.
4   Private support.
5   Metropolitan community.
6   Specific problems.

However, we should note Bergman's conclusion that 'to determine
which ones prevail and what composite is both necessary and sufficient
would require a calculus of human motivations far more sophisticated
than any yet devised.'

The general principles identified by Bergman can be perceived in other
metropolitan government reform programmes in the US, for example,
Dade County, Florida, Nashville–Davidson County and Seattle. They
also apply to Thunder Bay, Ontario, a new city created by amalgamating
Fort William and Port Arthur on 1 January 1970. To add further support
to these findings it should be noted that an attempt to produce a metropolitan government in St Louis in the fifties failed. At that time there was
no formal inter-municipal agreements of any importance, the economic
leaders felt no need to support a metropolitan government, few activities

were organized on a wide scale, and few crucial problems faced the area. Also St Louis crossed a state line, between Mississippi and Illinois, and this served to separate parts of the city.

Smallwood (1970) has reviewed government reorganization plans in North America and Britain, and he claims that, 'the metropolitan government movement in the US has languished in a post-war state of suspended animation for a full quarter-century.' He sees three basic reasons for this: tough opposition from local municipalities, the lack of effective government and the lack of a consistent set of urban and metropolitan development goals. The situation in the US contrasts sharply with similar experiences in Britain and Canada where strong regulatory powers have been used effectively to bring about local government reforms. However, while central governments are playing a more important part in the organization of local government affairs by increasing their redistribution of the nation's wealth, at the local level great emphasis is still placed upon public participation. Smallwood concludes that 'it looks as if we may be in for a continuously more tumultuous tug-of-war between the forces of centralization and decentralization.'

Finally, we should recognize that problems of reorganizing service district boundaries in and around urban areas are faced by citizens outside North America and the United Kingdom. Recent publications by the United Nations (1970) and the World Bank (1972b) emphasized the need for research in this field to improve organizational principles for improving the quality of services while taking into account different demands and varying levels of financial ability, as well as the rapid urbanization which is a characteristic of the Third World.

7 Conclusions

Empirical evidence suggests that single units rarely come into being and completely take over the functions that were traditionally provided by the smaller autonomous units, even though it is widely recognized that many of these small units are inefficient and the quality of services provided varies considerably between units. Unless citizens are made more aware of the purposes of reorganization, and the central government and public and private agencies are prepared to take strong initiative, local resistance is likely to perpetuate the current patterns. A compromise arrangement is often worked out whereby among municipalities services are exchanged. But as Morando (1968) points out, if services such as police protection, libraries and water are inadequate then inter-municipal cooperation is a reasonable solution to the problem. However, if the problem is 'segregation, inadequate housing and municipal tax resource inequities created by the multiplicity of government jurisdictions' then cooperation only serves to exacerbate the situation. Much more information is needed on people's perceptions of the quality of services, the efficiency with which different methods of representation transmit the preferences of citizens and the attributes of alternate methods for financing services, for example, local income taxes, grants-in-aid, user charges and property taxes. Once this information becomes available it should be widely circulated so that voters can be fully informed before making a choice.

Notes on further reading

Many books which deal with urban problems touch on the topics of inter-governmental relations, municipal taxation and provision of public services, for example Curran (1963), Chinitz (1964) and Martin (1967) provide useful summaries of the relationships between classical urban problems and the structure of local governments.

The analysis of patterns of inter-municipal cooperation is clearly discussed in Morando (1968) using data for Detroit. The classic studies in this field are by Williams (1963a and b; 1965) and Jacob and Toscano (1964).

Notes

1 Plunkett (1972) suggests that in Canada expenditures double every 5 years and education absorbs over 50 per cent of local tax revenues.

2 Proposals for Regional Government in the area considered Stoney Creek and Saltfleet a single unit (*Urban Focus*, 1973).

3 Unaccounted percentage refers to 'don't know' group.

4 See Yeates & Garner (1971, 493–494).

5 Alliance of Minnesotans to Preserve Local Entities.

7 The evolution of service districts

1 Introduction

In this chapter we will consider the influence of changes over time on the provision of public services. In particular we will examine the large-scale changes which complement the smaller scale ones we examined in Chapter 5. The general problem of evaluating the impact of variations over time on the location of facilities has rarely been treated in the literature on location theory. However, there is a large body of literature in geography which provides many cases studies from which general principles can be extracted. With regard to location theory *per se* Deighton (1971) notes the comment by Revelle *et al.* (1970) on the problem of defining the optimum position for facilities: 'Are locations set in order to be most efficient with today's population, ten years hence or twenty years hence or an average of all three?' If we are to use rigorous procedures for making recommendations for the positioning of facilities in space then we should take account of the influence of temporal variations. In a later section of this chapter we will examine this topic under the heading Simulation and Time Variations. However, first we will present a conceptual section on a general typology of the evolution of service districts over time. This will be clarified by reference to empirical examples drawn from Western Europe, North and South America and China. The analysis of the evolution of the spatial configuration of service centres will be examined in a separate section.

Perhaps the most characteristic feature of the evolution of service districts over time is the amalgamation of units into larger administrative or service districts. The processes corrected with amalgamations and unification within and near urban areas were discussed in Chapter 6 and we will complement this by examining the phenomenon on a larger scale later in this chapter. In that section we will concentrate upon the changing spatial configuration of service districts and the significance of these changes on functional efficiency, organization and control.

In general terms the development of administrative districts is closely related to the overall growth of settlement in an area. With repsect to Britain, for example, Mitchell (1963) has documented the evolution of parish boundaries since the middle ages. Her approach depends largely upon careful and intensive examination of documentary evidence. At the beginning of the nineteenth century the civil parish in the UK was used for rating purposes, and Mitchell notes that it was essentially co-extensive with the ecclesiastical parish. However, after a series of Acts dating from 1832 the spatial arrangement was modified in response to the growth of new centres. But Mitchell point out that: 'These adjust-

124

ments were by no means universal; the majority of rural districts remained untouched' (p. 91). Further, 'the parishes of the beginning of the nineteenth century may have existed for a long time. In many areas they do not differ from the parishes listed in the Valor Ecclesiasticus of 1534–35 or even from those in Pope Nicholas' Taxation of 1291.' She claims that the origin of the parish is obscure, though it has persisted for several centuries and has served as the basic spatial unit for the provision of different services at different points in time. The relationship between the shape and size of parishes in the UK was discussed in Chapter 2 and we particularly noted that the form has been strongly influenced by topography, drainage and vegetation patterns. 'The great variety of villages and parishes is then no chance occurrence, but is the outcome of the way in which man has worked over many centuries in harmony with the great variety of nature' (Mitchell, p. 117). However, with the growth of large urbanized areas, the demand for high quality standard public services and the development of rapid means of communication and travel, the form of the contemporary service district should consider these elements, rather than the terrain features cited above. We find though that the traditional spatial units frequently persist and generate a sentiment of local comfort for the residents. The range of functions these districts perform is however minimal so there is little incentive to modify the patterns. Rather, new larger spatial service districts are created to encompass several parishes and it is the search for principles for the establishment of these in Britain that occupied the Redcliffe–Maud Commission in the later 1960s.

Other geographers who have examined the evolution of parishes include Boots (1972) and Newcomb (1970; 1973). Boots applied shape measures to parishes in selected areas of Britain in order to discover the underlying processes of spatial organization. Basically, he tried to evaluate the hypothesis that parishes are randomly arranged. To do this he compared different processes for generating shapes, with the shapes of parishes in two selected regions: central Dorset (47 parishes) and Cornwall (35 parishes). This procedure differs from that used by Mitchell, yet both seek for a better understanding of the principles of spatial organization of parishes. In Newcomb's 1970 paper he attempted to reconstruct the evolution pattern of Danish parishes using historical documents. More recently (1973) he has employed pattern measures to examine the arrangement of churches, which he considered the parish nuclei. Also, he used the Contact Number to describe the shape of parishes. The results are close to 6·0 which is predictable in the light of the comments offered in Chapter 2. Like Baker (1971) he suggests that historical geographers should complement their documentary and archaeological evidence with quantitative indices, and Newcomb argues that: '(spatial pattern measures) . . . might be an inexpensive way whereby to provide some clues, to sketch some genetic possibilities or to rule out some unprofitable lines of speculation'.

In summary we should note that the traditional units, such as parishes, are often no longer suitable as service districts. New ones must therefore be created. However, inertia is powerful and frequently it is not easy to demonstrate forcefully the explicit disadvantages of the old units and the advantages of the new ones. Usually we have to wait until gross inefficiencies are evident, then new patterns can be introduced without too much resistance.

One of the most important factors which leads to reorganization of service districts involves improvements in transportation. Janelle (1969) has used the phrase *time–space convergence* to characterize the impact of transportation innovations, and he provides evidence to show that the sphere of influence of places as defined by travel-time has increased considerably over the last 100 years. Thus the townships of North America, cantons of France or parishes of England which could be traversed in a day in the nineteenth century can now usually be crossed in less than one hour. Clearly the units are no longer large enough to enclose a reasonable sphere of influence. In most western nations accessibility has reached a high level and it is difficult to imagine improvements in personal mobility, on a day-to-day basis, which compare with the improvements that followed the widespread use of the automobile. In fact, with an increase in the number of cars on highways, accessibility may again decrease and we may see a slowing down in the trends of the spatial organization of districts. However, the impact of other technological changes, such as the transmission of information, will probably manifest themselves on the spatial configuration of districts for some services. For example, in remote areas, education could be given via television and computer consoles, and pupils and teacher need never leave their homes. Potentially the service districts could be immense.

If we turn to a different cultural environment, China, and examine the evolution of administrative units over time, there are remarkable similarities with other countries even though there are features which are peculiar to that country. The general problem of dividing space and population into districts for taxation, representation, defence and trading purposes has occurred many times in Chinese history as it has in the history of western and third world countries.

The changing administrative geography of China has been examined in great detail by Whitney (1970) who notes that: 'Since the Ch'in dynasty there have been numerous changes in the number of echelons of the Chinese territorial–administrative hierarchy and great secular and spatial variations in the size of areas at any particular level.' Whitney goes on to claim that: 'Much of the waxing and waning of echelon growth can be traced to the problems of bureaucratic control and coordination . . . reforming and unifying dynasties have usually attempted to start their rule with a clean administrative slate by abolishing most of the echelons between the centre and the counties, only to find with the passage of time and the exigencies of bureaucratic and regional control that they

were forced to reassemble them again, or even to create new supra-
provincial ones in addition.' Whitney cites as examples of this the Ch'in
and Sui Dynasties, and the First Republic, and to a lesser extent the
Ming Dynasty. A detailed example is provided by considering:

> Sui Wen-ti (AD 589–605), who unified China after a long period of division,
> abolished the complex and diverse administrative hierarchies that had devel-
> oped during the preceeding two hundred years and created a two-tier one
> consisting of *chou*, averaging about 5000 square miles [12, 950 km²] each,
> and a lower one consisting of *hsien* or counties. By AD 605, however, only sixteen
> years after the beginning of the dynasty, it became necessary to establish areas
> of about the same size as the present day province, also called *chou*. . . . Again
> in the Ming period (AD 1368–1643) an attempt was made to reduce the number
> of echelons to three and to simplify and standardize the extremely complex
> system of administrative areas that had developed during the Yüan dynasty
> (p. 80).

The rise and fall of administrative structures in China is discussed in
detail by Whitney, and will not be repeated here. It is sufficient to note
that writers in the western world often ignore China's efforts to overcome
many of the spatial organization problems that are faced by all countries.
Planners and others interested in the role of space and location in the
provision of social services should improve their awareness of develop-
ments in a country which has such a long tradition of human settlement,
is operating with a political, social and cultural system which is quite
different from that of other countries and which contains almost a third
of mankind.[1] In an attempt to summarize the complexities of the evolution of administrative districts in China, table 7.1 has been constructed.

2 A general typology of the evolution process

The evolution of administrative districts can be examined from two
main standpoints. The first is specifically concerned with the spatial
pattern of areas and the second considers temporal changes in the control
and organization of the system. Though as geographers we tend to place
greater emphasis on the first we should recognize that changes in the
spatial pattern over time are often strongly related to the way the system
and the control mechanism is organized, as has been noted in the examples
from China. At a local level in a western society we may find, for example,
a powerful individual at the head of a government agency who feels that
school districts should be amalgamated and enlarged. During his period
in office, therefore, we note this trend in the evolution of the spatial
form. At another time local citizen groups and parents' associations
may be able to marshal support for a plan to maintain local control of
small school boards. During this period, therefore, we note the persistence
of many small school boards. In reality the competition is often between
several groups, not just citizens against one government official. This
competitive framework underlies most decision-making, and it is felt

Table 7.1 Development of administrative districts in China

		1	2	3	4	5*	6	7
Chin	221 BC			36:27		1,000		
Han	206–143 BC			116:14		1,587		
Han	143–220 AD		13:10	125:10		1,180		
W. Chin	265–313		19:9	173:7		1,232		
Sui	589–601				310:5	1,524		
Sui	605–618		15:13	190:7		1,255		
Tang	627–712	10:36			358:4	1,551		
	713–908		15:22		338:4	1,235		
Sung	997–1077		15:21		321:4	1,230		
	1085–1128		23:14		297:3	1,235		
	1280–1367	8:	15:13			1,113		
Ming	1368–1643		18:5	196:7		1,384		
Ching	1644–1911	6:	18:94	95:3	249:6	1,443		
Republic	1912–1913		18:4	76:22	1,663	1,685		
	1914–1927		18:91			1,685		
	1928–1933					1,650		
	1934–1949		18:11	190:9		1,663		
Peoples' Republic	1949–1954	5:4	19:8	156:10	1,604:9	1,604	14,200:15	47,000 (Hsiang) 220,466 (Hsiang)
	1955–1966	6:3	18:7	124:11	1,296:20	1,296	26,518 (communes)	74,000 (Hsiang–1957) 78,000 (Communes–1961)

Key

1 150,000 + (388,500 +)
2 60,000–125,000 (155,400–323,750)
3 8,000–25,000 (20,720 64,750) ⎫
4 4,000–6,000 (10,360–15,546) ⎪ Size of districts : square miles (km²)
5 900–1,400 (2,331–3,676) ⎬
6 100–200 (259–518) ⎪
7 5–30 (12·9–77·7) ⎭

* hsien

13:10 average number of units :
      average number of units
      controlled in next lower level

(After Whitney, 1970. 75–8).

by social scientists to be so important that if we are to understand and explain how decisions are reached we must frame the decision-making process into a type of competition or game. However, because it is usually very difficult to find suitable data to reconstruct how decisions to alter the form of service districts were made we often concentrate upon the spatial aspects and try to infer some of the reasons for spatial reorganization. This usually allows us to discover the most obvious reasons, but it does not throw light on the details of the decision-making process: the personal conflicts, the alternatives that were evaluated, the goals and strategies of those involved and the political, social and economic climate of the day. For this kind of information we have to depend upon the valuable work of other social scientists particularly historians. There is a rich tradition in this area, Mitchell (1963) and Darby (1926; 1953) for the UK; East (1966) for Western Europe; and Brown (1948) for the US, which unfortunately tends to be overlooked by some contemporary location theorists. We have already mentioned, for example, that for a clearer understanding of the evolution of parishes in the UK Mitchell's work (1963) should be consulted. We could also add Darby (1926), Webb and Webb (1960) and Tate (1946). In the context of North America the works of Brown (1948) and Harris (1966) serve a similar function. For the third world Whitney's work (1970) on China is most valuable as is Prescott's (1965) study of political organization in West Africa.

Let us now turn to some of the purely spatial aspects of service districts. At the outset we note that their shapes and sizes tend to vary over time. Our first problem is to try and classify these trends which are exhibited by empirical data. Examples of such data include Haggett's study (1965) of municipalities in Brazil: in 1950 there were over 1,760 municipalities and by 1960 the number had increased to about 3,000. An example of a decrease in the number of districts is provided by the amalgamation of school boards in Ontario, Canada. In 1945 there were over 5,600 public, separate and secondary school boards in the province, but by 1967 this had been reduced to slightly less than 1,500. A similar example is provided by the independent school districts in America where consolidations have reduced the number of independent districts by about 75 per cent since 1942. Clearly we could cite numerous examples of these amalgamation and decentralization processes but our objective is rather to offer a general typology into which the case studies can be placed. For this purpose we can divide the evolution of service districts into a series of stages. These are summarized in table 7.2.

The stages outlined in the conceptual framework can be treated as a sequence of results in a competition between a completely centralized service system, with a single service or administrative centre and no local subdivisions, and complete decentralization, whereby each individual provides all the goods and services he requires.

While such a typology serves to unite many studies from different parts

Table 7.2   A typology for the evolution of service districts

Time	State of the region in which districts are located	Stage of evolution
t_1	Unknown and unsettled	No spatial units
t_2	Explored, but unsettled	Some boundaries may be shown on maps to claim sovereignty of area
t_3	Settled in part	The settled part may be sub-divided into distinct districts
t_4	1 Expansion of settlement	New districts defined
	2 Density of settlement increases	Sub-division of existing districts to maintain small units.
t_5	3 Density of settlement increases	Amalgamation of small units to take advantage of economics of scale
	4 Communication systems improve with transportation innovations	Centralization and standardization in the quality of the service
t_6	Modification of demand and supply as values change, population density changes and distribution mechanisms change	Districts may be modified to amalgamate different functions. Districts may be kept at a level with *explicity* does not take advantage of scale, but provides local standards of service. Affluent communities may encourage quality to dominate cost considerations of strict economic reasoning

of the world and to search for regularities, it is restrictive in the amount of rigour which is used for analysing each study area. In the next section we shall put more emphasis on the rigorous analytical approaches which have been applied to specific types of service districts.

3   Simulation and time variations

One of the first writers to draw attention to the need for computable models to solve public facility location problems was Teitz (1968). He was concerned specifically with urban areas, but the principles he enunciated have much wider currency. We should note that public services play an important role in determining the quality of life for individuals and with our finite budgets we therefore wish to produce the most advantageous returns. However, if we locate facilities without reference to changes over time we may fail to achieve this objective. Teitz (p. 48) has noted that: 'Facility systems are usually built quite slowly, reacting to changes both in the size and the broader systems they serve and in technology and social preferences. . . . there may be the conflict between static and dynamic system optima.' This problem can be readily appreciated if we consider the following situation. Three service centres (for example, fire stations) are to be built over the next three years at the rate of one per year. We wish to locate these fire stations so that average response-time is minimal. The problem is to decide on the locations that achieve this objective while at the same time taking into account the sequential building programme. If the service area is of the form shown in figure 7.1 then we can argue that the best location for the first station

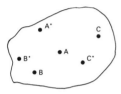

Figure 7.1 Sample district for a fire station problem

is at the point of minimum aggregate travel, A. However, when we locate B and C, the overall average distance is usually greater than if we first find the best location for A, B and C, call these A^*, B^*, and C^*, then find the best sequence in which to build them so that the overall average response-time is minimized. If this second strategy is adopted then with only one fire station the location A^*, B^*, or C^* is less efficient than A However, in the long run the second arrangement is more efficient. Scott (1971) has formally examined these two strategies for tackling location problems over time. Using an artificial set of data he showed clearly that over a planning horizon of several years it is more efficient to solve the problem according to the second strategy outlined above. This is technically known as a backward recursive procedure. The two basic steps in this procedure are outlined below:

1   Define objective function and the number of centres to be located – for example, three depots – to minimize aggregate distance travelled, with each centre serving an equal work-load. (There was discussion of this static problem in Chapter 4.)
2   Once the best set of depots is located the next task is to find the best sequence for locating them. This is usually done by evaluating all possible sequences if only a few (approximately ten) are to be located. Dynamic programming is normally used to search for this best sequence.

The first approach which finds the optimal location at the first time-period is known as a forward recursive procedure. Scott (1971b) calls this the myopic approach; as more centres are located the arrangement become increasingly sub-optimal. Scott generated a set of forty random points to evaluate these strategies, and considered that each point had

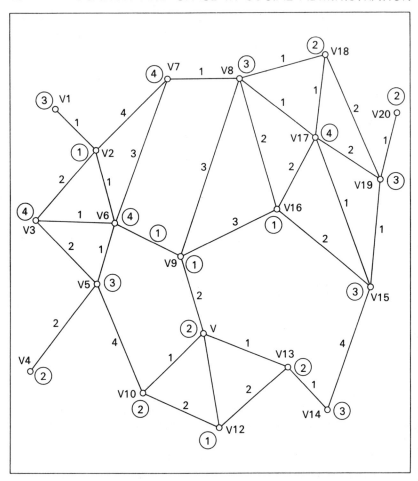

Figure 7.2 A sample network
(Whitaker, 1971, 66)

the same weight. He also assumed that transportation was feasible in all directions. The myopic approach is the better when less than nine centres are located. However with more than this number the dynamic programming procedure gives better results. These are shown in table 7.3. Whitaker (1971) has considered the same problem on a network with weighted nodes. The study network is shown in figure 7.2. He attempted to find the best sequence to locate three centres such that overall transportation distance from nodes to the nearest centres was minimized. By using a forward recursive procedure he identified two possible sequences, these are shown in table 7.3.

Table 7.3 Table of cumulated costs

Time-period	Myopic system	Dynamic programming System
1	1087·7	1136·0
2	1894·3	1945·1
3	2495·7	2584·8
4	3030·2	3129·6
5	3511·5	3587·5
6	3992·7	4045·4
7	4473·9	4503·4
8	4955·1	4961·3
9	5436·4	5419·2
10	5917·6	5877·1
11	6398·8	6334·9
12	6880·1	5792·9

(*Scott, 1971b, 153, table 8.1*)

Table 7.4 Forward recursive procedure

	Centres	Costs	
1	9.	184	
2	9.17	115	Total cost 380
3	9.17.6	81	
1	8.	184	
2	8.6	108	Total cost 360
3	8.6.13	68	

If we compare these results with those derived from the backward recursive procedure we again notice the utility of this latter approach. The values for this are shown in table 7.5.

Table 7.5 Backward recursive procedure

	Centre		
1	6.11.17	63	
2	6.17	100	Total cost 350
3	6.	187	

When the first centre is located we should choose 6 rather than 9 or 8, though they are cheaper by 3 units. With centres 6 and 17 there is a saving of 5 or 12 units over either of the other two solutions, and when all three centres are located the savings could amount to 10 or 30 units. With more centres the value of the backward recursive approach becomes increasingly noticeable. (See Whitaker 1971[2]).

Though we have not used real-world data to illustrate the strategies it seems that potentially we may be able to make savings by long-term planning. While this may appear true under the restrictive assumptions of our models, when we examine the real world it is rarely possible to construct a centre at exactly the optimum location. Furthermore, the data we use to summarize the demand at nodes and the accessibility is also subject to errors. With these points in mind it is appropriate that we now consider the sensitivity of a location to changes in the data which are used to define an optimum location. To examine this problem we will use a simulated data set of thirty-six points on a 300 by 300 grid. This is shown in figure 7.3. The points were located by a stratified random procedure, placing four points in each of nine equal grid squares; this method provided good areal coverage, while adhering reasonably closely to the assumption of a homogeneous surface of randomly occurring demands for a service offered at a central depot M. Demand was varied in the course of this study by altering the weights at the points.

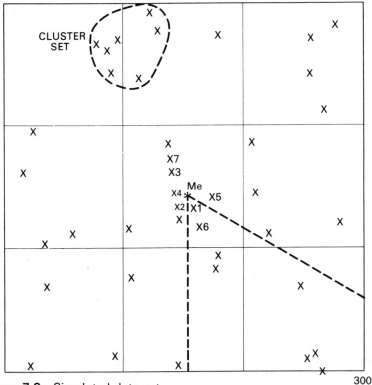

Figure 7.3 Simulated data set

The first step was to calculate the point of minimum aggregate travel using Cooper's (1967) algorithm under the assumption that all the points were equally weighted. This point, M_e, was used as the reference point from which departures under other assumptions were measured. Several systematic weighting changes were made in order to observe the change in M when various specific assumptions regarding the weights attached to points were made. Finally, the point of minimum aggregate travel was generated for thirty sets of random weightings to provide a criterion for evaluating the changes in M which occurred under the systematic weighting assumptions.

Seven systematic weighting schemes were used:

1   Peripheral points (more than 140 units from M_e) weighted 3; others weighted 1.
2   Central points (less than 100 units from M_e) weighted 3; others weighted 1.
3   Intermediate points (100–140 units from M_e) weighted 3; others weighted 1.
4   Points weighted as the reciprocal of their distance from M_e.
5   Points weighted according to function increasing linearly and horizontally from a value of 2 at the left-hand edge of the map to 8 at the right-hand edge.
6   One 60° sector (in the lower right-hand sector of the map) weighted 3; other points weighted 1.
7   One off-centre cluster (upper left-hand area of map) weighted 3; other points weighted 1.

The positions of the point of minimum aggregate travel for each scheme are shown on figure 7.3. The distribution of these M_i's suggests that those for which the weighting involves no significant 'unbalancing' of the point set (eg weighting of central points) cluster close to M_e, whereas those generated by an 'unbalanced' weighting (eg the off-centre cluster) have a directional basis from M_e. The only exception to this generalization is M_5, generated by the intermediate-point weighting. The eccentricity of M_5 can be explained by directional bias in the particular inter-mediate point set used, and does not affect the overall conclusions.

In the next stage, the points of minimum aggregate travel, M_r, for the above point set with thirty different random weightings were generated, and the distance from each of these to M_e calculated. These are shown in figure 7.4. A histogram of the frequency distribution of distances suggests that the distribution of distances is normal. The mean and standard deviation of these distances were calculated, and circles representing the mean distance and one standard deviation beyond it were super-imposed on the pattern of M_i's, M_r's, and M_e in figure 7.4.

From statistical theory, it is to be expected that approximately half the M_r's would fall within the mean distance circle, and a further 34 per cent within the first standard deviation circle. In actual fact, 17 out of 30 M_r's fell within the mean distance circle, and a further 7 (23 per cent) within the first standard deviation circle; these results were reasonably close to expectations, considering that the number of M_r's was the minimum required for the application of normal statistics.

Among the systematically generated points of minimum aggregate

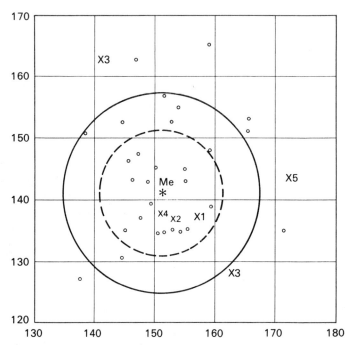

Figure 7.4 Distribution of depots using random weighting (1–100):
X₁–X₁ refer to figure 7.3; depot locations (dots); mean distance cycle
(broken line); 1 standard deviation circle (continuous line)

travel, those generated by weightings centred on M_e (ie using M_e as a
reference point at the centre of the weighted area) tended to fall well
within the mean distance circle, close to M_e. Those defined by off-centre
weightings fell outside the mean distance circle. The closest of the latter
group was M_6, from the sector weighting which by definition contained
some heavily weighted central points, followed by M_5 (from the 'inclined
surface' weighting) and M_7 (from the off-centre cluster weighting).

From this small study we can conclude that the point of minimum
aggregate travel appears to be rather insensitive to changes in demand
which occur under the seven different rules examined. These changing
demand patterns may occur over a period of time and because there is a
clustering of best locations we can feel reasonably sure that our centre
remains highly efficient, in a spatial sense, even though demand patterns
vary. Specifically, the circle of mean deviation covers only 0·18 per cent
of the study area and the mean distance of an M_r to M_e is approximately
3·5 per cent of a side of the study area. This general finding of insensi-
tivity is similar to the one by Goodchild (1972a) with respect to a location

problem in the private sector and the comments by Larson and Stevenson (1971) in their study of emergency services in New York, referred to in Chapter 5.

Clearly, further research is needed in the area of sensitivity analysis of location patterns, before we can be sure that our efforts to find the perfect location for depots are really worth while. Also, we should not confine ourselves to examining only the spatial aspects. In an attempt to broaden the view Deighton (1971) has suggested that accounting for rental costs associated with opening and closing centres could be used to determine a policy for long-run planning. This topic has not, as yet, been developed in the literature.

4 A spatial analysis of amalgamation

In this section we will use empirical studies to consider the general problem of identifying and explaining trends in the spatial organization of service structures over time. At a single point in time we can characterize a structure by a map of the district boundaries. Thus if we examine this map over time we may be able to make statements about the trends. Such a map often contains limited information. It may not show, for example, the location of the demand for services, the position of supply points or the transportation system and though large-scale aggregate conclusions can be made with some confidence, it is often difficult to apply these to individual districts. These points will be clarified in the following paragraphs when we examine some of the aggregate trends in the spatial organization of service districts.

Let us consider the two maps shown in figure 7.5. They depict spatial patterns in 1948 and 1967 and it is clear that between these two dates the number of areas has decreased, and the average size of the areas has increased. This general trend is typical of many spatial administrative systems. The earlier phase, showing an increase in the number of areas as noted in the early stages of the conceptual typology, is embedded in this gross trend. The maps in figure 7.6 illustrate this process in Santa Catarina state, Brazil, between 1872 and 1960. They show that as population density increases the number of areas increases. The relationship between the size of administrative units and population density has been examined in China by Whitney (1970). He found an inverse relationship between size and population density which has persisted through time. The differences between the number of units in the north and the south can also be partly explained by differences in population density. The ratio of number of basic administrative units (*hsein*) is similar to the ratio of population density, and since the late Ming period the latter ratio has been about 1 : 0·75 (north : south). The ratio of *hsien* has been about 1 : 0·70 for the same period. Turning back to figure 7.5 if we examine all the maps in the intervening period we can produce the graph shown in figure 7.7. Comparing this to the conceptual typology, 1948 can be

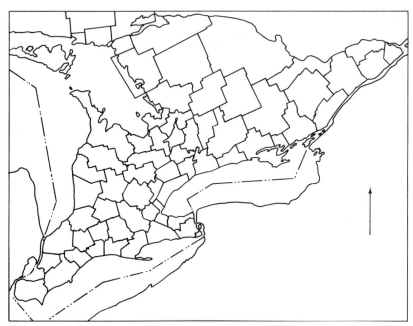

Figure 7.5a   Ontario hydro rural operating areas, 1967

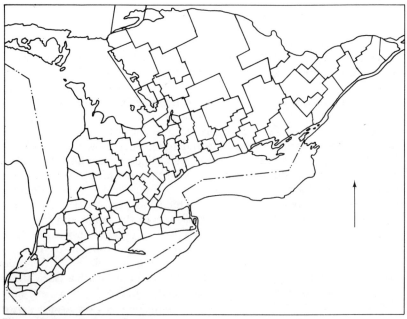

Figure 7.5b   Ontario hydro rural operating areas, 1948

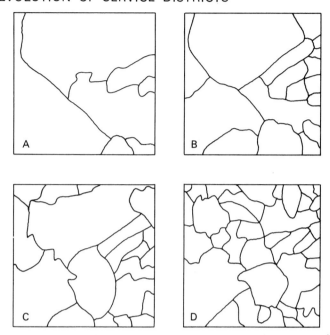

Figure 7.6 Progressive territorial subdivision of sample quadrat in Santa Catarina state. Brazil: *A*: 1872; *B*:1907; *C*: 1930; *D*: 1960 (*After Haggett, 1965*)

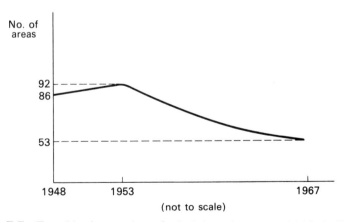

Figure 7.7 Trend in the number of administrative areas, 1948–1967

taken to represent stage t_3 ,and 1953 stage t_4; from 1953 to the present we see stage t_5 and the beginning of t_6.

We can use the maps as a basic data set and calculate shape measures of the districts. Massam and Goodchild (1971) have calculated shape (*S*) and spatial efficiency measures (E) for these districts for all years between 1948 and 1967. The S and E measures used were discussed in Chapter 2. In summary the closer the value of S and E are to 1·0, the more compact is the shape of the district (ie if $S = $ 1·0, the district is circular in shape) and the higher is the spatial efficiency.

The values for all areas at each point in time were calculated and the average value taken to represent a static description of the spatial organization for each year. It was known that once a year the authority had the option of redefining the spatial organization; the districts could be amalgamated, new ones could be created or centres could be relocated. If we plot a graph of S and E, see figure 7.8) for the twenty-year period we notice that the S index increases consistently for the period 1948–1955, then it is unchanged for three years. This is followed by two smaller cycles of five years each. The E index follows an approximately horizontal trend from 1948 to 1955, after this date it fluctuates with a marked increase from 1962 until 1967.

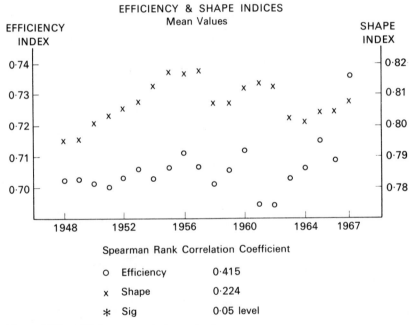

Figure 7.8   Efficiency and shape indices

The values for the two indices are fairly high, though we should note that in this part of the analysis we are using average values. For example, in 1967 the E index is approximately 0·74. However, there may be districts in 1967 which have values close to 1·0 and others with inefficient shapes reflected in low values, such as, 0·3 and 0·4.

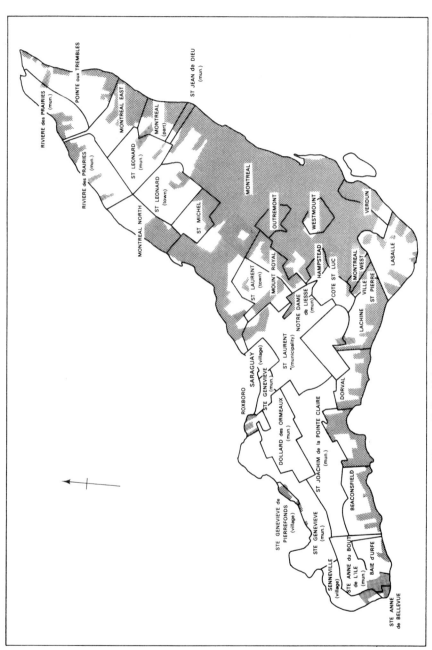

Figure 7.9 Urbanized area : Montréal 1952

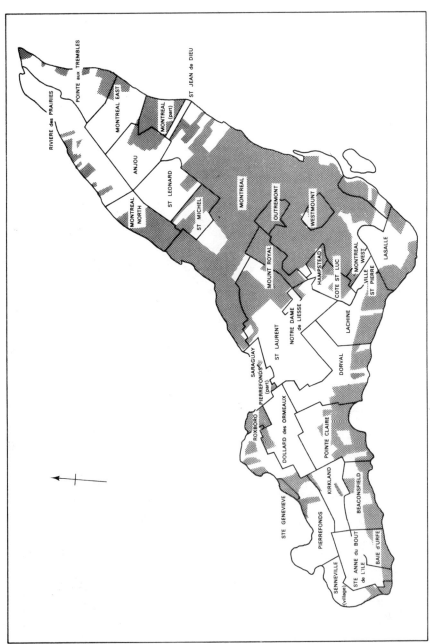

Figure 7.10 Urbanized area Montréal 1962

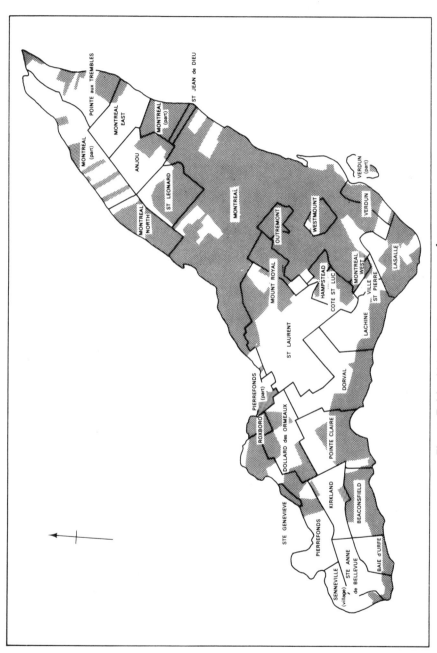

Figure 7.11 Urbanized area Montréal 1970

If we examine the variation in the E index over time we find that it decreases, thus we can conclude that the districts are becoming similar in spatial efficiency and this complements our conclusion that the overall level of efficiency appears to be inproving. We can conduct a similar analysis for the size of the districts and we find that the variation is decreasing over time. Similarly, we notice that the number of customers per district is become more equitable over the study period.

On a smaller scale we notice that similar trends emerge. Let us consider, for example, the configuration of municipalities on Montréal Island at three points in time; 1952, 1962 and 1970. These are shown in figures 7.9, 7.10 and 7.11.

These maps show the municipal boundaries on the Island of Montréal at three points in time. These boundary changes have occurred largely as a result of unincorporated areas being absorbed into existing municipalities. From 1962 to 1970 there were few evident boundary changes, though numerous variations of a few acres appear in data on the size of each municipality.

For each municipality at each of the three times, the shape index, S, was calculated for the form of the built-up area within each municipality. For summary purposes, the mean and standard deviation for the two types of shapes were calculated. The mean municipal shape index decreased from 0·69 in 1951 to 0·65 in 1962, indicating a modest decline in spatial compactness. In 1971 the value was 0·66. The standard deviation remained fairly stable with a slight increase in 1962. It should be noted that half the municipalities (15 out of 30) did not change area or shape appreciably between 1952 and 1971, so that the above changes are in fact accounted for by only 15 municipalities. The trend towards less spatial compact municipal shapes is probably accounted for by the placing of much land in the West Island under municipal administration before 1962, apparently without regard to municipal needs, efficiency of servicing, or the current state of development of the land.

By contrast, the statistics for the shape of the urbanized areas reveal a marked increase in the mean shape index ($\bar{S}$) over the years 1952–1971 and a marked decrease in the standard deviation of the shape index (SD) over the same period. These results, shown in table 7.6, indicate that actual urban growth, as opposed to changes in political boundaries, has tended towards increasing the spatial efficiency with which the urbanized area of municipalities can be serviced. Inspection of the maps suggests that this increase has been effected by linking previously separate blocs of urbanized land and by filling in interstitial areas of undeveloped land.

In most western countries with well-integrated transportation facilities the trends identified above tend to occur. However, in the developing parts of the world we frequently find that the major social services are concentrated in a few large centres and the majority of the population in the more isolated rural districts receive the poorest quality of services.

Table 7.6 Summary indices for Montreal data

		S	SD
Municipal areas	1951	0·69	0·18
Municipal areas	1962	0·65	0·20
Municipal areas	1971	0·66	0·19
Urbanised areas	1951	0·51	0·25
Urbanized areas	1962	0·53	0·25
Urbanized areas	1971	0·64	0·19

Attempts to decentralize and set up regional centres for education, health, welfare, banking and advisory services are a feature of many government policies in countries in the third world. We will examine some of these features in the following section on the evolution of the spatial configuration of service centres.

5   Evolution of the spatial configuration of centres

There is a well-defined body of literature in geography which focuses upon the evolution over space of man and his activities. This diffusion literature, discussed by Brown (1968) and Gould (1969), includes several studies on the evolution of the spatial arrangement of social services over time and in this section we will consider two examples fron Africa. The first by Riddell (1970), is from Sierra Leone, and the second is from Uganda. In 1896 Sierra Leone was declared a protectorate by Britain and a system of indirect rule was imposed. The concern of the five district officers 'was not the imposition of an immediate control over the native peoples . . . but rather the securing of conditions conducive to European trade and enterprise' (p. 49). Riddell argues that this simple form of rule was not appropriate for instigating basic social and economic improvements and so in 1937 following a report on Native Administration by Fenton (p. 51) a new system of government was created. This system encouraged local chiefdoms to establish treasuries, to set up local taxes and to pass by-laws for projects for social services and development schemes. Two model units were established in 1936, and by 1944 over 100 chiefdoms had adopted the scheme. During the next twenty years the number rose to over 140. In order to summarize this spatial diffusion process Riddell considered the data as a set of spatial and temporal locations. The locations fix the point in space which adopts the innovations and the time is defined by a vertical axis proportional in height to the date of adoption. We can think of these vertical axes as a set of poles projecting from a surface, the latter is the study area which in this case is Sierra Leone. If all places adopt the innovation at the same date, then if we fit a surface on to the top of the poles, the surface will be parallel to the plane of the study area, and no poles will either project through the surface or fall beneath it. We say therefore that the surface completely explains the distribution pattern. Clearly as the configuration of poles becomes more complex, the shape of the surface which fits on to the poles will also become complex. It will be like a contour map of a mountainous district. If this occurs then we say that a high order surface is needed to fit the distribution. So if we try to fit a linear (plane) surface onto the poles and we find that many poles project through or fall beneath, clearly the surface has a low degree of explanation for the diffusion pattern.

Recent attempts to fit surfaces to diffusion data have been summarized by Gould (1969). He comments on Riddell's work and shows that a

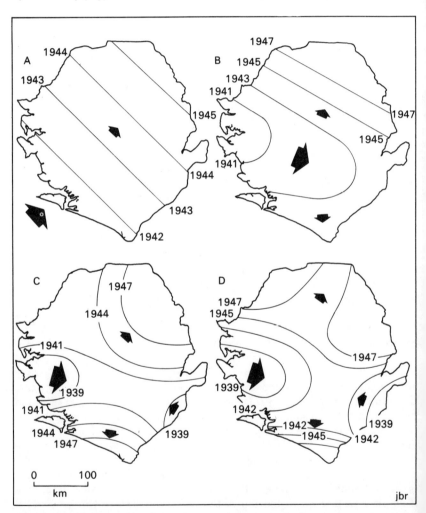

Figure 7.12 Diffusion of native administrations: *A* – Linear trend Surface; *B* – Quadratic trend Surface; *C* – Cubic trend Surface; *D* – Quartic trend Surface. (*Riddell, 1970, 53*)

simple linear surface fitted to the data points illustrates the basic diffusion direction from the south west to the north east (see figure 7.12). However, as we examine higher order surfaces we note that:

> From the eastern and western core areas of model chiefdoms the innovation of local administration spread rapidly through the area where the demonstration effect was strongest, and where the news could be carried quickly by people travelling over the main railway line that forms a major axis of development in the country. From this east–west alignment the idea diffused south, until by 1945 nearly every chiefdom had adopted the innovation. In the strongly Moslem and more conservation North, resistance was much greater except for a sudden thrust that used a branch of the railway as a main line of penetration (Gould, 1969, 66).

The spatial link between transportation and the spread of ideas in a developing area is strong. This contrasts with developed areas in which transportation may be well established and details of new structures for social organization may be diffused by television, radio, the press or publications of professional organizations. A good example of the latter is provided by the annual report of the City Managers Association of America in which new ideas for improving the quality of urban government receive wide and rapid diffusion. However, in parts of the world which do not have some of these 'modern' attributes it is instructive to examine the spatial evolution of innovations in the public sector, for at least two reasons. First, to build up a body of case studies for individual countries, institutions, innovations and environments, and second, to search for general principles and systematic variations. If these can be identified then they may help in formulating policies for national planning. For example, do people adopt new modes of education or health care because they hear about them via newspapers and radio, or is it more effective to start model schools and clinics and let people observe directly? Are large centres of population more likely to adopt before rural districts, and how long is the lag? If we can identify a period of lag then this may possibly influence the government's policy and cause greater investments in rural areas to overcome stronger traditional views and conservatism. The field of evolution, change, conservatism and the diffusion of innovations is treated in several recent books and papers (Soja, 1968) and clearly, a statistical analysis of the trend surface type of the spread of a public service is only the starting-point. Porter (1973) has drawn attention to the problem of defining modernization and he suggests that 'It might be worth our while to look at the concept of "modernization" from a number of angles to try to discover the assumptions which underlie the idea in its various definitions and the consequences which follow from these assumptions.'

Let us now examine Hirst's Uganda study (1971). He attempted to use an objective methodology to describe the development of the spatial pattern of district administrative centres in Uganda from 1900 to 1970.

In 1900 there were seven centres and by 1914 the number had increased to fifteen. Since then the figures have fluctuated between eighteen and fourteen, with the longest stable period between 1942 and 1961 using fourteen centres. It is particularly interesting to note that 'Districts change in shape and size, new districts were carved out of existing ones, and other districts disappeared; established district centres were relocated, some lost their administrative status and some were re-established after a lapse of a few years.' Specifically only four of the eighteen used in centres in 1970 have been in existence since 1900. Hirst notes that 'this continual flux in the spatial expression of the internal administrative structure' is a common feature of spatial evolution of a state and 'here lies a fruitful avenue for the geographical analysis of the functional integration of space.' In an attempt to determine the spatial arrangement of centres at different points in time Hirst used nearest-neighbour analysis. This allowed him to compare the observed arrangement with a uniform pattern which, it could be argued, offered the spatial arrangement which was most efficient in terms of minimizing the distance between any part of the state and the nearest centre. The early phase of development, until about 1914, is characterized by a concentration of centres in the southern portion of the country. The nearest-neighbour index for the patterns during this period is approximately 1·2, which suggests the pattern has limited spatial efficiency as defined according to the criterion noted above. In fact, centres which are distributed at random would have a value of 1·0, whereas the perfect uniform pattern could have a value of 2·15. During the period from 1914 to 1941 Hirst shows that the process of locating centres was essentially completed. The pattern index rose during this period to approximately 1·66. However, it seems that in the long period of stability between 1942 and 1961 'the search for an efficient spatial structure was successful.' Hirst makes this claim on the basis of data on the number of centres and the ideal number if the arrangement was uniform. During this period the ideal number would be twenty-one. At other times the difference between the actual number and an ideal number is greater than the ratio of 14 : 21. Also between 1942 and 1961 the pattern index rises to 1·74. Further evidence for the success of the spatial arrangement was provided by Hirst's intuitive attempts to improve the arrangement of the fourteen centres and he notes that his improvements were slight. If we search Hirst's data for a trend in the pattern index over time then we can show that the pattern is tending towards the uniform value and this trend is greater than we would expect to occur by change. This is confirmed by calculating Spearman's rank correlation coefficient, r_s; this takes on a value of approximately 0·8 for Hirst's data.

The conclusion from this study is that the first task in the spatial integration of the state was to cover the whole territory as efficiently as possible and then to make adjustments for regional needs. This conclusion is similar to the one reached by Witthuhn (1968) who used the same technique to analyse the spatial diffusion of post offices in Uganda between

1909 and 1965. This pattern appeared 'to progress first in the long movements needed to assure maximum (spatial) coverage and then in small steps [to adjust to local needs] . . .' (p. 19).

Simple analysis of the spatial diffusion process of district centres or post-offices using nearest-neighbour statistics must be followed by a detailed examination of the decision-making process, the alternate sites that were available, their relative merits and the goals of those in positions of authority who made the final choice. These data are hard to find and we thus tend to rely heavily on purely spatial data from which to infer process. This is a dangerous practice because many processes can cause the same spatial configuration, and conversely the same process may not always generate the same spatial pattern.

6 Conclusions

There is a large body of literature on the evolution of service districts, in a variety of social, economic, political and physical environments. Most of this literature is based on careful and detailed searching of historical documents, libraries, archives and local archaeological records. Recently attempts have been made to complement this approach by using pattern indices, and while little new information is usually provided, these indices may help to highlight specific problems if we follow Newcomb's argument. Thus we may hope to be in a stronger position to identify regularities in the evolution of service districts. The anomalies deserve individual attention once the gross trends have been isolated.

Since Teitz made his remarks in the late sixties on the need for models which could be solved to aid in making prescriptive statements for locating public facilities over time, significant technical advances have been made. In particular, algorithms have been tested which will handled fairly large sets of points. While work continues on this front it should be noted that much remains to be done to introduce the public and the policy-makers to the objectives of these new procedures. In the final analysis the spatial configuration of service districts and the location of centres is usually determined by some form of political organization, and the pattern which is adopted is likely to be the one which conforms most, accurately with the goals of the policy-makers. These goals are diffuse, and it would be naïve to claim that the policy-maker was not concerned about his own political future, that of his group or party, and the reactions of any opposition. It is within this larger organizational framework that the evolution of service districts should be viewed. In the next chapter we will attempt to turn attention to organization, control and political organization.

Notes on further reading

A clear presentation of the problem of locating facilities over time is provided by Teitz (1968), and the technique for solving the problem using dynamic programming is summarized in non-technical language in Scott (1971*b*).

There is a vast body of literature on diffusion studies, concise reviews are provided by Brown (1968) and Gould (1969). The latter is carefully illustrated with empirical examples, the material in this paper also occurs in Abler, Adams and Gould (1971).

A quick overview of the geography of modernization can be obtained by examining Soja (1968) and Porter (1973).

Whitney (1970) presents a fascinating review of spatial–temporal organization in China over a period of 2,000 years.

Notes

1 These points were forcefully presented to me in correspondence with Professor Norton Ginsburg. I am grateful for this.

2 Whitaker (1971) develops dynamic programming methods by which smaller problems with 10 or less time periods can be explicitly optimized. For larger problems heuristic methods are appropriate, for example the backward recursive approach described here.

8 Control and organization: the role of decision-makers

1 Introduction

Several times in earlier chapters we have stressed the role of decision-makers in the process of locating public facilities and implementing changes. However, because of the difficulty of determining precisely their role we have tended to concentrate on other aspects of the organization of social services, especially the importance of space, location and size. In this chapter we will try to introduce some concepts and principles which are more particularly concerned with those in control. We will also consider the styles of decision-making and some of the general problems of control and organization. In a single chapter we will only be able to scratch the surface of this growing and important field but it is to be hoped that by being introduced to some of the ideas, the reader will have a more balanced view of the organization of the public sector than if attention was only focussed upon space and location as seen, for example, through allocation–location models.

The provision of public services operates within a complex social–economic–political structure. Attempts to explain real-world patterns should thus take note of the milieu in which the service is provided. Also, prescriptive statements and suggestions for modifying the arrangement of public facilities are not likely to be readily adopted unless the planner is cognizant of the political scene. While much of the material presented in earlier chapters relies upon objective measurement and statements of goals in terms which allow us to build models which can be solved numerically, in the real-world decisions and policies are determined by the interplay of variables which not infrequently defy clear definition. Rarely are we able to measure them. However, if works in the fields of politics and administration are examined, it may be possible to identify problem areas on which to concentrate. The broad fields of politics, government and administration have generated a vast literature primarily of an empirical nature, but running parallel to this have been normative models of government and political organization. The latter range from the writings of Plato, Aristotle, Machiavelli and More to Marx, Mao and Galbraith, while on a more modest scale we should include such workers as Fesler (1949), Heady (1966), Self (1972), Maas (1959) and Pugh *et al.* (1971). These workers have tried to unravel the complexities of political and organizational structures in order to search for underlying principles. One focus of attention in these searches has been the decision-making process, and the particular type under examination here is usually referred to as non-market decision-making. A recent surge of publications in this field has been generated, and the journal *Public Choice* was created in 1971 to handle some of this material and give a focal point for the scholars in this field.

The main contributors to the field of government and political organization have come from political science yet the substance of examination is of interest to many disciplines that are concerned with man's organization. The breadth of the field of politics is interpreted thus by Lockard (1969): 'politics is involved in most of what goes on in the governing of human society, for people are constantly trying to influence those who can lay down and apply the rules.' Government, Lockhard suggests, can be thought of as ordering a society: 'Government refers to the people and institutions that make and enforce rules for a given society'. Clearly, politics and government interact for they are both concerned with public policy-making and as such they generate sentiments and prejudices which can interfere with objective analysis. In many cases ethical values held by a community influence the way the community is organized and the institutions which cater to the social needs. Also the same values can influence the distribution of power to influence the formulation of policies. The institutions and the distribution of power may be highly structured, but not infrequently the strategies and the interplay of roles, and the goals of the participants do not conform to written formalized codes, they tend to be *ad hoc*.

We should also note that government institutions may not be equally important for all parts of a state, and as has been shown in earlier chapters, their functions tend to vary over time. With respect to spatial variation, the county in the US varies in importance. For example, in New England its role is insignificant whereas in the South and and West it is an important spatial political unit. Further, counties have disappeared in Connecticut and Rhode Island, and they never existed in Alaska. Another example of spatial variation is provided by Lockard with respect to the extent to which party politics enters local affairs. In the eastern part of US political parties play an important part in state and local affairs. In some western states, however, a completely different role is assigned to the party. In Canada the national parties are not involved in local government and this is a major distinction between American and Canadian local government. In Britain the national parties are represented in local elections.

Spatial variations in political phenomena should be seen against the background of the variation in other aspects of the environment. For example, the physical environment, climate, vegetation, and water, the occurrence of natural hazards, the socio-economic attributes of the population, the distribution of wealth and the historical evolution of the pattern of development. It is not unreasonable to suggest that patterns of behaviour and sets of priorities among needs evolve in relation to these attributes and as a consequence institutional structures evolve. The stability of the institutions is often disturbed by changing priorities and we should recognize that the diffusion of information has probably accelerated this process. The flow of information may disturb long-held value systems enjoyed by communities which previously existed in isolation. This information revolution was perhaps the single most important contributory factor in causing reforms in the structures for providing public goods and services in the mid-twentieth century. We should not, however, claim that only now are new systems of administration being invented. Public administration has existed as long as political organizations, ever since man began to organize himself into groups. However, Heady (1966) has suggested that it was not until the eighteenth century that concern with the systematic management of government affairs really took hold following the interest shown by German scholars in Western Europe. He offers an overview of public administration in a variety of national states, and claims that we should examine the various administrative devices developed abroad as they may prove worthy of consideration for adoption or adaptation at home. He notes the influence of Western patterns of administration in developing areas but stresses that there are also exchanges of administrative styles between small and large nations. With this in mind he cites the example the office of Ombudsman, which is found in Scandinavian administration with the task of protecting the public from governmental injustice. Western Europe, North America and some of the newer states are rapidly acquiring their Ombudsmen. References to such a position have occurred, for example, in the speeches of Kaunda (1966) particularly in the mid-sixties, when Zambia was just setting out as an independent nation, and Kaunda was appealing for a just system of administration.

The exchange or standardization of administrative procedures among countries has been encouraged by the growth of international organizations, the European Economic Community for example. East (1968) has focused attention upon the development of these supra-national government bodies and it is clear that as soon as a country joins such an organization it sacrifices some of its sovereignty, because there is a certain loss in control over national affairs. The consequences of the growth of organizations such as the EEC rest not only in the direction of modifications to administrative procedures but also changes in the political relations within and between nations. Administrations and politics are linked. However, in a wide-ranging review of literature on public choice, Ostrom and Ostrom (1971) summarize Woodrow Wilson's concept (1887) that politics and administration should be separated. The latter can function satisfactorily under a variety of different political constitutions or principles. Successful administration, he claimed, depends upon hierarchical order: direction is provided by political heads of departments whereas operational aspects are dealt with by professional administrators and civil servants. This framework has been widely accepted as the most satisfactory compromise between politics and administration. At the international level it enjoys popularity[1] and at the national level it is used extensively, for example, in Britain[2] and as a format for local government reforms in urban areas it is incorporated into the city-manager plan which is particularly popular in North America.

Like most large organizations those in the public sector are characterized by specialization of responsibility and functions and this usually fits within an hierarchial structure. Heady (1966, 23) notes that 'this process of departmentalization has occurred in a remarkably uniform way in countries that vary greatly in their political orientation and in other aspects of their administrative systems.' The fundamental unit of organization is the department or the ministry and Chapman (1959) has identified five basic fields of national government. They are, foreign affairs, justice, finance, defence and war, and internal affairs. Over time these have spawned other ministeries and departments. In particular internal affairs has been subdivided in to departments, for example, of transportation and communications, education, health, welfare and social security. Meyer (1957) has examined the patterns of development in various countries, and he notes that the number of ministeries ranges from about twelve to thirty. Clearly, a small group is more likely to work more rapidly and reach a consensus without the protracted debates which could ensue if a large number of ministers met together. We have no law which suggests that a cabinet of twelve is more efficient than one of fifteen, but we have a general principle that a *modus operandi* can be appropriately established with from ten to twenty ministers. Smaller groups tend to be under-representative of the department of state and larger groups are more unwieldy in terms of reaching day-to-day decisions on affairs of state.

2 The development of theories of organizations

Traditional organizational theory is based on two schools of thought (March and Simon, 1958, Chapter 2). Both were developed in the literature and gained acceptance in the earlier part of the twentieth century though the fundamental principles and philosophy underlying them can be traced to classical and biblical writings. The first school is derived from the work of Taylor (1911) who studied the role of man as a complement to machines. He looked upon man as a mechanism for performing tasks within an organization and suggested that time and motion studies were the key to defining roles for workers so that efficiency could be maximized. While this approach may have some merit for standard repetitive tasks it provides little help in the higher levels of organization where major decisions have to be made.

The second school of thought turns its attention to the division of work and responsibility between departments and the forms of cooperation between levels. The general problem of so assigning workers to jobs that maximum efficiency is achieved is similar to the spatial allocation problem treated in an earlier chapter in that we should ideally examine all possible assignments and select the one that best fits our objective function. However, we should note the comment of March and Simon (p. 25) that: 'A study of the mathematical structure of the assignment problem suggests that there is little to be hoped for in the way of global generalizations beyond the propositions . . . that are already to be found in the nonmathematical literature on the subject.' The early writings of Gulick and Urwick (1937) provide a good example of this second school.

In order to give a more complete overview of the subject of organization theory we should recognize the contributions of March and Simon. They feel that the more traditional viewpoints do not take sufficient note of human motivations and man's ability to process information and make decisions. They feel there is a creature which they call 'administrative man' and he differs from 'economic man' of classical location theory. The latter acts deterministically to maximize a well-defined objective function, for example, profit, whereas 'administrative man' operates in an environment in which there are three types of consequences, certainty, risk and uncertainty, and his objective is often a composite of personal, institutional and social desires. While we cannot argue with these basic claims we should recognize that we are still not in a position to make definitive statements concerning the way men act within organizations. Also we lack precise analytical procedures for defining the best kinds of organizations. Our notions of best are often coloured by the traditions of our heritage and the attributes of alternatives which are dictated to us by parties with vested interests.

In the late fifties Simon (1959) argued for a new view of administration, based upon empirical facts and the formulation of hypotheses and ultimately aimed to develop a theory. He was particularly concerned with defining efficiency in order to provide a standard for comparing alternative administrative arrangements. A prerequisite for this was the need to measure and scale the efforts and effectiveness of all administrative organizations. It is not readily obvious why a hierarchical structure should be the most efficient and further, we lack a clear procedure for evaluating alternate hierarchial structures. The search for the best arrangement is usually through empirical trial and error; there is a continual evolution of allocation of responsibilities and positions, and these tend to operate within traditional norms, union regulations, specific needs, evolving technology and expanding information flows. Perhaps the best we can hope to do is to provide a framework which can adapt rapidly to changes, rather than to establish a rigid optimum structure that fits the needs at a single point in time, in the belief that this will always be the best arrangement. Ridley and Simon (1938) were among the first to define procedures for measuring activities; Coombs (1967) attempted to tackle theoretical problems of measurement of data and some empirical examples of measuring parts of administrative structures were offered in earlier chapters, for example, the work on the relationship between the quantity of service produced and the cost per unit of the service. At a more general level we should note Smith's work (1973) on the problems of measuring social satisfaction. He stresses the point that if we are to attack social problems then we need measures of social well-being so that we can observe trends over time and compare the effectiveness of alternate policies. This notion of monitoring the social state of a nation involves the development of *social indicators* which we can use in conjunction with the more usual *economic indicators*, such as gross domestic product, *per capita* income and level of unemployment. Smith notes that several national governments are beginning to respond to this desire to monitor the social health of their countries and he cites recent reports in the US[3] and Britain.[4]

Let us now turn to some recent attempts by Pondy (1969) and Indik (1964) to examine the relationship between the number of personnel and the size of an organization. Specifically they were concerned with the ratio of administrators to workers needed to produce different quantities of goods. Ideally if we are able to evaluate the efficiency with which different-sized work loads can be handled, then we may be able to determine an optimum level, and this in turn could possibly be used to define optimum-sized service districts. Adler (1960) has examined the relationship between the size of an organization and the level of efficiency. He was concerned with 'technical' organizations and based his analysis on the amount of documentation produced. He claimed that efficiency increases, at a decreasing rate, as the size of an organization grows. We will now look at the relationship between the number of administrators and the efficiency of an organization. We will begin by dividing administrators into two classes, supervisors and non-supervisors. The first group can be thought of as those who make major decisions while the second group contains the clerical and ancillary staff. At the outset we should recognize the difficulty of assigning workers to separate categories when this is frequently an artificial division. Comments on this general problem are made in McWhinney (1965, 348) in his critique of the work of Haire (1959) who divided members of an organization into categories according to their job description or department titles.

Pondy (1969) has attempted to analyse the structure of organizations by examining their administrative efficiency. The latter he considered in relation to the number of employees in the two categories defined above. He argues the general case for this type of study in the following terms:

> A theory of organization structure ought to explain why the relative size of the administrative component [supervisors] varies so widely across organizations – and should have something to say about the optimum administrative intensity [ratio of employees in the two categories] for a given industry or organization, i.e. optimum in terms of maximum efficiency or profit for a given level of operation.

Pondy examines the relationship between the size and complexity of an organization and administrative intensity. He defines administrative intensity as the number of managers, professionals and clerical workers divided by the number of craftsmen, operatives and labourers employed by the organization. We could replace this by the number of supervisors divided by the number of clerical and ancillary staff. Supervisors and administrative personnel are, in Pondy's paper, considered to be a factor of production, together with the traditional inputs, labour and capital. This can be stated in the form of the functional relationship $Q = f(K, L, A)$ where Q is the total output of the organization, L is the number of production personnel, K is the capital and A is the number of supervisors, f tells us that the value of Q is related to the values of K, L and A. After the rigorous formulation of a model of a production process which included K, L and A and maximized Q, the output, Pondy tested it against empirical data for forty-five organizations in America. He concluded that, 'administrative intensity is found to decrease with organization size'. This finding agrees with that of the psychologist Indik (1964). He studied five sets of organizations and found that the relationship between organizational unit size and supervision ratio is logarithmic in form and negative in slope. The supervision ratio was defined as the ratio of supervisors to total employees, and organizational unit size was measured by the total number of employees. We should recognize that the merit of these studies lies in the construction of a theoretical logical basis for relationships between efficiency and administrative intensity and the careful testing of these relationships against real-world data. We should, however, be wary of the statistical procedures adopted.

This point has been very forcefully summarized by McWhinney (1965) in a review of the works of Haire (1959), Levy and Donhowe (1962), Draper and Struther (1963) and Chapin (1957). McWhinney analysed the data used in the studies and demonstrated that the relationships posited by Haire and his followers Levy, Donhowe, Draper and Struther to describe the ratio of employees who dealt with people outside an organization (E) to those who were primarily concerned with internal organization (I) can be handled equally well by several simple forms of equations whereas Haire suggested that the relationship $(\sqrt{E} = a + b \sqrt[3]{I})$ was the best one. There seems to be no theoretical justification for Haire's equation though he has argued that there is an analogy with solid bodies: 'the relation of measures of the surface and the interior of an organization would be the same as the relation of the surface and interior of a compact solid' (McWhinney, 1965, 348). He derives this notion from the claim that organizations may have properties similar to those found in the biological world. While we may be sympathetic to the general principle of isomorphism between complex systems, we should not be naïve enough to imagine that simple Euclidean properties in each system are sufficient to identify the isomorphism.

In a paper on the optimum size of an organization Chapin attempted to identify a numerical ratio which related to the viability of an organization, and he argued that healthy organizations would be characterized by a typical ratio of components of the membership of the organization. This ratio, F, can be written symbolically $F = A/(A + C)$ where A is the number of 'mature' persons and C is the number of 'young' persons. Chapin claims that ideally F should be 0·618. This, he noted, was the ratio found for many natural phenomena in the biological world. McWhinney examines the data used to test this relationship and he concludes from these studies that '. . . in both cases, the biological analogy is superficially established. In the first case, [Haire] it was based on a loose literary simile and permitted to persist by inappropriate analysis of data; in the second, [Chapin] a coincidence of two numerical values permitted a suggestive parallelism to be taken as a condition for organizational optimality' (p. 361).

In conclusion we should accept that drawing analogies between different kinds of organizations is useful, but before we transfer properties from one to another we must establish a set of basic equivalents. Essentially there are three aspects to this: first, we need a set of components or elements; second, we must identify the relations which link the components; and third, we must decide a law to measure the relationships and the form of the structure. McWhinney suggests that of these the essential connection to the real world, the measure, is still missing. Until this can be firmly identified it is unlikely that there will be any significant progress in comparing organizational structures and identifying similarities among different types.

The problem of defining viable efficient organizations concerns all

Table 8.1 Illustrative set of workload measures, quality factors, and local condition factors that should be considered in productivity measurement[a]

Selected service functions[b]	Illustrative "workload" measures[c]	Illustrative quality factors (ie measures of citizen impact) that should be considered in interpreting productivity	Illustrative local condition factors that should be considered in interpreting productivity[d]
1 Solid waste collection	Tons of solid waste collected	Visual appearance of streets 'Curb' or 'back-door' collection Fire/health hazard conditions from solid waste accumulation Service delays	Frequency of collection Private versus public collection Local weather conditions Composition of the solid waste (including the residential–commerical–industrial mix: type of waste, etc)

Table 8.1 *continued*

2 Liquid waste treatment (sewage)	Gallons of sewage treated	Quality level of effluent, eg, 'BOD' removed and remaining after treatment Water quality level resulting where dumped	Initial quality of waterway into which the sewage effluent is released Community liquid waste generation characteristics
3 Law enforce-ment (police)	No. of surveillance-hours No. of calls No. of crimes investigated	Reduction in crime and victimization rates Crime clearance rates, preferably including court disposition Response-times Citizen feelings of security	Per cent of low-income families in population Public attitude towards certain crimes
4 Law enforce: ment (courts)	Number of cases resolved	Number of convictions/ Number of plea-bargain reduced sentences Correctness of disposition Delay time until resolution	Number and types of cases
5 Health and hospital	Number of patient-days	Reduced number and severity of illnesses Conditions of patients after treatment Duration of treatment and 'pleasantness' of care Accessibility of low-income groups to care	Availability and price of health care Basic community health conditions
6 Water treatment	Gallons of water treated	Water quality indices such as for hardness and taste Amount of impurities removed	Basic quality of water supply source
7 Recreation	Acres of recrea-tional activities Attendance figures	Participation rates Accessibility to recreational opportunities Variety of oppor-tunities available Crowdedness indices	Amount of recreation pro-vided by the private sector No. of individuals without access to automobiles ; and the available

(continued on page 160)

Table 8.1 *continued*

		Citizen's perceptions of adequacy of recreational opportunities	transit system Topographical and climate characteristics Time available to citizens for recreation activities
8 Street maintenance	Square yards of repairs made	Smoothness/ 'bumpiness' of streets Safety Travel time Community disruption: amount and duration Dust and noise during repairs	Density of traffic Density of population along roadway Location of residences, homes, shopping areas, recreational opportunites, etc.
9 Fire control	Fire calls Number of inspections	Fire damage Injuries and lives lost	Local weather conditions Type of construction Density of population
10 Primary and secondary education	Pupil-days Number of pupils	Achievement test scores and grade levels Continuation/ drop-out rates	Socio-economic characteristics of pupils and neighbourhood Basic intelligence of pupils Number of pupils

[a] More extensive lists of workload measures and quality factors (often called measures of effectiveness or evaluation criteria) can be found in references 1, 6, 9, 10, 16, 17 and 26 of the Bibliography in *Improving Productivity and Productivity Measurement in Local Governments*.

[b] Numerous sub-functions each with its own sub-measures could also be identified. However, care should be taken to avoid going into excessive, unuseful detail.

[c] Dividing these by total dollar cost or by total man-days yields workload-based productivity measures.

[d] Such local conditions as population size and local price levels are relevant to all service functions.

(*Improving productivity and productivity measurement in Local Governments*, by Harry P. Hatry and Donald M. Fisk, The National Commission on Productivity, 1971, p. xvi–xvii.)

sectors of the economy. With regard to government services a symposium on *Productivity in Government* was reported by the *Public Adminstration Review* in 1972 and one of the most interesting papers, from our point of view, discussed the measurement problem in public services (Hatry, 1972). The author constructed a table (table 8.1) to show measures of workload, quality of services and local conditions.

Clearly the decision-maker should consider all these elements before offering a policy for the supply of a particular service. However, as we mentioned in Chapter 3, emphasis has traditionally been placed on analysing the quantity of service and the cost per unit, and the argument for a particular level of service has been couched in economic terms. More recently the emphasis has shifted towards the quality of the service and the evaluation of the perceived level of satisfaction. However, as Hatry states, 'Many new productivity improvement approaches need to be tried out in local governments if productivity is to be improved. . . . However, without adequate measurement, so-called evaluations are likely to be little more than public relations stories by the sponsors and of minimal practical use.' Measurement is one of the keys to improving the provision of services. Among the others we should include the dissemination of information about alternate approaches.

In an attempt to capture the totality of an organization there have been several recent studies of the systems type. Perhaps the most celebrated and widely-publicized has been the Program Planning Budgeting System (PPBS) which was introduced into government organization in the US by President Johnson in the mid-sixties following its adoption in the Department of Defence. Emphasis in this approach is on capturing the direction and strength of relationships between the major components of an organization so that the impact of alternative policies can be evaluated, prior to implementation. Reviews of PPBS are provided by Hartley (1968), Hovey (1968) and Hinricks and Taylor (1969). While this is the aim of several planning tools, rarely are we able to determine the form of the linkages and their rates of change over time. Thus, while PPBS may be thought of as offering us a useful conceptual tool, it seems that we are still some way from making it fully operational. Assessing PPBS, Botner (1970) suggested that while it has not yet lived up to original expectations it will probably become increasingly effective in the future.

The systems approach to public policy-making has recently been appraised by Hoos (1972). She claims that:

Systems analysis requires serious contemplation because of its central role in public planning, the vast expenditures of human and financial resources it has occasioned, and the mythology that surrounds it. Full of contradictions, a curious mixture of sweeping comprehensiveness and arbitrary eclecticism, systems analysis in its various forms has become the dominant methodology for managing the present and designing the future (p. 1).

Although the dominant methodology systems analysis is not necessarily the most successful in terms of achieving an harmonious society. As Forrester (1969) points out, there are considerable risks in applying this method to the solution of social problems. These risks stem from our imperfect understanding of human behaviour and value systems. Only when until our understanding is improved will we be able to predict accurately the outcome of alternative policies. Consequently systems

analysis, if we are to believe Hoos, is of little use in solving human and
social management problems at this time.

In recent geographical literature we have another conceptual system
arrangement in which government and administration, under the title
of legislative structure, form a component of a system in which man
interacts with the physical environment (Figure 8.1). The link between

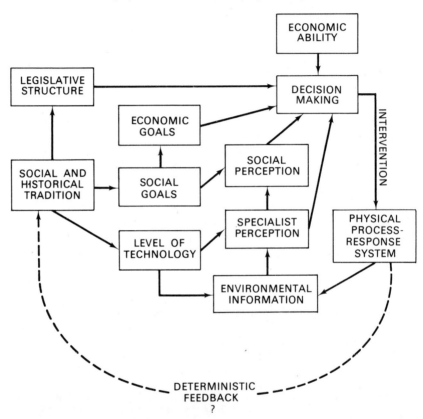

Figure 8.1   Some schematic elements of a decision-making system.
On the right the human intervention in the process-response system.
(After Chorley and Kennedy. 1971, 300)

social and physical environments should be studied more closely especially
in the light of the present concern with environmental degradation,
population control and other aspects of ecological balances. The statis-
faction of public needs must be related to the earth's potential and policy-
makers should be concerned with the long-term as well as the short-term
local effects of their actions on both social satisfaction and natural resource
bases.

3 The ecological view – a case study

In human geography and particularly in the branch concerned with the organization of societies there is a large body of literature devoted to ecological studies. Basically this literature examines man's relationship to his environment. These responses can be examined in spatial terms, for example, population distribution over the earth's surface, or they can be examined in institutional terms. Heady (1966, 24) notes that '... bureaucracies, as well as other political and administrative institutions, can be better understood if the surrounding conditions, influences, and forces that shape and modify them are identified and ranked to the extent possible in the order of relative importance.'

In this section we will consider a particular form of administrative organization, the city-manager plan, and examine the environment which tends to produce it. The detailed characteristics of the city-manager form of local government have been discussed by Plunkett (1969) and Madgwick (1970), and they will not be repeated here. However, some of the salient features will be highlighted as this section develops.

A theoretical basis for this type of local government was developed by Banfield and Wilson (1963). They argue that the form of local government is directly related to the ethos which is valued by the community, and the ethos is linked to the socio-economic attributes which obtain. More specifically they suggest that in the US the municipalities which are characterized by high socio-economic levels generate a public-regarding ethos and this favours the city-manager form of local government with its emphasis on the separation of politics and administration. Political questions are dealt with by the elected representatives, namely the mayor and council, while administrative problems are tackled by a professional – the city-manager. He is responsible for the technical problems of management following policy directives from the elected representatives. To complement the high socio-economic communities we have a second category which have a private-regarding ethos. These municipalities tend to favour an overlap between politics and administration particularly if voters can be directly repaid for their political support with jobs and security.

Several workers, particularly in political science, have examined the relationship between the form of local government and the socio-economic characteristics of municipalities. In general, their findings support the ethos theory outlined above.[5] In order to test this theory socio-economic data are correlated with the form of government. The general procedure has been to rank the value of a particular attribute, such as *per capita* income, and to note that the higher ranking municipalities have the city-manager system. This exercise is repeated for other variables, such as years of education and percentage house ownership; the set of variables which relate to socio-economic level have been discussed by Shevky and Bell (1955). We should note that while this type of analysis appears to be fairly objective, it does overlook several problems. For example:

1   Socio-economic variables interact to produce an overall ethos.
2   Adoption of the city-manager plan may be restricted by legislation. In Canada, for example, only cities and towns have the option.
3   Adoption has occurred over time, thus we should look at the ethos levels over time.
4   Adoption has been influenced by proximity to municipalities already using the system.

In order to tackle some of these aspects of the adoption of the city-manager plan some recent studies have employed factor analysis (Mercer, 1972) and discriminant analysis (Massam, 1973). Factor analysis was used to combine a set of 45 variables for 384 census tracts of the 1961 Montréal metropolitan area, and Mercer found that 17 of the 19 city-manager communities were strongly related to two factors he called 'economic achievement' the first with respect to the English-speaking group and the second the French-speaking group. These factors summarized a set of socio-economic variables and particularly they identified the high socio-economic status communities. In an attempt to look at variations over time, Mercer examined the population growth of Montréal suburban municipalities and found that those which adopted the plane had often experienced high rates of population growth before the decision to adopt was taken. The temporal aspects of the problem in Montréal have also been examined by Massam (1973). I divided municipalities into two groups, city-manager and other, at eight points in time (1911, 1921, 1931, 1941, 1951, 1961, 1966 and 1971), and, using a set of variables which described the size and the social and economic attributes of each municipality, I attempted to find a combination of the variables which predicted the two groups. The primary conclusion was that socio-economic variables can be used with a fairly large degree of success to classify municipalities into city-manager or other types. Out of a total of 201 classifications only 11 were misplaced. The direction of the relationship is harder to distinguish, though in the first period (until 1931) the value of taxable real estate appears to have a direct correlation with the city-manager group, and in 1931 British origin shows a strong link. However, in this same year, a negative relationship between the value of new factories and the city-manager plan is suggested and the direction of this link appears to remain the same when 1941 data is used. In the second period (1941 and 1951) discrimination is of a high order, though almost twice as many variables are needed in each function. In 1941 the size of the municipality measured by the population appears to be a significant variable, as is general prosperity measured by assets, value of new houses and the number of new constructions: all correlate with the city-manager form of local government. By 1951 the ethnic character which was hardly noticeable in 1941 is beginning to be of some significance. British origin together with high medium earnings, high tax per $100 and large liabilities typify the city-manager municipality. The linguistic variables (English only or French only spoken) show weak links with the mayor-council municipality form. By 1961 the language spoken in a municipality and the income allow fairly good discrimination, revenues and expenditures are of less importance, though they are incorporated into statistically significant discriminant functions. During the last period (since 1966) the use of socio-economic or size variables, provided little help in explaining the form of local government, and it is in this period that the classification system breaks down. The implication is clear. The forms of local government currently used reflect a mélange of factors of varying importance over time. In the early days of the city-manager plant it was the more prosperous municipalities which opted for it, later the larger, faster-growing municipalities. Superimposed upon this sequence is the spatial contiguity notion: the explanation of the diffusion pattern can be partially explained by a neighbourhood effect. In the study area 60 per cent of the municipalities which adopted the plan were congituous to municipalities which had previously adopted it.

Finally, though it has been argued that the socio-economic and growth attributes of a municipality appear to be statistically related to the form of local government, we have no deep understanding of the desicion-making process which brings a particular type of government into being. We are unable to answer questions about the power of various groups in a community, the influence of the incumbents, and the role of governments outside the locality as well as the perception of the relative merits of alternative forms of local government. Traditionally it was thought that the mayor-council local government structure lacked the expertise to handle the complex organizational, financial and technical problems of modern municipalities. However, the validity of this claim should be examined in precise terms since consulting agencies with particular skills can be called in on an *ad hoc* basis and many local government officials now have qualifications in technical, legal or financial fields. Clearly, much more work is needed before we can fully understand the diffusion patterns over space and time of specific types of administration.

4 Conclusions

For analytical purposes we often try to collapse the complexities of social, economic, political and physical environments into a set of discrete boxes. Then we try to define the links between them by taking into account institutions, power and influence and the level of social services produced. Unfortunately we lack well-defined procedures for measuring the phenomena and thus much of our research depends upon intuitive experience. While this frequently stands the test of time, from a purely scientific standpoint we need to be more objective. Some of the studies which have used widely recognized quantitative methodologies are weak because of logical inconsistencies in the basic arguments. Intuitively we recognize the systemic nature of human organization, but it is a difficult step to move to a precise model which links together all components in such a way that we can evaluate the utility of alternative policies and strategies for providing public services.

While we should not abandon the systems models our immediate task is to gain a better understanding of parts of the system, and hopefully in the future the parts will be brought together. Perhaps the key to this lies in improvements in our procedures for measuring attributes and events. With this in mind we should not restrict ourselves to traditional scales and metrics, rather we should search for new ones and evaluate those employed in related disciplines with which we are less familiar. A good example of this is the recent use that some geographers[6] have made of scaling procedures which were developed by psychologists. We do not need more conceptual systems diagrams, we need more empirical studies with a firm logical basis using sound measurement techniques.

Notes on further reading

The classic books on the relationships between politics, administration, power, and space are by Fesler (1949) and Maas (1959).

With respect to organization theory the historical perspective is provided by Wilson (1887) and Taylor (1911), and excellent reviews of the field are provided by Simon (1959) and March and Simon (1958).

Organizations have been examined by some workers using simplistic geometrical measurements, a useful critique of this approach is provided by McWhinney (1965).

Research into the topic of decision-making in the public sector is reported in the journal *Public Choice*.

A very useful review of the difficulties and some of the ways for evaluating the productivity of a government is provided in a special issue of *Public Administration Review* (1972).

References

1 See *Public Administration Review* (1970).
2 See Chapman and Dunsire (1971) and Hanson and Walles (1970).
3 United States Department of Health, Education and Welfare (1969).
4 Central Statistical Office (1970).
5 See, for example, Schnore and Alford (1963), Kessel (1962), Sherbenou (1961) and Hawkins (1971).
6 See Golledge and Rushton (1972).

9 Conclusions and further work

The aim of this book was to describe and attempt to explain the influence of space and location on social administration. The principal conclusions have already been set out at various stages in the study. This chapter serves to provide an overview of these conclusions and also indicates lines of research that might prove profitable in the future. The basic premise of this study rests on the belief that to comprehend political organization of space and the provision of public services it is necessary to understand interaction over space. This is summarized by Wolfe (1963) who claims that 'one fact underlies political events and political institutions; they always involve men interacting over distance. Ultimately political organization is spatial organization.'

With this in mind, this study has attempted to illustrate the use of procedures for analysing the spatial organization of social services. In particular, we have concentrated upon the rationale for dividing states into smaller units for administrative purposes. It is argued that Acts, passed by the state legislature, can be more easily and more satisfactorily enforced by dividing the state area into semi-autonomous units. Ease and satisfaction are defined in terms of spatial and political accessibility to policy-makers and financial viability.

Political scientists, economists and geographers, among others, have all been drawn to study the size, shape and functions of spatial units. Political scientists have focused attention on political process and behaviour, and in their study of areal relationships some emphasis has been placed upon the socio-economic characteristics of the population of a particular location. Fesler (1943–44) noted that the number and average size of units deemed desirable for the administration of a given agency is most closely related to the magnitude of the activity to be carried on in the field. This point is amplified in Johnsrud's (1958) study of Wisconsin agencies. Fesler provides a summary of the five factors which should be given greatest weight in determining the number and size of units.

1   The magnitude of field work.
2   The localization of the objects to be administered.
3   The capacity of the headquarters to supervise the regional chiefs.
4   The comparative results to be expected from large-scale and small-scale administration.
5   The implications of political influence on appointment of regional personnel.

He also notes that the determination of the exact boundaries of the units should be based upon a consideration of the following four criteria:

167

1   Equalization of the burden of work.
2   The nature of the distribution of the objects to be administered.
3   The administrative areas to be used by cooperating agencies.
4   The disadvantages of changing existing boundaries.

Finally he states that the location of administrative centres must take into account the following factors:

1   The location of objects of administration within the region.
2   The location of the headquarters of other agencies.
3   The availability of office space.
4   The need for frequent personal contacts between the headquarters and the regional offices.

Attempts to formulate some of these basic principles into numerical models are best illustrated in the sections dealing with static and dynamic allocation–location models. Implicit and explicit references are also made in other sections, for example, with regard to economies of scale, spatial justice, and local sentiment and control.

Some political scientists have begun to move away from the spatial aspects of administration. Ostrom (1956), for example, expresses the complexity of a regional analysis of politics in terms of an intimate connection between behaviour and policy-formulation. He considers that the traditional institutional referents used in political science such as councils, agencies and departments, cannot serve as a basis for investigating the activities, relations and behaviour involved in policy formulation in the non-corporate region. With this in mind the geographer can serve a very useful purpose in examining the spatial aspects of political units, and so add to the general understanding of political activities.

Economists have maintained their traditional view towards administrative areas, that is they use cost analysis techniques to evaluate the efficiency of administrative functions which occupy a defined space. We should note that considerable attention is now being placed upon evaluating the quality of services provided and the cost of ensuring this quality in the social and physical environments. The wide range of variables which influence the form of administrative units has been summarized by the geographer Christaller (1965): 'consider features of the terrain, the network of natural waters, densities of population, existing settlements, traffic routes, and last but not least, the anticipated trends of future development and politically desirable planning objectives.'

Tests of the influence of some of these variables have been provided by Johnsrud (1958), Whebell (1961) and Lewis (1966). The latter emphasizes the changing role of transportation and communication through time. In the 1940s Dickinson (1947) attempted to explain how administrative areas varied through space and time. He concentrated on some spatial administrative functions in France, Germany and Britain. His work is dated mainly because it was completed before the large-scale introduction of inter-municipal cooperation which has been a feature of politics since 1945.

Fundamental to both empirical and theoretical studies of administrative units is the concept of transportation cost. Several times in this study we have offered working definitions in order that our models could be made operational. In general the power of this variable has changed over time. Where the system of transport is underdeveloped, only a limited area around a village or town can come under its political influence. The growth of city states, in classical times, was largely a result of parochial forces. These forces continued in Europe in medieval times and even today several city states remain. During the colonial period in Canadian history a similar phase was in evidence, a phase during which centres grew and developed as road communication with nearby farms improved. The growth and delimitation of townships depended primarily on the accessibility of centrally located villages or towns. With improved systems of communication, growth of pooulation, the increased cost of providing social services because of the rise in the quantity, quality and variety of services the small traditional units have been replaced by larger units.

Explicit definitions for the optimal arrangement of administrative areas have been outlined by Dickinson (1947, 34–5). He considered that the local administrative area,

> should be determined primarily on the basis of accessibility to a town. The leading idea in the creation of new units is that they should be compact, with a rough equality in area and population, each with its chief administrative centre in the geographical centre and with its frontiers in thinly populated areas which are divided by local associations.

More recently Prescott (1965, 173) stated that boundary reorganization should be guided by the following principles:

1   All government areas should be composed of aggregates of the smallest basic unit, in such a way that the boundaries are multi-functional.
2   Conurbations should be constituted into single administrative areas capable of coordinating development.
3   Boundaries should follow watersheds, to avoid unnecessary divisions of water, roads and sewage services, which usually follow valleys.
4   The boundary should be drawn to cater for local sentiment and regional patriotism.

In an attempt to move from the general principles enunciated by Dickinson and Prescott this book has offered some operational methods for evaluating accessibility, compactness and centrality by examining some of the geometrical properties of service units. It is hoped that future work will provide firmer bases for defining objectively the spatial attributes of different shapes and sizes for administrative units. We can only echo

Prescott's plea (1965, 179) that '. . . it is hoped that precise statistical data, associated with internal boundaries, will make it possible to develop methods for their analysis.'

Finally, an attempt to summarize aims and objectives for future work is offered in table 9.1. Though we have divided the overall work into a series of discrete entities for the practical purpose of developing specializations, workers must in the long run exchange ideas and methodologies if we are to make full use of knowledge and present our findings to the public in order that they may take a meaningful role in policy-making. The provision of public services is vital for the health, comfort and satisfaction of mankind. Scientists, both physical and social, have a duty to study different modes of production and distribution and their efforts will, it is hoped, help to improve the world we live in.

Table 9.1 Summary of future work on public services

1   Greater concern with measurement of attributes of public services, values, human behaviour.
2   Development of analytical techniques to evaluate alternate structures.
3   Integration of partial studies, eg allocation – location models and economies of scale models.
4   Study of the relationships between space and location, and cultural and physical environmental conditions.
5   Analysis of specific problem areas.
   (i)   Restructuring out-dated systems, eg, Western Europe, China, ex-colonies.
   (ii)   Restructuring due to rapid technical changes, especially in transportation, eg Third World.
   (iii) Restructuring due to population growth, outdated political patterns and urbanization, eg metropolitan areas.
   (iv)   Restructuring due to changes in financial arrangements, eg taxation, user-changes, spillovers, transfer payments.
6   Improvement in diffusion of findings among researchers to avoid duplication and to speed up analyses, and to the public and policy-makers to aid in evaluating alternative strategies for providing social services. Clarity in the expression of empirical findings is imperative.

References

ABLER, R., ADAMS, J. S., GOULD, P. R. 1971: *Spatial organization*. Englewood Cliffs, New Jersey: Prentice Hall.

AD HOC COMMITTEE, 1965: *The science of geography*. Washington, DC: NAS–NRC, publication **1277**.

ADLER, E. P. 1960: Relationships between organization size and efficiency. *Management Science* **12** (1), 80–84.

ALESCH, D. J. and DOUGHARTY, L. A. 1971: *Economies of scale analysis in state and local government*. Santa Monica: Rand Corporation, **R–748–CIR**.

ALESCH, D. J. and DOUGHARTY, L. A. 1971: *The feasibility of economies-of-scale analysis of public services*. Santa Monica: Rand Corporation, **R–739–CIR**.

APPLEBAUM, W. 1970: *Shopping centre strategy*. New York: International Council of Shopping Centres.

AUSTIN, M., SMITH, T. E. and WOLPERT, J. October 1970: The implementation of controversial facility–complex programs. *Geographical Analysis* **2** (4), 315–329.

BAILEY, N. T. J. 1954: Queuing for medical care. *Applied Statistics* **3**, 137–145.

BAKER, A. R. H. 1971: Some shape and contact characteristics of French rural communes. In Dossart, F. (ed.) *L'Habitat et les Paysages Ruraux d'Europe. Comptes rendus du symposium tenu à l'université de Liège* **58** 13–23.

BAKER, A. R. H. (ed.) 1972: *Progress in Historical Geography*. Newton Abbott: David and Charles. (Chapter 1.)

BANFIELD, E. C. and WILSON, J. Q. 1963: *City politics*, Cambridge, Mass.: Harvard University Press.

BERGMAN, E. F. 1971: *Metropolitan political geography: achieving area-wide systems*. PhD thesis, Dept. of Geography, University of Washington.

BERRY, B. J. L. 1967: *Geography of market centres and retail distribution*. New Jersey: Prentice Hall.

BERRY, B. J. L. and GARRISON, W. L. 1958: A note on central place theory and the range of a good. *Economic Geography* **34**, 304–311.

BERRY, B. J. L. and HORTON, F. 1970: *Geographic perspectives on urban systems*. New Jersey: Prentice Hall.

BERRY, B. J. L. and PRED, A. 1965: Central place studies. *Bibliography Series* **1**. Regional Science Research Institute, Philadelphia.

BIRD, F. L. 1960: *The general property tax*. Washington, DC: US Bureau of the Census, Census of Governments.

BLAIR, D. J. and BISS, T. H. 1967: The measurement of shape in geography: an appraisal of methods and techniques. *Bulletin of Quantitative Data for Geographers*, Dept. of Geography, Nottingham University.

BOADEN, N. 1971: *Urban policy-making: influences on county boroughs in England and Wales*. Cambridge: Cambridge University Press.

BOLLENS, J. C. and SCHMANDT, H. J. 1965: *The metropolis: its people, politics and economic life.* New York: Harper and Row.

BOOTS, B. N. 1970: An approach to the study of patterns of cellular nets. *Discussion Paper* 1, Dept. of Geography, Rutgers University.

BOOTS, B. N. 1972: *The study of cellular nets.* PhD thesis, Dept. of Geography, Rutgers University.

BOTNER, S. B. 1970: Four years of PPBS: an appraisal. *Public Administration Review* 2, 423–431.

BROOKFIELD, H. C. and BROWN, P. 1963: *Struggle for land.* London: Oxford University Press.

BROWN, L. 1968: *Diffusion processes and location: a conceptual framework and bibliography.* Philadelphia: Regional Science Research Institute.

BROWN, L. A. 1972: Metropolitan spatial injustice: some comments on the research perspective. *Annual Meeting, Association of American Geographers,* Kansas. (Mimeo.)

BROWN, R. H. 1948: *The historical geography of the United States.* New York:

BUNGE, W. 1962: Theoretical geography. *Lund Studies in Geography, Series C* 1, Lund: Gleerup. (Revised edition, 1966.)

BURSTALL, R. M., LEAVER, R. A. and SUSSAMS, J. E. 1962: Evaluation of transport costs for alternate factory sites. *Operational Research Quarterly* 13 (4), 345–354.

BUTTIMER, A. 1972: Inequality, inefficiency and spatial injustice. *Annual Meeting, Association of American Geographers,* Kansas. (Mimeo.)

CARTER, G. M., CHAIKEN, J. M. and IGNALL, E. 1971: *Response areas for two emergency services.* New York: Rand R–532–NYC/HUD.

CARTER, H. 1972: *The study of urban geography.* London: Arnold, Boston: Crane Russak.

Central Statistical Office 1970: *Social Trends.* London: HMSO.

Centre de Recherches sur l'Opinion Publique. 1973: *Attitudes towards regroupment in six municipalities on the Island of Montreal.* Montreal.

CHAIKEN, J. M. and LARSON, R. C. 1971: *Methods for allocating urban emergency units.* New York: Rand Corporation, P-4719.

CHAPIN, F. S. 1957: The optimum size of institutions: a theory of the large group. *American Journal of Sociology* 62, 449–460.

CHAPMAN, B. 1959: *The Profession of government.* London: Allen and Unwin.

CHAPMAN, R. A. and DUNSIRE, A. 1971: *Style in administration.* London: Allen and Unwin.

CHINITZ, B. (ed.) 1964: *City and suburb.* Englewood Cliffs, New Jersey: Prentice Hall.

CHRISTALLER, W. 1965: The advantages of space economical theory for the practice of regional planning. *Ekistics* 20 (119), 223–227.

CHRISTOFIDES, N. and EILON, S. 1969: Expected distances in distribution problems. *Operations Research Quarterly* 20, 347–443.

CHORLEY, R. J. and KENNEDY, B. A. 1971: *Physical geography: a systems approach.* London: Prentice Hall.

CLARK, R. 1972: *In them days.* PhD thesis, Dept. of Geography, McGill University.

CLOVER, Y. T. 1966: *Property tax on houses and concept of justice.* Dept. of Economics, School of Business Administration, Texas Technological College.

COLE, J. P. and KING, C. A. M. 1968: *Quantitative geography.* London: Wiley.

Coleman Report, 1966: *Equality of educational opportunity*. US Office of Education, Dept. of Health, Education and Welfare, Washington, DC.

COLENUTT, R. 1970: Bu¦lding models of urban growth and structure. In Board, C. *et al.* (eds.) *Progress in Geography* **2**. London: Arnold; New York: St Martin's Press.

Committee for Economic Development, 1968: *Modernizing local government*. New York.

COOK, G. C. A. 1969: Public service provision in metropolitan areas. In Feldman, L. D. and Goldrick, M. D. (eds.) *Politics and Government of Urban Canada*, Toronto: Methuen, p. 93.

COOMBS, C. H. 1967: *A theory of data*. London: Wiley.

COOPER, L. 1963: Location–allocation problems. *Operations Research* **11** (3), 331–343.

COOPER, L. 1967: Solutions to generalized locational equilibrium models. *Journal of Regional Science* **7** (1), 1–8.

COOPER, L. and STEINBERG, D. 1970: *Introduction to methods of optimization*. London: W. B. Saunders.

COX, K. 1965: The application of linear programming to geographic problems. *Tijdshrift voor Econ. en Soc. Geografie* **56**, 228–236.

COX, K. 1973: *Conflict, power and politics in the city: a geographic view*. New York: McGraw-Hill.

COYLE, R. G. and MARTIN, M. J. C. 1969: Case study: the cost minimization of refuse collection operations. *Operational Research Quarterly* **20**, 43–56.

CURRAN, D. J. 1963: The metropolitan problem: solution from within? *National Tax Journal* **16**.

DARBY, H. C. (ed.) 1926: *The historical geography of England before 1807*. Cambridge: Cambridge University Press.

DARBY, H. C. 1953: *Domesday geography of eastern England*. Cambridge: Cambridge University Press.

DAVIES, B. 1968: *Social needs and resources in local services*. London: Michael Joseph.

DAWSON, D. A. 1972: Economics of scale in the Ontario public secondary schools. *Canadian Journal of Economics* **5** (2).

DEE, N. V. 1970: *Urban playgrounds: an optimal location model*. PhD thesis, Dept. of Geography and Environmental Engineering, Johns Hopkins University.

DEIGHTON, D. M. 1971: A comment on location models. *Management Science, Theory* **18** (1), 113–115.

DEVISE, P. 1971: Cook County Hospital: Bulwark of Chicago's Apartheid Health Service and Prototype of the Nation's Public Hospitals. *Antipode: Access to Essential Public Services* **3**, 9–20.

DICKINSON, R. E. 1947: *City, region and regionalism*. London: Routledge.

DRAKE, A. W., KEENEY, R. L. and MORSE, P. M. 1972: *Analysis of public systems*. Cambridge, MIT Press.

DRAPER, J. and STRUTHER, G. 1963: Testing a model of organization growth. *Human Organization* **22**, 180–194.

EARICKSON, R. November 1971: Poverty and Race: The Base of Access to Essential Public Services. *Antipode: Access to Essential Public Services* **3** (1), 1–8.

EAST, W. G. 1966: *An historical geography of Europe.* London: Methuen.
EAST, W. G. 1968: Political organizations at higher ranks. In Fisher, C. A. (ed.) *Essays in Political Geography.* London: Methuen.
EILON, S. 1972: Goals and constraints in decision-making. *Operational Research Quarterly* **23** (1), 3–15.
EILON, S. WATSON-GANDY, C. D. T. and CHRISTOFIDES, N. 1971: *Distribution management: mathematical modelling and practical analysis.* London: Griffin.
ELIOT-HIRST, M. 1972: *A geography of economic behaviour.* Belmont, California: Duxbury Press.
ELSHAFFI, A. N. 1972: *Facilities location: formulations methods of solution, applications and some computational experiences.* **Memo No. 276**, Insitute of National Planning, the Arab Republic of Egypt, Cairo.
EWING, G. O. 1970: *An analysis of consumer space preferences using the method of paired comparisons.* PhD thesis, Dept. of Geography, McMaster University.
FAIRTHORNE, D. 1965: The distance between pairs of points in towns of simple geometrical shapes. *Proceedings of the 2nd International Symposium on the Theory of Road Traffic Flow.* OECD, London.
FESLER, J. 1949: *Area and administration.* Alabama: Alabama Press.
FESLER, J. W. 1943–44: Criteria for administrative regions. *Social Forces* **22** (1), 26–32.
FITCH, L. C. 1964: *Urban transportation and public policy.* San Francisco: Chandler.
FORRESTER, J. 1969: *Urban dynamics.* Cambridge, Mass.: MIT Press.
GARRISON, W. et al. 1959: *Studies of highway development and geographic change.* Seattle: University of Washington Press.
GIBBS, J. 1970: A method for comparing the spatial shapes of urban units. In Gibbs, J. (ed.) *Urban research methods.* Princeton: Van Nostrand.
GLASGOW, J. A. 1971: *Changes in the governmental geography of the urbanized areas of the United States, 1950 to 1960.* PhD thesis, Dept. of Geography, Clark University.
GODLEY, W. and RHODES, J. (no date): *The rate support grant system* Dept. of Applied Economics, Cambridge University. (Mimeo.)
GOODCHILD, M. F. 1972a: The trade area of a displaced hexagonal lattice point. *Geographical Analysis* **4** (1), 105–107.
GOODCHILD, M. F. 1972b: *Properties of some stochastic partitioning processes.* Dept. of Geography, University of Western Ontario, Mimeo.
GOODCHILD, M. F. and MASSAM, B. H. 1969: Some least-cost models of spatial administrative systems in Southern Ontario. *Geografiska Annaler* **52** (2), 86–94.
GORDON, G. and ZELIN, K. 1968: *A simulation study of emergency ambulance service in New York City.* New York: IBM Scientific Center Report, 320–2935.
GOULD, P. R. and LEINBACH, T. R. 1966: An approach to the geographic assignment of hospital services. *Tijdschrift Voor Econ. en Soc. Geografie* **57**, 203–206.
GOULD, P. R. 1969: Spatial diffusion. *Resource Paper* **4**, Washington, DC: Association of American Geographers.
GULICK, L. H. and URWICK, L. (eds.) 1937: *Papers on the science of administration.* New York: Institute of Public Administration.

HAGGETT, P. 1965: *Locational analysis in human geography*. London: Arnold; New York: St Martin's Press.

HAGGETT, P. 1972: *Geography: a modern synthesis*. London: Harper & Row.

HAGGETT, P. and CHORLEY, R. J. 1969: *Network analysis in geography*. London: Arnold; New York: St Martin's Press.

HAIRE, M. (ed.) 1959: *Modern organization theory*. New York: Wiley.

HALEY, K. B. 1963: Siting of depots. *International Journal of Production Research* **2**, 41–45.

HALL, E. T. 1969: *The hidden dimension*. New York: Anchor.

HAMPSON, A. 1971: *The influence of territorial shape on municipal expenditures: England and Wales*. MA thesis, Dept. of Geography, Uniersity of Denver.

HANSON, A. H. and WALLES, M. 1970: *Governing Britain*. London: Collins.

HANSON, N. W. 1966: Economy of scale as a cost factor in financing public schools. *National Tax Journal*, **17**, 70–83.

HARRIS, B. 1968: Quantitative models of urban development: their role in metropolitan policy-making. In Perloff, H. S. and Wingo, L. (eds.) 1968 *Issues in urban economics*. Baltimore: The Johns Hopkins University Press.

HARRIS, R. C. 1966: *The seigneurial system in early Canada*. Madison: Uniersity of Wisconsin Press.

HARTLEY, H. J. 1968: *Educational planning-program and budgeting: a systems approach*. Englewood Cliffs, New Jersey: Prentice Hall.

HARVEY, D. 1969: *Explanation in geography*. London: Arnold; New York: St. Martin's Press.

HARVEY, D. 1972: *Society, the city and the space-economy of urbanism*. Resource Paper **18**, Washington, DC: Association of American Geographers.

HARVEY, D. 1973: *Social justice and the city*. London: Arnold; Baltimore: The Johns Hopkins University Press.

HATRY, H. P. 1972: Issues in productivity measurement for local governments. *Public Administration Review* **32** (6), 776–784.

HAWKINS, B. W. 1971: *Politics and urban policies*. New York: Bobbs-Merrill.

HAWLEY, A. H. and ZIMMER, B. H. 1971: Resistance to unification in a metropolitan community. In Jackson, W. A. D. and Samuels, M. S. (eds.) *Politics and Geographic relationships*. Englewood Cliffs, New Jersey: Prentice Hall, 414–430.

HEADY, F. 1966: *Public administration: a comparative perspective*. Englewood Cliffs, New Jersey: Prentice Hall.

HESS, S. W. and SAMUELS, S. A. 1971: Experiences with a sales districting model: criteria and implementation. *Management Science*, **18** (4), Part II, 41–54.

HILLIER, F. 1963: Economic models for industrial waiting line problems. *Management Science* **10**, 119–130.

HINRICKS, H. H. and TAYLOR, G. M. 1969: *Program budgeting and benefit-cost analysis*. California: Goodyear.

HINMAN, J. 1970: *Controversial facility-complex programs: coalitions, side-payments, and social decisions*, Discussion Paper **8**, Regional Science Association, University of Pennsylvania, Philadelphia.

HINMAN, J. 1971: *A location model for public facilities with neighborhood effects*. Discussion Paper **13**, Regional Science Association, University of Pennsylvania, Philadelphia.

HIRSCH, W. Z. 1964: Local versus area-wide urban government services. *National Tax Journal* **17** (4).

HIRSCH, W. Z. 1965: Cost functions of an urban government service refuse collection. *The Review of Economics and Statistics* **47**, 356–367.

HIRSCH, W. Z. 1968: The supply of urban public services. In Perloff, H. and Wingo, L. (eds.) *Issues in urban economics*, Baltimore: The Johns Hopkins University Press. 477–525.

HIRSCH, W. Z. 1973: *Urban economics analysis.* New York: McGraw Hill.

HIRST, M. A. 1971: The changing pattern of district administrative centres in Uganda, since 1900. *Geographical Analysis* **3**, 90–98.

HOGG, J. 1968: The siting of fire stations. *Operations Research Quarterly* **19**, 275–287.

HOGGART, R. 1957: *The uses of literacy.* Harmondsworth: Penguin.

HOLMES, J. WILLIAMS, F. B. and BROWN, L. A. 1972: Facility location under a maximum travel restriction: an example using day-care facilities. *Geographical Analysis* **4** (3), 258–266.

HOOS, I. R. 1972: *Systems analysis in public policy.* London: University of California Press.

HOVEY, H. A. 1968: *The PPB approach to government decision-making.* New York: Praeger.

HUDSON, J. C. and FOWLER, P. M. (no date): The concept of pattern in geography. *Discussion Paper Series* **1**, Dept. of Geography, University of Iowa.

INDIK, B. P. 1964: The relationship between organization size and supervision ratio. *Administrative Science Quarterly* **9**.

ISARD, W. 1960: *Methods of regional analysis: an introduction to regional science.* Cambridge, Mass.: MIT Press.

JACKSON, R. R. P. and ADELSON, R. M. 1962: A critical survey of queuing theory, Part I. *Operational Research Quarterly* **13**, 13–22.

JACOB, P. E. and TOSCANO, J. U. 1964: *The integration of political communities.* New York: Lippincott.

JANELLE, D. G. 1969: Spatial reorganization: a model and concept, *Annals, Association of American Geographers* **59** (2), 348–364.

JOHNSON, J. H. 1970: Reorganization of local government in Northern Ireland *Area* **2** (4), 17–21.

JOHNSRUD, R. O. 1958: *Areal relationships in the functioning of Wisconsin state agencies.* PhD thesis, Dept. of Geography, University of Wisconsin, Madison.

KAISER, H. F. 1966: An objective method for establishing legislative districts. *Midwest Journal of Political Science* **10**, 80–96.

KATZ, I. N. and COOPER, L. 1973: *An always-convergent numerical scheme for a random locational equilibrium problem.* Technical Report, Computer Science and Operations Research Centre, Southern Methodist University, Texas.

KAUNDA, K. 1966: *Zambia: independence and beyond. The speeches of Kenneth Kaunda.* London: Nelson.

KEENEY, R. L. 1972: A method for districting among facilities. *Operations Research* **20** (3).

KESSEL, J. H. 1962: Government structure and political environment. *American Political Science Review* **56**, 615–620.

KIESLING, H. J. 1966: Measuring a local government service: a study of school districts in New York State. *The Review of Economics and Statistics*, **48**, 139–154.

KRIESEL, K. M. 1971: The thresholds of public services provided via service contract *Proceedings Association of American Geographers* **3**, 105–109.

LANKFORD, P. 1971: The Changing Location of Physicians. *Antipode: Access to Public Services* **3** (1), 68–72.

LARSON, R. C. 1971: *Response of emergency units: the effects of barriers, descrete streets, and one-way streets.* New York: Rand Corporation, **R–675–HUD**

LARSON, R. C. and STEVENSON, K. 1971: *On insensitiveness in urban redistricting and facility location.* New York: Rand Institute, **R–533–NYC/HUD.**

LEVY, S. and DONHOWE, G. 1962: Explorations of a biological model of industrial organization. *Journal of Business* **35**, 335–342.

LEWIS, J. E. 1966: *Functional regions of the US South: their expansion in relation to transportation change.* PhD thesis, University of Georgia.

LINEBERRY, R. L. and SHARKANSKY, I. 1971: *Urban politics and public policy.* New York: Harper and Row.

LINTACK, F. and DAWSON, P. 1964: *Police amalgamation feasibility study.* In the minutes of the combined meeting of Stoney Creek and Saltfleet Councils, Sixth Council.

LITHWICK, N. H. 1970: *Uraban Canada: problems and prospects.* Ottawa: Central Mortgage and Housing Corporation.

LLOYD, P. E. and DICKEN, P. 1972: *Location in space: a theoretical approach to economic geography.* London: Harper and Row.

LOCKARD, W. D. 1969: *The politics of state and local government.* London: Macmillan.

LORENZ, K. 1963: *On aggression.* New York: Harcourt.

MAAS, A. (ed.) 1959: *Area and power: a theory of local government.* New York: Glencoe.

MADGWICK, P. J. 1970: *American city politics.* London: Routledge and Kegan Paul.

MARTIN, R. C. 1967: Government adaptation to metropolitan growth. In Dye, T. R. (ed.) *Politics in the Metropolis.*

MARANZANA, F. E. 1964: On the location of supply points to minimize transport costs. *Operational Research Quarterly* **15**, 261–270.

MARCH, J. G. and SIMON, H. A. 1958: *Organizations.* New York: Wiley.

MARKLAND, R. E. *et al.* 1972: Design and evaluation of police patrol beats using a political districting algorithm. *Proceedings 3rd Annual Meeting, American Institute Decision Sciences.*

MASSAM, B. H. 1970: A note on shape: *The Professional Geographer*, **22** (4), 197–199.

MASSAM, B. H. 1970a: An analysis of inter-municipal co-operation. *Ontario Geographer* (**6**), 9– 6.

MASSAM, B. H. 1971b: A test of a model of administrative areas. *Geographical Analysis* **3** (4), 402–406.

MASSAM, B. H. 1972a: Construction de modèles urbains. *METRA* **11** (2), 279–292.

MASSAM, B. H. 1972b: *The spatial structure of administrative systems. Commission on College Geography.* Resource Paper 12, Association of American Geographers, Washington, DC.

MASSAM, B. H. 1973: Forms of local government in the Montreal area: 1911–1971: a discriminant approach. *Canadian Journal of Political Science.*

MASSAM, B. H. and BURGHARDT, A. F. 1968: The administrative subdivision of Southern Ontario: an attempt at evaluation. *Canadian Geographer* **12** (3), 125–134.

MASSAM, B. H. and GOODCHILD, M. F. 1971: Temporal trends in the spatial organisation of a service agency. *The Canadian Geographer* **15** (3), 193–206.

MCMAHON, T. 1973: Size and shape in biology. *Science* **179** (4079), 1201–1204.

MCWHINNEY, W. H. 1965: On the geometry of organizations. *Administrative Science Quarterly* **10**, 347–363.

MERCER, A., O'NEIL, J. S. and SHEPHERD, A. J. 1970: The churching of urban England. *Proceedings, International Federation of Operations Research Societies*, 725–739.

MERCER, J. 1972: *Local government in the Montréal metropolitan area.* Dept. of Geography, University of Iowa. (Mimeo.)

MEYER, P. 1957: *Administrative organization: a comparative study of the organization of public administration.* London: Stevens.

MICHAELSON, W. 1966: An empirical analysis of urban environmental preferences. *American Institute of Planners Journal* **32**, 355–360.

MILLS, G. 1967: The determination of local government electoral boundaries. *Operations Research Quarterly* **18** (3), 243–255.

MITCHELL, J. B. 1963: *Historical geography.* London: English Universities Press.

MONROE, C. B. 1972: *A spatial simulation of ambulance service in Madison Wisconsin.* Dept. of Geography, Pennsylvania State University. (Mimeo.)

MOORE, P. G. 1968: *Basic operational research.* London: Pitman.

MORANDO, V. L. December 1968: Inter-local co-operation in metropolitan areas: Detroit. *Urban Affairs Quarterly* **4** (2), 185–200.

MORRILL, R. L. and EARICKSON, R. 1969: Influence of race, religion, and ability to pay on patient to hospital distance. In de Vise, P. *et al.* (eds.) 1969: *Slum medicine: Chicago's apartheid health system.* Chicago: University of Chicago Press.

MOWITZ, R. J. 1965: Evaluating costs and benefits of intergovernmental relations. In Buck, R. C. and Rath, R. A. (eds.) *Community development: problems and prospects*, 65–72.

NETZER, R. 1966: *Economics of property tax.* Washington, DC: The Brookings Institute.

NEWELL, G. F. 1971: *Applications of queuing theory.* London: Chapman and Hall.

NEWCOMB, R. M. 1970: A model of a mystery: the medieval parish as a spatial system. *Skrifter fra Geografisk Institöt ved Århus Universitet.* (Mimeo.)

NEWCOMB, R. M. 1973: *Settlement patterns in Northern Juthand: pattern versus Genesis.* Dept. of Geography, University of Århus. (Mimeo.)

OLSSON, G. 1965: *Distance and human interaction: a bibliography and review.* Philadelphia: Regional Science Institute.

OSTROM, V. 1956: The political dimensions of regional analysis. *Papers and Proceedings of the Regional Science Association* **2**, 85–97.

OSTROM, V. and OSTROM, E. 1971: Public choice: a different approach to the study of public administration. *Public Administration Review* **31**, 203–216.

PALMER, D. S. 1973: The placing of service points to minimise travel. *Operational Research Quarterly* **24** (1), 121–123.

PANICO, J. A. 1969: *Queuing theory*. New Jersey: Prentice Hall.

PEDERSEN, P. O. 1967: *On the geometry of administrative areas*. Dept. of Geography, University of Copenhagen (unpublished report).

PIELOU, E. C. 1969: *An introduction to mathematical ecology*. London: Wiley.

PLUNKETT, T. J. 1969: *Urban Canada and its government*. Toronto: Macmillan.

PLUNKETT, T. J. 1972: *The financial structure and the decision-making process of Canadian municipal government*. Ottawa: Central Mortgage and Housing Corporation.

PONDY, L. R. 1969: Effects of size, complexity and ownership on administrative intensity. *Administrative Science Quarterly* **14** (1), 47–60.

PORTER, P. W. 1973: Review of Soja (1968). *Geographical Analysis* **5** (1), 67–73.

POUNDS, N. J. G. 1963: *Political geography*. New York: McGraw-Hill.

PRESCOTT, J. R. V. 1965: *The geography of frontiers and boundaries*. London: Hutchinson.

Public Administration Review 1970. Special issue on the international civil service.

PUGH, D. S. HICKSON, D. J. and HININGS, C. R. 1971: *Writers on organizations*. Harmondsworth: Penguin.

RAMSAY, A. S. 1959: *Dynamics*. Cambridge: Cambridge University Press.

REVELLE, C. D., MARKS, D. and LIEBMAN, J. C. 1970: An analysis of private and public sector location models. *Management Science* **16** (1).

RIDDELL, J. B. 1969: *Structure, diffusion and response: the spatial dynamics of modernization in Sierra Leone*. PhD thesis, Dept. of Geography, Pennsylvania State University.

RIDDELL, J. B. 1970: *The spatial dynamics of modernization in Sierra Leone*. Evanston, Illinois: Northwestern University Press.

RIDLEY, C. and SIMON, H. 1947: *Measuring municipal activity*. New York: Institute of Public Administration.

RIEW, J. 1966: Economics of scale in high school operation. *The Review of Economics and Statistics* **48**.

ROBERTS, P. D. 1971: Some comments concerning Revelle, Marks and Liebman's article on facility location. *Management Science* **18** (1), 109–111.

ROSS, J. H. 1972: *A measure of site attraction*. PhD thesis, Dept. of Geography, University of Western Ontario.

Royal Commission on Local Government in England 1966–69. Cmnd **4040**, 1969. London: HMSO.

RUSHTON, G. 1969: Analysis of spatial behaviour by revealed space preferences. *Annals, Association of American Geographers* **59**, 391–400.

SACKS, S. and HARRIS, R. 1964: Determinants of state local government expenditures and intergovernmental flows or funds. *National Tax Journal* **17**, 338–355.

SAVAS, E. S. 1969. Simulation and cost-effectiveness analysis of New York's emergency abulance service. *Management Science* **15**, B-608-B-628.

SAVAS, E. S. 1971: A computer-based system for forming efficient election districts. *Operations Research* **19**, 135–155.

SAVAS, E. S. *et al*. 1972: Letters to the editor. *Operations Research* **20** (1), 46–48.

SAWYER, W. W. 1955: *Prelude to mathematics*. Harmondsworth: Penguin.

SCHMANDT, H. J. 1961: *The municipal incorporation trend* 1950–1960. Madison: University of Wisconsin Press.

SCHNEIDER, J. B. 1967: The spatial structure of the medical care process. *Discussion Paper Series* **14**, Regional Science Research Institute, Philadelphia.

SCHNEIDER, J. B. 1971: Solving urban location problems: human intuition versus the computer. *Journal, American Institute of Planners* **37**, 95–98.

SCHNORE, L. F. and ALFORD, R. R. 1963: Forms of government and socio-economic characteristics of suburbs. *Administrative Science Quarterly* **8**, 1–17.

SCOTT, A. J. 1971*a*: An introduction to spatial allocation analysis. *Resource Paper* **9**, Association of American Geographers, Washington, DC.

SCOTT, A. J. 1971*b*: *Combinatorial programming, spatial analysis and planning*. London: Methuen.

SCOTT, S. and FEDER, E. L. 1957: *Factors associated with variations in municipal expenditure levels: a statistical study of California cities*. University of California, Berkeley.

SELF, P. 1972: *Administrative theories and politics*. London: Allen and Unwin.

SELIGMAN, E. R. A. 1925: *Essays in taxation* (10th edition). New York: Macmillan.

SERCK-HANSSEN, J. 1970: *Optimal patterns of location*. Amsterdam: North-Holland.

SHEA, A. 1966: Determining of the optimal location of depots distributive systems session. *Proceedings 4th International Conference Operations Research*. Boston.

SHERBENOU, E. L. 1961: Class, participation and the council manager plan. *Public Administrative Review* **21**, 131–135.

SHEVKY, E. and BELL, W. 1955: *Social area analysis*. Stanford Sociological Series, Stanford, Calif: Stanford University Press.

SILVA, R. 1965: Reapportionment and redistricting. *Scientific American* **213** (5), 20–27.

SIMON, H. A. 1959: *Administrative behavior*. New York: Macmillan.

SMALLWOOD, F. 1970: Reshaping local government abroad: Anglo-Canadian Experiments. *Public Administration Review* **30**, 521–530.

SMEED, R. J. 1962: The space requirements for traffic in towns. *Urban Survival and Traffic* **6**, 136–162.

SMEED, R. J. 1963: The effects of some kinds of routing systems on the amount of traffic in the central areas of towns. *Journal, Institute of Highway Engineers* **10** (1), 5–30.

SMEED, R. J. 1964: The traffic problem in towns: a review of possible long-term solutions. *Town Planning Review* **35** (2), 133–158.

SMITH, D. M. 1973: *The geography of social well-being in the United States*. New York: McGraw-Hill.

SNYDER, R. D. 1971: A note on the location of depots. *Management Science* **18** (1), 97.

SOJA, E. W. 1968: *The Geography of modernization of Kenya*. Syracuse, NY: Syracuse University Press.

SOJA, E. W. 1971: The political organization of space. *Resource Paper* **8**, Washington, DC: Association of American Geographers.

STAMP, L. D. 1964: *Man and the Land*. London: Collins.

STEINMETZ, N. 1972: *The use of hospital emergency rooms and outpatient departments in Montréal*. Dept. of Epidemiology and Health, McGill University, Montréal. (Mimeo.)

STIDHAM, S. 1970: On the optimality of single-server queuing systems. *Operations Research* **18**, 708-732.

STIDHAM, S. 1971: *Stochastic design models for location and allocation of public service facilities*. Ithaca, New York: Dept. of Environmental Systems Engineering, Cornell University.

SUSSAMS, J. E. 1969: *Industrial logistics*. London: Camelot Press.

TATE, E. W. 1946: *The parish chest: a study of the records of parochial administration in England*. Cambridge: Cambridge University Press.

TAYLOR, F. W. 1911: *The principles of scientific management*. New York: Norton.

TAYLOR, J. L. 1971: Urban gaming simulation systems. In Board, C. *et al.* (eds.) *Progress in Geographer 3*. London: Arnold; New York: St. Martin's Press.

TAYLOR, P. J. (undated): Distances within shapes: an introduction to a family of finite frequency distributions. *Discussion Paper* **16**, Department of Geography, University of Iowa.

TAYLOR, W. L. 1971: *Hanging together: equality in an urban nation*. New York: Simon and Schuster.

TEITZ, N. B. 1968: Toward a theory of urban public facility location. *Papers, Regional Science Association* **21**, 35-51.

TEMPERLEY, M. N. V. 1953: *Properties of matter*, London: Universities Tutorial Press.

TERREIN, F. W. and MILLS, D. L. 1955: The effect of changing size upon the internal structure of organizations. *American Sociological Review* **15** (1), 11-13.

THOMPSON, W. R. 1965: *A preface to urban economics*. Baltimore: The Johns Hopkins University Press.

TIEBOUT, C. M. October 1956: A pure theory of local expenditures. *Journal of Political Economy* **64**, 416-424.

TOREGAS, C. and REVELLE, C. 1972: Optimal location under time or distance constraints. *Papers, Regional Science Association* **28**, 133-140.

TÖRNQUIST, G., NORDBECK, S., RYSTEDT, B. and GOULD, P. R. 1971: *Multiple location analysis*. Lund: Gleerup.

TOSCANO, J. V. 1964: Transaction flow analysis in metropolitan areas. In Jacob, P. E. and Toscano, 1964: *Integration of political communities*, New York: Lippincott.

United Nations, 1970: *Administrative aspects of urbanization*. New York: UN ST/TAO/M/51.

United Nations Technical Assistance program, 1962: *Decentralization for national and local development*. New York: UN.

United States, Department of Health, Education and Welfare 1969: *Toward a Social Report*. Washington, DC.

Urban Focus I 1973: Queen's University, Kingston, Canada.

Urban Study and Action Committee, September 1966: *Report*. Saint Paul: Chamber of Commerce, cited in Bergman (1971) footnote 84.

VERGIN, R. C. and ROGERS, J. D. 1967: An algorithm and computational procedure for locating economic facilities. *Management Science* **13** (6), 8–240.

WARD, R. A. 1964: *Operational research in local government.* London: Allen and Unwin.

WASHIN, G. J. 1971: Municipal decentralization: little city halls and other neighborhood facilities, in *Municipal Yearbook*, Washington, DC: International City Managers Association, **38**, 8–12.

WATSON-GANDY, C. D. T. 1972: A note on the centre of gravity in depot location. *Management Science* **18** (8), B–478–481.

WEBB, S. and WEBB, B. 1924: *English local government from the revolution to the municipal corporations act: the parish and the county.* London: Longman.

WEAVER, J. B. and HESS, S. W. 1963: A procedure for non-partisan districting: development of computer techniques. *Yale Law Journal* **73**, 288–308.

WESOLOWSKY, G. O. 1973: Location in continuous space. *Geographical Analysis* **5** (2), 95–112.

WHEATON, W. L. C. 1964: Integration at the urban level, in Jacob, P. E. and Toscano, J. V. 1964. *Integration of political communities.* New York: Lippincott.

WHEBELL, C. F. J. 1961: *The geographical basis of local government in Southern Ontario.* PhD thesis, University of London, Ontario.

WHEELER, R. H. 1965: Annexation law and annexation success. *Land Economics* **56**, 354–360.

WHITAKER, R. A. 1971: *An algorithm for estimating the medians of a weighted graph subject to side constraints.* PhD thesis, Dept. of Geography, University of British Columbia.

WHITNEY, J. B. R. 1970: China: Area, administration and nation building. *Research Paper* **123**, Dept. of Geography, University of Chicago.

WHITTINGTON, G., BEAVON, K. S. O. and MABIN, A. S. 1972: Compactness of shape: review, theory and application. *Occasional Paper 7*, Dept. of Geography and Environmental Studies, University of Witwatersrand, Johannesburg.

WILKINSON, P. 1973: Neighbourhood parks and their use. *The Bulletin of the Conservation Council of Ontario* **20** (1), 1–5.

WILLIAMS, A. 1966: The optimal provision of public goods in a system of local government. *Journal of Political Economy* **74**, 18–33.

WILLIAMS, P. O. *et al.* 1963*a*: Social status, tax resources, and metropolitan co-operation. *National Tax Journal* **16**, 56–62.

WILLIAMS, O. P. *et al.* 1963*b*: Differentiation and Co-operation in a metropolitan area. *Midwest Journal of Political Science* **7**, 145–155.

WILLIAMS, O. P. *et al.* 1935: *Suburban differences and metropolitan policies.* Philadelphia: University of Pennsylvania Press.

WILSON, W. June 1887: The study of administration. *Political Science Quarterly* **2**, 197–222.

WISEMAN, H. V. (ed.) 1970: *Local government in England, 1958–1969.* London: Routledge.

WITTHUHN, B. O. 1968: *The spatial integration of Uganda as a process of modernization.* PhD thesis, Dept. of Geography, Pennsylvania State University.

WOLDENBURG, M. J. 1970: The hexagon as a spatial average. *Harvard Papers in Theoretical Geography* **42**.

WOLFE, R. I. 1963: *Transportation and politics.* New Jersey: Van Nostrand.

WOLFINGER, R. E. and FIELD, J. O. 1966: Political ethos and the structure of city government. *American Political Science Review* **60**, 306–326.

WOLPERT, J., MUMPHREY, A. and SELEY, J. 1972: Metropolitan neighborhoods: participation and conflict over change. *Resource Paper* **16**, Washington, DC: Association of American Geographers.

WOOD, R. C. 1958: *Suburbia: its people and their politics.* Boston: Riverside Press.

World Bank, June 1972a: *Urbanization.* Sector Working Paper. Washington, DC.

World Bank, 1972b: *Sectoral programs and policies, Urbanization.* Baltimore The Johns Hopkins University Press.

YEATES, M. 1963: Hinterland delimitation – a distance minimizing approach. *Professional Geographer* **15** (6), 7–10.

YEATES, M. 1968: *An introduction to quantitative analysis in economic geography.* London: McGraw-Hill.

YEATES, M. and GARNER, B. J. 1971: *The North American city.* New York: Harper and Row.

ZIMMERMAN, J. F. 1970: Metropolitan reform in the US: an overview. *Public Administration Review* **30**, 531–543.

Author Index

Subject Index